MODERNISM, FICTION AND MATHEMATICS

Edinburgh Critical Studies in Modernist Culture
Series Editors: Tim Armstrong and Rebecca Beasley

Available

Modernism and Magic: Experiments with Spiritualism, Theosophy and the Occult
Leigh Wilson

Sonic Modernity: Representing Sound in Literature, Culture and the Arts
Sam Halliday

Modernism and the Frankfurt School
Tyrus Miller

Lesbian Modernism: Censorship, Sexuality and Genre Fiction
Elizabeth English

Modern Print Artefacts: Textual Materiality and Literary Value in British Print Culture, 1890–1930s
Patrick Collier

Cheap Modernism: Expanding Markets, Publishers' Series and the Avant-Garde
Lise Jaillant

Portable Modernisms: The Art of Travelling Light
Emily Ridge

Hieroglyphic Modernisms: Writing and New Media in the Twentieth Century
Jesse Schotter

Modernism, Fiction and Mathematics
Nina Engelhardt

Forthcoming

Modernism, Space and the City
Andrew Thacker

Slow Modernism
Laura Salisbury

Primordial Modernism: Animals, Ideas, Transition (1927–1938)
Cathryn Setz

Modernism and the Idea of Everyday Life
Leena Kore-Schröder

Modernism Edited: Marianne Moore and The Dial *Magazine*
Victoria Bazin

Modernism and Time Machines
Charles Tung

Visit our website at: edinburghuniversitypress.com/series-edinburgh-critical-studies-in-modernist-culture.html

MODERNISM, FICTION AND MATHEMATICS

Nina Engelhardt

EDINBURGH
University Press

Edinburgh University Press is one of the leading university presses in the UK. We publish academic books and journals in our selected subject areas across the humanities and social sciences, combining cutting-edge scholarship with high editorial and production values to produce academic works of lasting importance. For more information visit our website: edinburghuniversitypress.com

© Nina Engelhardt, 2018

Edinburgh University Press Ltd
The Tun – Holyrood Road, 12(2f) Jackson's Entry, Edinburgh EH8 8PJ

Typeset in 10/12.5 Sabon by
Servis Filmsetting Ltd, Stockport, Cheshire

A CIP record for this book is available from the British Library

ISBN 978 1 4744 1623 8 (hardback)
ISBN 978 1 4744 1624 5 (webready PDF)
ISBN 978 1 4744 1625 2 (epub)

The right of Nina Engelhardt to be identified as the author of this work has been asserted in accordance with the Copyright, Designs and Patents Act 1988, and the Copyright and Related Rights Regulations 2003 (SI No. 2498).

CONTENTS

Acknowledgements   vi
Series Editors' Preface   viii
List of abbreviations   ix

Introduction: All that Counts – Modernism, Fiction, Mathematics   1
1 Mathematics and Politics: Thomas Pynchon, *Against the Day*   24
2 Mathematics, Language, Structure: Hermann Broch, *The
   Sleepwalkers*   59
3 Mathematics, Epistemology, Ethics: Robert Musil, *The Man
   without Qualities*   93
4 Mathematics and Fiction: Thomas Pynchon, *Gravity's Rainbow*   126
Conclusion: Modernism, Fiction and Mathematics   157

Glossary   164
Bibliography   170
Index   186

ACKNOWLEDGEMENTS

I am thankful for and would like to acknowledge those who contributed to shaping this research project. First of all, I would like to thank Randall Stevenson from whose ideas and support I have profited enormously in the course of this project. The insightful comments and suggestions on chapters and presentations were immensely helpful in framing my ideas, and the general support, advice and encouragement were invaluable, both in the imaginary heights and along the real axis of the project. Simon Malpas and Paul Crosthwaite also offered much appreciated support over the years. I would like to thank the series editors Tim Armstrong and Rebecca Beasley as well as Adela Rauchova at Edinburgh University Press for their patience and support. For offering time and space to exchange ideas, work together, and find rest and diversion, I particularly thank Christin Höne, Julia Hoydis, Kelly Kawar, the PhD community at the University of Edinburgh, my colleagues from the a.r.t.e.s. research lab, and the mathematicians and scientists who generously offered information and criticism, most of all Harald Engelhardt and Michael Harris. For providing events, encouragement and inspiring conversations along the research process, I thank the British Society for Literature and Science, the International Pynchon Week and, not least, the Work in Progress Seminars at the Department of English Literature at the University of Edinburgh where this project began.

Rather predictably, these acknowledgements, too, end with more private thanks. If the general fact is not unusual, my individual experience has been singular and so are the people that have made it so. While writing this book, a couple of forks in the path have changed my life for the better: my brother who taught the valuable lesson that things are what they are and that it never is too late; and forming a small, temporary community with S., helping each other along a part of our ways. From the first to the very last, my family has been with me in this: most directly involved with this book was my father in whom, with his interest, dedication, mathematical understanding and literary curiosity, I have had a much valued 'Doktorvater' over the years. But this research has been interrelated with other parts of my life that also demanded attention, put up 'real' challenges, and were the source of much motivation and happiness, and yes, sometimes grace. My biggest thanks lie here and go to my parents and my sister: for continuous support and opening up singular chances, for helping realise what began as possibilities and wild flights of fancy, and for being there in the complexities of life. For my own, singular case, my family – real, complex, sometimes purely improbable, and remaining delightfully surprising in their anarchical behaviour – is the best of all possible families.

I wish to thank the following publishers for permission to quote:

From *The Sleepwalkers* by Hermann Broch, published by Martin Secker. Permission granted by Penguin Random House Group Limited.

From *Gravity's Rainbow* by Thomas Pynchon, published by Jonathan Cape. Reprinted by permission of The Random House Group Limited.

From *Against the Day* by Thomas Pynchon, published by Vintage, 2007. Copyright Thomas Pynchon, 2006. Permission granted by Melanie Jackson Agency, LLC.

Part of Chapter 4 appeared, in different form, in *Orbit: A Journal of American Literature*, 2.2 (2014) as 'Gravity in *Gravity's Rainbow* – Force, Fictitious Force, and Frame of Reference; or: The Science and Poetry of Sloth'. DOI: http://doi.org/10.7766/orbit.v2.2.80

SERIES EDITORS' PREFACE

This series of monographs on selected topics in modernism is designed to reflect and extend the range of new work in modernist studies. The studies in the series aim for a breadth of scope and for an expanded sense of the canon of modernism, rather than focusing on individual authors. Literary texts will be considered in terms of contexts including recent cultural histories (modernism and magic; sonic modernity; media studies) and topics of theoretical interest (the everyday; postmodernism; the Frankfurt School); but the series will also reconsider more familiar routes into modernism (modernism and gender; sexuality; politics). The works published will be attentive to the various cultural, intellectual and historical contexts of British, American and European modernisms, and to interdisciplinary possibilities within modernism, including performance and the visual and plastic arts.

Tim Armstrong and Rebecca Beasley

LIST OF ABBREVIATIONS

AD   Thomas Pynchon, *Against the Day*
DSW   Hermann Broch, *Die Schlafwandler*
GR   Thomas Pynchon, *Gravity's Rainbow*
MM   Robert Musil, 'The Mathematical Man'
MoE   Robert Musil, *Mann ohne Eigenschaften*
MwQ   Robert Musil, *Man without Qualities*
SW   Hermann Broch, *The Sleepwalkers*

To my parents
Für meine Eltern

INTRODUCTION: ALL THAT COUNTS – MODERNISM, FICTION, MATHEMATICS

'Mighty are numbers; joined with art, resistless.'[1] The quotation from Euripides' play *Hecuba* joins the two elements at the heart of this book, and it expresses the pleasure resulting from the combination of mathematics and literature – domains that are often regarded as alien or opposed to each other. The context of the quotation reveals, however, that it does not refer to the relation between maths and fiction, but is a threat that, with cunning, Hecuba's numerous fellow Trojan women will help her 'master men' and avenge her son.[2] The suggestion that number bears power also relates to the argument of this book: mathematics is generally regarded as certain and true and believed to constitute authoritative knowledge; yet, literature draws on the privileged position of number and calculation for its own purposes and in the course thereof questions the established power structure of the disciplines.

If mathematics and literature are often viewed as diametrically opposed, a focus on modernist interrelations between these fields might appear particularly surprising: science and modernism can seem mutually contradictory, since modernism is commonly understood to react against a modernity rooted in the scientific revolution and Enlightenment valuation of reason. And as Isaac Newton's immensely influential *Principia Mathematica* (1687) signals in its very title, early modern inquiries into nature allocated a central role to mathematics and established its place at the extreme end of scientific rationality. On the other hand, however, the abstractness of maths has provoked questions about its relation to reality, and it has been understood to deal with ideal constructs that escape the restrictions of the given world. This book explores how literature draws on the contradictory image of maths and reflects the sometimes surprising relations between the fields. With this focus, I seek to help redress an imbalance in scholarship: mathematics has received far less attention in the humanities than other sciences. While scholars from a range of disciplines have explored Charles Darwin's work on evolution, the principles of quantum mechanics or Albert Einstein's theory of relativity and their connections with modernist literature and the arts, similarly decisive developments in mathematics are less widely remembered. But these also shaped modern worldviews, and reverberations in the works of philosophers, artists and literary writers suggest that we have to pay greater attention to the cultural relations of mathematics and more closely consider its place among manifestations of modernism.

In what follows, I explore the meeting of modernism and mathematics from the perspective of history of maths and with a main focus on literature, that is, on works of fiction that engage with modern maths as part of broader developments in the first half of the twentieth century. In Hermann Broch's novel trilogy *The Sleepwalkers* (1930–32), Broch's integrated essay introduces 'research into first principles of modern mathematics' as 'the clearest example' of a 'sweeping revolution in the style of thinking', and Robert Musil's *The Man without Qualities* (1930/32) establishes maths as 'the new method of thought itself, the mind itself, the very wellspring of the times' (SW 481, MwQ 35).[3] Thomas Pynchon's novels *Gravity's Rainbow* (1973) and *Against the Day* (2006) take the exploration of the period to a postmodern vantage point. The latter novel echoes the exemplary role that maths occupies in Broch's and Musil's assessments of the early twentieth century, when Yashmeen, one of a number of characters practising maths, suggests to her colleague Kit to view the time in terms of a connection between their field and the First World War: 'The political crisis in Europe maps into the crisis in mathematics. [. . .] The connections lie there, Kit – hidden and poisonous' (AD 668). Taking a longer temporal perspective, *Gravity's Rainbow* places maths at the core of a transformation of the modern Western world that begins with Newton's work in the scientific revolution and reaches its culmination in the Second World War. The novels by Pynchon, Broch and Musil, considering the twentieth century from perspectives that can be roughly distinguished into modern and postmodern, also reflect their engagements with maths in their literary forms. Taking a closer look at the maths will thus help us appreciate modernist and postmodernist innovations in literary style and form. At the same time, when the texts interrelate mathematical and literary developments, they point to characteristics shared between these fields and advance the notion of mathematical modernism: they support the idea that maths does not only become modern but modernist, that apart from undergoing a process of modernisation, it is part of modernist culture.

The field of modernist studies has opened up to diverse alternative modernisms in recent years, strengthening the focus on international and interdisciplinary perspectives and situating literary modernism within its cultural, social and institutional contexts. Scholars also pay increasing attention to the scientific environment and have overturned the well-rehearsed view that modernist writers were generally opposed to scientific ideas. 'Although the modernists' unsympathetic representations of science are significant, they are only half of the story', Michael Whitworth argues, and a growing body of work emphasises that writers traditionally viewed as opposed to science, such as Joseph Conrad, D. H. Lawrence, Virginia Woolf and T. S. Eliot, respond to its modern development with enthusiasm as well as antipathy.[4] Other modernist writers openly celebrate science and advocate its method as a way to modernise literature. In a 'Meditatio' of 1916, for instance, Ezra Pound pits notions of impersonality, objectivity and authority in science against a moribund literature:

> [I]f we can't write plays, novels, poems or any other conceivable form of literature with the scientist's freedom and privilege, with at least the chance of at least the scientist's verity, then where in the world have we got to, and what is the use of anything, anything?[5]

He explicitly laments literature's belatedness: 'Literature in the nineteenth and the beginning of the twentieth centuries was and is where science was in the days of Galileo and the Inquisition.'[6] Pound's suggestion to remake literature according to the model of the sciences corresponds to the last out of the three kinds of literary response to scientific developments that Tim Armstrong discerns in *Modernism: A Cultural History*: 'texts which register shock; texts which incorporate the new science into their depiction of the world; and texts which deploy science at the level of poetics'.[7] The novels by Pynchon, Broch and Musil each include elements of all three categories: they reflect the enormous changes brought about by science and technology, integrate new science in the depiction of their worlds, and revaluate literary form in view of modern mathematics.

Scholarship on modernism is surprisingly underrepresented in literature and science studies, as the field continues to be dominated by a focus on Victorian literature that the pioneering works of Gillian Beer and George Levine established in the 1980s. Even regarding this well-explored era, Alice Jenkins notes a lack of scholarship on mathematics: 'Very little attention indeed [. . .] has been given by literary scholars to the workings of *mathematics* in Victorian culture. This is a problematic absence from both Victorian studies and literature and science studies.'[8] Whitworth points to the special characteristics of mathematics that partly explain its similarly marginal position in studies of modernist literature and science: in contrast to the applied sciences and their close ties to technology, maths seems 'removed from the conventional concerns of literature, allowing the fewest possibilities for metaphorical exchange'.[9] Yet Whitworth concludes that modernist writers employ models and metaphors from pure science not primarily in terms of theme but that engagement with it manifests in literary form, and in this practice mathematics appears as an apt interest of modernist writers: as a formal science that works with abstract concepts and not with the empirical methods of the natural sciences, it precisely lends itself to considerations of structure and form.[10] As we shall see, the novels by Pynchon, Broch and Musil engage with maths as topic and metaphor as well as on a structural level, and examining the texts affords an insight into the role of pure science in innovations in literary form. But, with its focus on maths, this book directs literature and science studies to a field that more generally puts into question the division between the two cultures: as a formal or structural science, mathematics holds an exceptional position in the relation of the (natural) sciences and the humanities. Where C. P. Snow in his talk 'The Two Cultures' (1959) famously laments a dangerous drifting apart of the disciplines, the physicist and philosopher Bernd-Olaf Küppers suggests that the structural sciences abstract from reality and are therefore best suited to building a bridge between the natural sciences and the humanities.[11] This proposition points us towards the specificity of mathematics and its unique place in the relationship between the disciplines that receives particular attention with its modern development.

MATHEMATICS AND ITS RELATION TO NATURE

'[T]he layman does not conceive it to be any part of his aesthetic and cultural duty to understand the least thing about mathematics', Norbert Wiener lamented in 1956.[12] If the hurdles for non-professional engagement with mathematics can be high, on the other hand, the discipline itself only very gradually opened up to non-mathematical considerations: historical, social and cultural studies of maths developed noticeably later than comparable examinations of the natural sciences. When such studies finally emerged in the mid-1970s, they had to overcome considerable difficulties. Conducting a sociological analysis of maths in *Knowledge and Social Imagery* (1976), David Bloor described it as 'perhaps the most difficult of all the obstacles to the sociology of knowledge', and he admitted that, compared to the natural sciences, there were few examples he could give.[13] Similarly, the field long remained overlooked in the history of science, and the few mathematicians writing on the development of their discipline tended to explain the roots of modern theories rather than examining historical material on its own terms. Ivor Grattan-Guinness asserts: 'they confound the question, "How did we get here?", with the different question, "What happened in the past?"'[14] This confusion arises from the exceptional epistemological status of mathematics, which also is a reason for its relative neglect in historical and cultural studies: mathematics is traditionally seen to aggregate eternal truths that are independent of exterior factors and therefore not in need of contextualisation.

The view that mathematics constitutes general and incontrovertible truth goes back to ancient Greece in the sixth century BC. Pythagoras and the brotherhood he founded held that numbers exist independently of the natural world, and the realisation that they describe many phenomena, from musical harmonies to planetary orbits, led them to proclaim that the universe itself was constructed of whole numbers. For the Pythagoreans, mathematical learning was therefore driven by the hope to discover fundamental truths and gain godly knowledge. Given that from Pythagoras onwards mathematics appeared essential to understanding the order of nature and the heavens, many philosophers and scientists agreed with the view that it was a human duty to pursue this discipline; a notion also expressed in a quotation ascribed to Plato: 'He is unworthy of the name of man who does not know that the diagonal of a square is incommensurable with its side.' Two thousand years after Pythagoras, Galileo Galilei similarly asserted that human beings could reach the highest truth and participate in God's knowledge through mathematics. In a well-known phrase, he echoes the ancient Greek belief in number as the key to nature:

> Philosophy is written in this grand book – I mean the universe – [. . .] but it cannot be understood unless one first learns to comprehend the language and interpret the characters in which it is written. It is written in the language of mathematics.[15]

When Galileo understands mathematics as the language of the Book of Nature, he takes it to represent the physical world and to derive its truth and meaning from this relation to reality. Following from this link is the assumption that everything written in the language of mathematics stems from nature and therefore exists. In the sixteenth century Nicolaus Copernicus was among the first to argue not only for the equivalence of maths and reality but to grant priority to mathematical truth: 'Copernicus only offered entirely abstract mathematical arguments. No matter how contrary to natural philosophy the motion of the earth may seem, Copernicus insisted, it must be true *because the mathematics demands it*. This was revolutionary.'[16] While Copernicus himself held maths to describe truths about the physical world, his contemporaries understood his heliocentric system as a model only and more generally regarded mathematics as merely an auxiliary construction to gain knowledge about nature. Thanks to this misreading the Catholic Church did not challenge Copernicus, while, when Galileo took up Copernicus's work and insisted on the physical reality of the mathematical description, he met with opposition and was put under house arrest by the Inquisition. Questions about the truth of maths and its relation to nature thus had far-reaching consequences in the sixteenth and seventeenth centuries as mathematics began to challenge the explanatory system of Christianity and rival physical reality itself.

Galileo's programme of a detailed study of nature based on mathematics began to replace the practices of natural philosophy and its aim to provide an explanation of the entire system of the world. Later, protagonists in the Enlightenment movement that highly valued reason and scientific method similarly accorded mathematics a prominent place: Thomas Hobbes developed the view that reason is calculation, and Immanuel Kant accounted for the successes of mathematical truths that described nature so adequately by creating for it a new category of knowledge: synthetic judgement a priori. Mathematical knowledge is synthetic as a calculation puts together different facts and arrives at new knowledge: for example, the elements 5 and 7 add up to 12, a new element.[17] And since mathematical knowledge is not derived from experience, it constitutes knowledge a priori. As such it is independent of context, and any mathematical description of the world could be regarded as absolutely certain and true. Pierre-Simon Laplace formulated the extreme consequences of believing in a mathematically describable world in 1814, when he asserted that theoretically an intellect – later called 'Laplace's demon' – could know all determinants of the universe and express it in a single formula according to which past, present and future could be calculated. A single mathematical formula would thus encompass the whole universe at all times, and mathematics as the description of all space and time would be the true language of reality.

The view of mathematics as the most certain science and perfect language of nature was dominant until the mid-nineteenth century. From the perspective of the early 1900s, the mathematician and philosopher Henri Poincaré summarised: 'Mathematical truths are derived from a few self-evident propositions, by a chain of flawless reasonings; they are imposed not only on us, but on Nature itself. By them the Creator is fettered.'[18] However, at the time of outlining this traditional understanding, Poincaré had witnessed the discovery of new concepts that drew attention to the fact that not all of mathematics has counterparts in nature and a rethinking of its relation to reality had begun to take place. In geometry, which had been based on five intuitively true axioms formulated by Euclid in the third century BC, mathematicians constructed new systems that contradicted the established rules: violating Euclid's parallel postulate, in these geometries there is no pair of straight lines that are at constant distance from each other. Farkas Bolyai warned his son János about the consequences of developing a non-Euclidean geometry, and his dramatic language illustrates that the failure of the seemingly self-evident parallel axiom affected not only mathematics but also the general sense of certainty:

> I have traversed this bottomless night, which extinguished all light and joy of my life. [...] I turned back when I saw that no man can reach the

bottom of this night. I turned back unconsoled, pitying myself and all mankind.[19]

Unabashed, János Bolyai published his findings of non-Euclidean geometry in 1832, and when Bernhard Riemann later showed that infinitely many geometries that are not Euclidean can be constructed, there was overwhelming proof that a fundamental premise of the field was not correct. Poincaré summarised the reactions: 'If several geometries are possible, they say, is it certain that our geometry is the one that is true?'[20] The coexistence of several systems showed that the traditional Euclidean geometry is not more true than other, equally possible systems, but that the definition of its axioms 'can only be more convenient'.[21] The discovery of non-Euclidean geometries thus gave rise to questioning mathematics as the language of nature that arrives at certain truths about the world.

If worrying concepts appeared in geometry, mathematicians even more readily identified fundamental questions in algebra. In 1831 William Rowan Hamilton stated that '[n]o candid and intelligent person can doubt the truth of the chief properties of *Parallel Lines*, as set forth by Euclid in his Elements', while in algebra 'it requires no peculiar scepticism to doubt, or even to disbelieve, the doctrine of Negatives and Imaginaries'.[22] The idea of debt renders the concept of negative quantities quite readily graspable, but the counter-intuitive 'existence' of imaginary numbers meant that their wide acceptance did not come about until well into the nineteenth century. The very term 'imaginary' points to questions about the reality and existence of these numbers – an issue we will further examine in Chapter 1. Since discoveries of alternatives to the taken-for-granted geometry and algebra suggested that reference to physical reality could not adequately prove mathematical existence, it came to be seen as relying on coherence in the system itself: 'mathematicians fashioned for themselves a new image of the subject: autonomous, abstract, largely axiomatic, and unconstrained by applications even to physics'.[23] The notion that maths does not have a direct representational relationship with nature is a main feature of its modern development, and the release from the constraints of realist representation had enormous implications for the discipline and beyond. The mathematician Marshall Stone even claims it to mark 'one of the most significant intellectual advances in the history of mankind'.[24] But the modern view also elicited great concern when a question arose from the realisation that mathematics does not rest on its relation to nature: what are the foundations of mathematics that guarantee its truth and meaning?

THE FOUNDATIONAL CRISIS OF MATHEMATICS

This question – what are the foundations of mathematics that guarantee its truth and meaning? – is at the core of the so-called 'foundational crisis of mathematics', which took place from the 1880s to about 1930. With notions of truth, meaning and existence at the root of debates, the upheaval was not purely mathematical but also marked by philosophical concerns. The sense of crisis accordingly registers in talk *about* mathematics, for example in philosophical works or in speeches and prose writing by practising mathematicians such as David Hilbert, whose description of the situation as 'intolerable' indicates what was at stake: 'If mathematical thinking is defective, where are we to find truth and certitude?'[25] The foundational questions also immediately impacted on the development of the discipline: it split into the schools of logicism, formalism and intuitionism, each attempting to set mathematics on new foundations. Logicism, founded by Gottlob Frege in 1884, views maths as part of logic; the formalist school around Hilbert understands it as a self-contained formal system; and intuitionism with its founding father L. E. J. Brouwer identifies human intuition as the foundation of maths.[26] All three schools share in the characteristic modern development: they do not claim a direct representational relationship between mathematics and nature. But an antagonism inside this modern movement incited the foundational crisis, which mainly played out between the schools of formalism and intuitionism. In a highly influential monograph from 1990, Herbert Mehrtens situates the mathematical conflict in a wider cultural and social context and advocates understanding it as part of modernist discourse: '"Modernism" and "counter-modernism" are the terms for two opposing forms of the self-understanding and style of mathematics.'[27] Before turning to relations between mathematical and literary modernism, a closer look at the formalist school, which Mehrtens equates with modernism, and at the counter-modernist intuitionist stance will bring into view wider implications of the opposed foundational positions.

Formalists and intuitionists drew fundamentally different conclusions from the independence of modern mathematics from physical reality and its consequent want of foundations. Intent on saving the progress made in the nineteenth century, formalists were prepared to circumvent problems by accepting looser notions of mathematical meaning and truth. When Hilbert describes maths as working with symbols that 'have no significance in themselves' in the manner of 'a game played according to certain rules with meaningless marks on paper', he takes existence and truth to reside in the absence of contradictions in the mathematical system.[28] Limited only by a rule against inconsistency, formalist mathematics is entirely free in its development: 'the *essence* of *mathematics* is its *freedom*', as Georg Cantor put it.[29] Unrestrained inside its own system, formalist mathematics claims no relation to any non-mathematical origin or meaning, and limited to manipulating its symbols, it is unresponsive to any demands for extra-mathematical truth or value. Thus, in the formalist understanding, mathematics always points back to itself: it 'has no "reason" apart from itself. "Truth" cannot be saved.'[30]

Counter-modernist intuitionism, as Mehrtens's term already implies, is a reaction against the modernist view, addressing precisely the question that formalism excludes: 'Where is the reference of mathematics to stable reality, which endows it with value and meaning?'[31] In his speeches and prose writing Brouwer, the figurehead of intuitionism, emphasises the moral dimension of mathematics: 'Let the motivation behind mathematics be the craving for the good.'[32] To ensure genuine value and meaning, he set out to construct the subject from scratch, claiming that 'man builds up pure mathematics out of the basic intuition of the intellect'.[33] This means that, in Brouwer's intuitionist view, maths is a construct of the mind, and the human being, as the link between maths and the world, justifies its truth and meaning. When positing intuition as the origin of mathematical truth, Brouwer compromises its relation to reason; indeed, he asserts: 'mathematics is independent of the so-called *logical laws* (laws of reasoning or of human thought)'.[34] Thus, while formalism attempts to build an independent mathematics on rational foundations, intuitionism abandons logic and traces maths to a human origin, which connects it to the world and allows advancing a moral practice. Hilbert complained about the resulting restriction of mathematical freedom and about the 'subjectivism [. . .] which, as it seems to me, finds it [sic] apex in intuitionism' and appeared, to him, to destroy and disfigure mathematics.[35] On the other hand, Brouwer objected to the abandonment of truth and value by the formalist school. As Mehrtens puts it: 'The difference between modernist and counter-modernist mathematics boils down to the question: reality and eternal truth or creative freedom and freedom from contradiction?'[36]

The speeches and prose writings of Hilbert and Brouwer show that the points of conflict between modernist and counter-modernist orientations were not purely mathematical but that they addressed philosophical questions and included moral arguments. In an overview of the crisis in maths and its split into conflicting schools, Ernst Snapper draws attention to the role of emotional reasons, contending that the arguments were ultimately 'grounded in a deep sense as to what mathematics is all about'.[37] Feelings about what mathematics ought to be dominated the last phases of the crisis in the 1920s, when the conflict between modernist and counter-modernist orientations came to a head in a personal clash between Hilbert and Brouwer and their supporters. By that time, intuitionism had gained philosophical support and the majority of mathematicians accepted it as a valid foundational theory. However, since intuitionism dismisses established theorems and introduces others that do not hold in classical mathematics, most practitioners, unwilling to sacrifice a substantial part of well-working traditional methods, rejected it and agreed with Hilbert's objection to Brouwer's programme: 'With your methods most of the results of modern mathematics would have to be abandoned, and to me the important thing is not to get fewer results but to get more results.'[38]

If intuitionism failed the practice test, Kurt Gödel proved the impossibility of accomplishing the formalist programme, demonstrating that Hilbert's aim to define a complete and consistent set of axioms as the foundation of mathematics cannot be realised. Gödel's incompleteness theorem refers to formal systems whose axioms allow doing arithmetic – a qualification that is often ignored in popular accounts of Gödel's theorem and its application to non-mathematical contexts. Yet, illustrating its structure in a non-technical example can clarify the argument: the truth value of the sentence 'This sentence is unprovable' is undecidable. If the sentence is taken to be true, it is unprovable, meaning that its correctness cannot be proven. If by contrast the statement is taken to be false, then it should be provable, but it can only be proven to be unprovable, thus leading to a contradiction. Gödel's incompleteness theorem uses a comparable metalanguage in maths to demonstrate that every foundational system contains undecidable sentences, and it follows that defining a complete and consistent foundation of mathematics is impossible. With this verdict, Hilbert's programme had failed, but when Gödel published his work in 1931 the sense of crisis had already subsided and most mathematicians were content to use the flawed but nevertheless well-working formalist approach rather than resort to the restrictive and inconvenient intuitionist framework. As the historian of mathematics Dirk van Dalen puts it, Hilbert 'won the conflict in the social sense' even though he 'had lost it in the scientific sense'.[39] The foundational crisis of mathematics thus did not end with a solution or clear winner, but its questions and the coexistence of contradictory positions ceased to be perceived as problematical. That the crisis was not resolved but simply faded from view further suggests that it was not a purely scientific upheaval but that much of the sense of uncertainty derived from its implications for notions of meaning, truth and value and could not be appeased with mathematical means. The philosophical and moral questions in modern mathematics connect it with similar concerns in other fields at the time and constitute a basis for locating maths in the cultural context of modernism.

Mathematical Modernism

Moritz Epple remembers the 1980s as a time when it was common in European maths departments to talk about a mathematical modernism and compare transformations in maths around 1900 with modernist developments in literature, painting or music.[40] The publication of Mehrtens's monograph in 1990 introduced the topic into scholarly discussion, and his comparison between characteristics of maths and modernist art continues to animate debate. Mehrtens writes: 'The two common traits of the various modernisms that I identify as central are, first, the autonomy of cultural production and, second, the departure from the vision of an immediate representation of the world of experience.'[41] The independence of mathematical development and the turn away from a direct representational relation to physical reality are regular features in definitions of mathematical modernism and its analogies with movements in the arts. Jeremy Gray draws on these characteristics to prepare the basis of his argument that modern mathematics relates 'to the rise of modernism in cultural spheres such as painting, music, and literature' and should be viewed as a cultural phenomenon:

> Modernism can be defined as an autonomous body of ideas, pursued with little outward reference, maintaining a complicated, rather than a naïve, relationship with the day-to-day world and drawn to the formal aspects of the discipline. It is introspective to the point of anxiety; and is the *de facto* view of a coherent group of people, such as a professional, discipline-based group, who were profoundly serious in their intentions. As a philosophy (taking the term in its broadest sense) it is in sharp contrast to the immediately preceding one in each of its fields.[42]

This definition of modernism, as carefully phrased as it may be, is indicative of a challenge: as the concept of modernism is far from clearly defined in any one discipline, how is it possible to identify common modernist characteristics across different fields? Leo Corry notes this problem in his contribution to the essay collection *Modernism in the Sciences*, where he also criticises searching for preconceived modernist characteristics rather than developing these from mathematics itself. The former is an explicit method in Mehrtens's approach; he explains that he 'chose the term "modernism" for mathematics to be able to embed the history of science into its cultural context', and Gray similarly draws on the already available framework of modernism to explore mathematical trends.[43] Working with fuzzy and changeable concepts and facing the difficulty of examining relations between fields without preconceptions is common in any interdisciplinary research, but it may be particularly challenging in view of the relatively short tradition of cultural and historical studies on mathematics.

Coming to the study of science and the arts from a literary perspective, Gillian Beer in her seminal essay 'Translation or Transformation?' includes mathematics, the field seemingly furthest removed from literature, when setting out her argument that the relations between the fields go beyond straightforward influence of science on literary subject matter but that there always is a two-way traffic between disciplines. So, while, for example, Marjorie Hope Nicolson in the mid-twentieth century did pioneering, if now largely forgotten, work on the effects of science on literary production, and Linda Dalrymple Henderson's influential examination of modern painters' engagement with non-Euclidean geometry similarly leans towards a one-way model of influence, Beer also considers exchange in the reverse direction. She uses Benoît Mandelbrot's fractal geometry to show that cultural influence affects the terminology and thereby the reaction to mathematical concepts: Mandelbrot employs Gothic terms to describe his fractals, and names such as 'Cross Lumped Curdling Monsters' or 'Knotted Peano Monsters, Tamed' represent the unsettling nature of the structures while also rendering them more familiar. Investigating mutual impact without granting precedence to either side as sole origin of the other is now the established standard in literature and science studies.

In cultural studies of mathematics the two-way traffic approach is not common and scholars distances themselves from any notion of influence: 'the mathematical [changes] described here and the better-known artistic ones happened independently', Gray insists.[44] He is wary of the temptation to overstate analogous developments in different fields, cautioning scholars 'not to collapse into the arms of a generalization so sweeping that Picasso sits on the page with Einstein and Noether'.[45] At the same time, researchers agree that the modernist transformation of mathematics is too pervasive to exclusively examine it in tightly focused analyses and that only broader strokes can do justice to its import and the similarities between developments in maths and modernist culture. Several historians favour an approach that explains these simultaneous movements by supposing an underlying field or general process, with Corry proposing to identify the common ground of various modernist developments by focusing on the historical processes shared across all fields.[46] It is not clear what such a process would look like or how it could be determined except by examining its concrete implementations, that is, the very phenomena it is supposed to occasion. However, scholars stress the importance of institutional and disciplinary changes in this context and point to the distinctiveness of German mathematics, in which much of the modernist transformation took place.

When William Whewell coined the word 'scientist' in 1833, it signalled the emergence of a community of professionals, and by the 1860s members of this profession were no longer expected to also be experts in literature and vice versa. The tendency towards specialisation also informed the development of mathematics, where practitioners paid increasing attention to differences between their field and the natural sciences. In nineteenth-century Germany the sciences and humanities similarly formed into separate domains, yet, though broadly similar to the British course in terms of specialisation, German mathematics took a distinct route in its institutional and disciplinary development. While British mathematics focused on application and thus maintained a closer connection to the natural sciences, the German counterpart was characterised by pure, abstract considerations and philosophical concerns: it was marked by 'the preference for a strictly theoretical orientation, the concentration on narrowly defined specialities or branches of mathematics, and in many cases a close attention to the philosophical presuppositions of the advocated theories'.[47] The University of Göttingen, the centre of mathematical research around 1900, profited from an unparalleled connection between mathematicians and philosophers, and this close contact productively informed the debate around notions of truth, meaning and existence that crucially informed the modernist transformation of maths. In the 1920s the close exchange between German-speaking philosophers and mathematicians continued in the Vienna Circle up to its disintegration in the politically charged climate of the 1930s. The respective focuses on applied and abstract mathematics and the different degrees of institutional proximity with philosophy also influenced the resources available to mathematically interested laypersons. At the close of the nineteenth century, the history of mathematics had a firm place in German mathematical culture, while it was side-lined in the British focus on empiricism and only received some modest attention after the Second World War with the foundation of the British Society for the History of Science.[48] The different institutional and disciplinary conditions in Britain and Germany go some way in explaining the leading role of German mathematics in its modernist transformation and, accordingly, in Pynchon's, Broch's and Musil's literary visions of maths in modernist culture.

Since the first publication on mathematical modernism in 1990, several scholars have proposed modifications to Mehrtens's approach. Where the pioneering study focuses on the German context, Gray extends the analysis across national and disciplinary lines. Epple also supports Mehrtens's interpretation but criticises his concentration on external historiography: 'His sources are mainly the programmatic declarations of the mathematicians involved and the documents of their institutional activities. Mehrtens [...] makes no claims about the internal construction of modern mathematics.'[49] He also points to the limitations of focusing on mathematics as a language and extends the analysis to concrete acts in mathematical practice, using the example of abstract and concrete writing to support Mehrtens's conclusions with a view to mathematical construction itself.[50] Calls for further studies mainly address scholars in the history of mathematics; yet, with this book I hope to show that literary studies also open up rewarding sources of inquiry and contribute a fruitful perspective to research on modernist mathematics.

Mathematics, Art and Fiction

'[M]athematics, though classified as a science, is equally an art.'[51] Brian Rotman's remark in *The Routledge Companion to Literature and Science* follows in a tradition of comparing mathematicians with artists, which received a boost with the realisation in the nineteenth century that it is possible to consciously construct new mathematical structures, for example non-Euclidean geometries. G. H. Hardy's *A Mathematician's Apology* (1940) gives a sustained account of this view when drawing heavily on the comparison with the arts to explain what mathematics is and why it should be pursued. 'I am interested in mathematics only as a creative art', Hardy declares and proclaims both to share a common aesthetics, claiming that '[t]he mathematician's patterns, like the painter's or the poet's, must be *beautiful* [. . .]. Beauty is the first test: there is no permanent place in the world for ugly mathematics.'[52] For Hardy, the aesthetic dimension is the main reason to practise pure mathematics: he praises its capacity to create '"[i]maginary" universes [which] are so much more beautiful than this stupidly constructed "real" one', and asserts that since it has no immediate connection to the real world, maths 'must be justified as art if it can be justified at all'.[53] Other practitioners in the early twentieth century similarly highlighted creativity in their field and suggested it to share qualities with the sphere of art: Poincaré held that 'mathematical reasoning has of itself a kind of creative virtue', and Hermann Weyl proposed that '"[m]athematizing" may well be a creative activity of man'.[54] Outside the discipline, too, the decades around 1900 saw the appearance of concepts that consider mathematics as a human construct and tool to deliberately create imaginary universes. I here introduce such views in the philosophical works of Friedrich Nietzsche, Oswald Spengler, Ernst Cassirer and Hans Vaihinger, before turning to the literary perspective on connections between mathematics and fiction in Chapters 1 to 4.

'This complete reliability of mathematics is an illusion, it does not exist, at least not unconditionally.'[55] The decidedly negative terms in which the mathematician Oskar Perron summed up the situation in 1911 express the sense of anxiety that marks the years of the foundational crisis. As the basic assumptions of maths were under revision, the 'growing appreciation of error leading to a note of anxiety, hesitant at first but persistent by 1900' tied in with feelings of a loss of confidence in other domains.[56] In the non-mathematical sphere, the sense of crisis and questioning of absolute certainty, finding their height in the First World War, were prominently associated with the nihilistic thinking of Friedrich Nietzsche: 'The present European War is [. . .] even called "Nietzsche in Action," or the "Euro-Nietzschean (or Anglo-Nietzschean) War"', William Salter asserted in 1917.[57] Nietzsche's writing resonated widely when it pronounces a crisis of the foundations of Western thought and the necessity for a *'revaluation of all values'*: 'the weight of all things must be determined anew'.[58] It also expresses a commonly held view when connecting the diagnosis of a decline of Christian faith with the demand for certainty in other areas, with the greatest hopes being invested in the scientific domain. Arguing that, together with faith, the rules of what is considered morally good and valuable disappear and trigger modern disintegration, Nietzsche proposes mathematics as best suited for establishing new grounds for truth. He demands to 'introduce the subtlety and rigour of mathematics into all sciences', with 'sciences' – from German *Wissenschaften* – encompassing both the natural sciences and the humanities.[59] The proposal that '[m]athematics is [. . .] the means to general and final knowledge of humanity' can be read as a celebration of its role in establishing a completely scientific view and an alternative to religion, but Nietzsche also discusses aspects of its modern development that are in conflict with this notion: he acknowledges that the most certain science is itself part of the modern crisis of foundational beliefs.[60]

Nietzsche qualifies his professed confidence in mathematics when he draws on it to rethink the very certainty of knowledge and develop the idea that reality cannot be perceived directly but is always interpreted. According to his perspectivism, 'facts is precisely what there is not, only interpretations. [. . . The world] has no meaning behind it, but countless meanings.'[61] Even mathematics is caught up in this process and produces interpretations rather than getting to the facts of reality directly: 'logic (like geometry and arithmetic) applies only to fictitious entities that we have created'.[62] Nietzsche thus does not take maths to constitute Truth or to stand in a representational relationship to nature, and elsewhere in his writing, he describes it to be not a language of fact but a language of fiction: 'The arithmetic formulas, too, are only regulating fictions which we use to simplify and arrange real events to our proportion.'[63] Indeed, he considers the 'fiction' of mathematics to be 'false' and to distort the world:

> [O]ur fundamental tendency is to assert that the falsest judgements (to which synthetic judgments *a priori* [e.g. mathematics] belong) are the most indispensable to us, that without granting as true the fictions of logic, [. . .] without a continual falsification of the world by means of numbers, mankind could not live.[64]

According to Nietzsche then, mathematics is not true, but it is claimed to be so because it is indispensable to life. It is consistent with this view of maths as a 'false' but necessary fiction that the foundational crisis subsided in the pragmatic practice of acknowledging the unsolved problems while holding on to the still beneficial tools. Influenced by Nietzsche, other philosophers further developed the idea of maths as a useful fiction.

Inspired by Nietzsche, Oswald Spengler connects the crisis in mathematics with a wider sense of deterioration in his controversial *The Decline of the West*, published in 1918 and 1922. He regards maths not as incontrovertible truth but as a field that evolves and changes in accordance with the spirit of the time and differs between cultures. So, while concepts such as irrational and imaginary numbers are deemed 'impossible, futile and senseless' in certain periods, in other cultures or times the same 'mathematical [. . .] way of thinking is right, convincing, a "necessity of thought"'.[65] From the changeableness of what is considered mathematically valid, Spengler concludes that '[t]here is not, and cannot be, number as such. There are several number-worlds as there are several Cultures'.[66] Following from the idea that 'there are more mathematics than one', any one instance of mathematics – any *mathematic* – cannot be said to be objective and absolute: mathematical '[t]ruths are truths only in relation to a particular mankind'.[67] With this verdict, Spengler declares maths to be a part of culture and subject to historical change, just like art, philosophy or politics. Indeed, he claims that all expressions of a period are interconnected: '[d]eep relations were revealed between political and mathematical aspects of the same Culture', and '[e]very philosophy has hitherto grown up in conjunction with a mathematic *belonging* to it'.[68] In Spengler's view, then, mathematics does not inhabit a special position among the disciplines; since it has styles and style-periods, he understands it as essentially belonging to the sphere of art: 'The mathematic, then, is an art.'[69]

Where taking up Nietzsche's perspectivism leads Spengler to claim that a monolithic '"Mathematics" is an illusion' and that any specific implementation is an art, Ernst Cassirer refers to the contemporary mathematical discussion itself to argue for considering maths not in terms of absolute truth but of language and art.[70] Viewing maths as a symbolic form that represents the 'ideal relations' of systemic structures, Cassirer situates his comparison with language and art in the re-examination of 'fundamental doctrines' and 'the conflict between "formalism" and "intuitionism" in its present acute form'.[71] If the former fields construct 'a peculiar and independent, self-contained world of meaning according to an inherent formative law of [their] own', mathematics is similarly characterised by adherence to its own rules that take precedence over physical reality: it 'builds up this [natural] world according to its structure and so teaches us to understand it through the laws that prevail in it'.[72] According to Cassirer, the introduction of ideal elements that have no empirical correspondence, such as points without extension or imaginary numbers, results in a detachment of mathematics and the real world but does not inhibit its usefulness. Rather, the 'unquestionable fruitfulness of the ideal elements' enhances the discipline.[73] With the notion of useful yet empirically non-existent ideal formations, Cassirer reflects Nietzsche's view of mathematics as a necessary fiction. However, he also proposes that since the concept of number expresses the rational method in general, the mathematical crisis impacts on the very foundations of knowledge: as modern maths limits itself to working inside its self-created structures, it is '[f]or the purposes of knowledge of nature, in the positivistic sense of the word, [. . .] a constant danger'.[74] Turning away from physical reality and 'let[ting] the empirical determinateness of being disappear into the freedom and caprice of thought', the discipline at the foundation of knowledge is at the core of a general epistemological crisis.[75]

Hans Vaihinger, one of the first academic philosophers to engage with Nietzsche's work, further examines the relation between mathematical ideals and fiction in *The Philosophy of 'As If'*, published in 1911. Claiming that 'all ideals, logically considered, are fictions', Vaihinger argues that the ideal elements of mathematics, such as '*negative* numbers, *fractions*, and *irrational* and *imaginary* numbers', are paradoxical fictions and that mathematics as a whole is 'based upon an entirely imaginary foundation, indeed upon contradictions'.[76] He portrays the twentieth century as a time that makes particularly heavy use of such elements: 'Modern mathematics is characterized specifically by the freedom with which it forms these fictional constructs.'[77] Due to its productive employment of imaginary and paradoxical properties, modern maths constitutes a model for other areas: Vaihinger responds to the statement 'Freedom is only an entity of thought' by declaring that living without the imaginary is impossible and that human beings have to retain the ideal of freedom 'just as the mathematicians, for example, retain imaginary ideal points in spite of their inner contradiction'.[78] Modern maths with its characteristic independence from physical reality thus provides an exemplar to areas of twentieth-century life that lose room for manoeuvre, for example when being increasingly dominated by processes of rationalisation. In this way, Vaihinger establishes the case of modern mathematics as a forerunner of a more general valuation of the fictional.

The works by Nietzsche, Spengler, Cassirer and Vaihinger are examples of philosophical engagement with mathematics at the time of its modernisation, and they form part of the modernist culture in which it is proposed to participate. Philosophers in the later twentieth century further develop the implications of viewing maths as based upon fictions, both for the field itself and in view of its exemplary status for other areas of knowledge and life. In 1980 Hartry Field introduced a sustained theory of mathematical fictionalism. Developed in *Science without Numbers*, fictionalism maintains that mathematical theories refer to objects that do not exist and that they therefore cannot be said to be true. Field compares the notion of mathematical truth to that of literary fiction where statements are correct according to the conditions set out in the text but not in reference to reality. For example, the statement 'Oliver Twist lived in London' is true when considered in the fictional universe of Charles Dickens's *Oliver Twist*, but it is not true in reality since Oliver Twist is a fictional character and never existed. Accordingly, Field explains:

> [T]he fictionalist can say that the sense in which '2+2=4' is true is pretty much the same as the sense in which 'Oliver Twist lived in London' is true: the latter is true only in the sense that it is true *according to a certain well-known story*, and the former is true only in that it is true *according to standard mathematics*.[79]

Field asserts that fictional mathematics can be useful despite its lack of truth and that maths is precisely an advantageous but not a necessary part of science. He demonstrates his conviction that maths is not indispensable but only facilitates formulating and working with scientific theories, by exemplarily reformulating Newton's gravitational theory without reference to mathematical entities. The proposition that there can be science without number challenges the view that mathematical theories must be true because they are so extremely useful in empirical science. This common contention is formally formulated in the Quine–Putnam indispensability argument, and Field's fictionalism was largely rejected precisely because it does not offer a convincing explanation of what Eugene Wigner calls the 'unreasonable effectiveness of mathematics'.[80] While Wigner accepts the 'miracle of the appropriateness of the language of mathematics [...] as] a wonderful gift which we neither understand nor deserve', the physicist and philosopher Gerhard Vollmer puts forward a combination of reasons for the applicability of mathematics to the world: mathematics describes structures; nature is structured; mankind is adapted to the structured world through evolution and can recognise some of these structures; and, finally, language, logic and mathematics are tools to formulate structures that cannot be recognised directly, for example because they are too large or too small.[81] Although mathematical fictionalism did not find wide acceptance, it triggered a lot of response and shows how early twentieth-century philosophical theories that relate mathematical existence with fiction can suggest general comparisons between the ontological status of maths and literature.

The French philosopher Alain Badiou explicitly takes mathematics to ontological concerns when he argues that number is not 'an operational fiction' but that '[n]umber is *a form of Being*'.[82] He develops this statement from the view that maths has no direct relation to reality and ultimately refers to and thus 'is' itself, so that '[i]n mathematics, being, thought, and consistency are one and the same thing'.[83] For Badiou, maths is thus not a fiction fruitfully employed to gain knowledge, but he claims that 'mathematics *is* ontology – the science of being qua being'.[84] The physicist Max Tegmark advances this notion from the scientific side: in his controversial Mathematical Universe Hypothesis, he argues that physical reality is a mathematical structure.[85] Badiou's and Tegmark's views can be summarised in Badiou's assertion 'mathematics=ontology', and they complete the transition from philosophical concern with the role of mathematical fictions for knowledge to examining maths in terms of being.[86] If, roughly speaking, over the course of the twentieth century epistemological questions regarding mathematics and fiction yield to ontological interests, Brian McHale has argued for a similar shift of dominant in view of modernist and postmodernist literary fiction. The possible relations between epistemological and ontological concerns in maths and in literature are the topic of Chapters 1 to 4.

MODERNISM AND MATHEMATICS: MODERNIST INTERRELATIONS IN FICTION

This book explores relations of mathematics and modernism with a focus on literary fiction and its negotiations of the place of maths in historical and cultural contexts and in innovations in literary form. Pynchon's *Against the*

Day and *Gravity's Rainbow*, Broch's *The Sleepwalkers* trilogy and Musil's *The Man without Qualities* all accord maths and the philosophical questions accompanying its modern development a central place in their visions, while their distinct temporal and cultural perspectives invite comparison. The works of the Austrian authors Broch and Musil are part of the modernist culture in which mathematics is understood to participate, and they are, moreover, produced and set in the German-speaking context in which much of its transformation took place. As a contemporary American writer, Pynchon presents the period of crisis from a temporal as well as spatial distance. His novels engage with discoveries in modern German mathematics and are partly set in the country, but *Against the Day* and *Gravity's Rainbow* also point to their times of production as periods of cultural and disciplinary redefinition. Each of the texts includes mathematics in an encyclopaedic attempt to present the assumptions underlying Western culture and compares it to modern and modernist movements in various other fields. Contrasting their different temporal perspectives and comparing Broch's and Musil's modernist stylistic experimentations and decisive developments in Pynchon's postmodernist practice will illuminate the role of mathematics in innovations in novelistic form.

The non-chronological order of the chapters taps into the productive comparative potential of combining texts that explore modernism and mathematics from different perspectives. Chapter 1 on Pynchon's *Against the Day* focuses on interrelations between mathematics and politics as domains that are both shaken by crises of fundamental beliefs and in need of review. From a postmodern vantage point, the novel explores diverse paths of development that were still open at the turn to the twentieth century, and, reactivating possibilities from an informed later position, it provides an almost ideal basis for the examination of Broch's and Musil's perspectives closer to the time's actual unfolding. Their works are similarly set against the background of the First World War, but, written when the legacies of the war could still be felt and the foundational debate of maths was just subsiding, the texts are themselves part of the modernist renegotiation of mathematical knowledge and its place in culture. Chapter 2 on Broch's *The Sleepwalkers* analyses relations between mathematics and turn-of-the-century scepticism of language and investigation of form, while the examination of Musil's *The Man without Qualities* in Chapter 3 focuses on the place of maths in epistemological and ethical questions. Chapter 4 sets the engagement with modernist mathematics into broader context when examining the rise, fall and transformation of Enlightenment thinking and science in Pynchon's *Gravity's Rainbow*. This last chapter also zeroes in on a subject that runs through all sections: the interrelations of mathematics and fiction.

Examining ways in which texts incorporate mathematics as part of modernist fiction and culture, this book adds a literary perspective to studies of mathematical modernism. The analysis and historicising of their relations also points to the specific conditions of studying mathematics in the wider field of literature and science: particularly in view of its modern transformation when its distinct characteristics gain prominence, the need for a more specialised study of mathematics becomes compelling. And, not least, exploring mathematics in the works of Pynchon, Broch and Musil affords deeper insights into their literary visions and allows us to appreciate that, indeed, '[m]ighty are numbers; joined with art, resistless'.

Notes

1. The quotation circulates in this form that associates mathematics and art, particularly among mathematicians; see, for example, the collection of mathematical quotations by Robert Moritz, *Memorabilia Mathematica; or the Philomath's Quotation-book* (New York: Macmillan, 1914), p. 246. However, a more common translation is: 'Numbers are a fearful thing, and joined to craft a desperate foe' (Euripides, *Hecuba. The Plays of Euripides II*, trans. Edward P. Coleridge (London: Bell, 1891), p. 157).
2. Euripides, *Hecuba*, p. 157.
3. 'the clearest example': 'am deutlichsten' (DSW 533). I quote from published English translations and occasionally amend a quotation and give the original in a footnote. Where texts are not available in English, I use my own translation and cite the original in a footnote.
4. Michael H. Whitworth, *Einstein's Wake: Relativity, Metaphor, and Modernist Literature* (Oxford: Oxford University Press, 2001), p. 130.
5. Ezra Pound, 'Meditatio' [1916], in *Pound/Joyce: The Letters of Ezra Pound to James Joyce, with Pound's Essays on Joyce*, ed. Forrest Read (London: Faber & Faber, 1967), pp. 69–74.
6. Ezra Pound, *Literary Essays of Ezra Pound*, ed. T. S. Eliot (London: Faber & Faber, 1954), p. 316.
7. Tim Armstrong, *Modernism: A Cultural History* (Cambridge and Malden, MA: Polity, 2005), p. 117.
8. Alice Jenkins, 'George Eliot, Geometry and Gender', in *Literature and Science*, ed. Sharon Ruston (Woodbridge: D. S. Brewer, 2008), pp. 72–90.
9. Whitworth, *Einstein's Wake*, p. 198.
10. Whitworth, *Einstein's Wake*, p. 234.
11. Bernd-Olaf Küppers, *Physik der Geschichte? Zur Annäherung von Natur- und Geisteswissenschaften* (Paderborn: Universität-Gesamthochschule Paderborn, 1991), p. 104.
12. Norbert Wiener, *I Am a Mathematician* (London: Gollancz, 1956), p. 62.
13. David Bloor, *Knowledge and Social Imagery* (London: Routledge & Kegan Paul, 1976), p. 2.
14. Ivor Grattan-Guinness, 'Does History of Science Treat of the History of Science? The Case of Mathematics', *History of Science*, 28.2 (1990), 149–73 (p. 157).
15. Galileo Galilei, et al., *The Controversy on the Comets of 1618*, trans. Stillman Drake and C. D. O'Malley (Philadelphia: University of Philadelphia Press, 1960), pp. 183–4.
16. John Henry, *The Scientific Revolution and the Origins of Modern Science* (Basingstoke: Palgrave, 2002), p. 17.
17. Immanuel Kant, *Critique of Pure Reason*, trans. Norman Kemp Smith, 2nd edn (Basingstoke: Palgrave Macmillan, 2007), pp. 52–3.

18. Henri Poincaré, *Science and Hypothesis*, trans. W. J. G. (London and Newcastle on Tyne: Walter Scott, 1905), p. xxi.
19. Jeremy J. Gray, *János Bolyai, Non-Euclidean Geometry, and the Nature of Space* (Cambridge, MA: Burndy, 2004), p. 51. Mathematical concepts not immediately relevant to the argument are explained in the glossary (see here the entry 'non-Euclidean geometry'). The glossary also holds definitions of frequently used mathematical terms.
20. Poincaré, *Science and Hypothesis*, p. 48.
21. Poincaré, *Science and Hypothesis*, p. 50.
22. William Rowan Hamilton, 'Theory of Conjugate Functions, or Algebraic Couples; with a Preliminary and Elementary Essay on Algebra as the Science of Pure Time', *The Transactions of the Royal Irish Academy*, 17 (1831), 293–422 (p. 294).
23. Jeremy J. Gray, *Plato's Ghost: The Modernist Transformation of Mathematics* (Princeton and Oxford: Princeton University Press, 2008), p. 305.
24. Marshall Stone, 'The Revolution in Mathematics', *The American Mathematical Monthly*, 68.8 (1961), 715–34 (p. 716).
25. David Hilbert, 'On the Infinite' [1925], in *Philosophy of Mathematics: Selected Readings*, ed. Paul Benacerraf and Hilary Putnam (Oxford: Blackwell, 1964), 134–51 (p. 141).
26. For a very readable description of the nature and respective failures of the three mathematical schools, see Ernst Snapper, 'The Three Crises in Mathematics: Logicism, Intuitionism and Formalism', *Mathematics Magazine*, 52.4 (1979), 207–16.
27. See Herbert Mehrtens, *Moderne Sprache Mathematik: Eine Geschichte des Streits um die Grundlagen der Disziplin und des Subjekts formaler Systeme* (Frankfurt am Main: Suhrkamp, 1990). Here quoted from: Herbert Mehrtens, 'Modernism vs. Counter-Modernism, Nationalism vs. Internationalism: Style and Politics in Mathematics, 1900–1950', in *L'Europe mathématique: histoires, mythes, identités*, ed. Catherine Goldstein, Jeremy Gray and Jim Ritter (Paris: Éditions de la Maison de l'homme, 1996), 518–29 (p. 519).
28. Hilbert, 'On the Infinite', p. 143; Hilbert qtd in David M. Burton, *The History of Mathematics: An Introduction* (Boston et al.: McGraw-Hill, 2007), p. 621.
29. 'das *Wesen* der *Mathematik* liegt gerade in ihrer *Freiheit*' (Georg Cantor, 'Über unendliche, lineare Punktmannigfaltigkeiten V', *Mathematische Annalen*, 21.4 (1883), 545–91 (p. 564)).
30. 'der Diskurs der Mathematik keinen "Grund" hat außer sich selbst. Die "Wahrheit" ist nicht zu retten' (Mehrtens, *Moderne Sprache Mathematik*, p. 520).
31. 'Wo also ist der Bezug der Mathematik zur festen Wirklichkeit, der ihr Wert und Sinn gibt?' (Mehrtens, *Moderne Sprache Mathematik*, p. 436).
32. Brouwer qtd in Dirk van Dalen, *Mystic, Geometer, and Intuitionist: The Life of L. E. J. Brouwer; vol. 1: The Dawning Revolution* (Oxford: Clarendon, 1999), p. 82.
33. Luitzen Egbertus Jan Brouwer, 'On the Foundations of Mathematics' [1907], in *L. E. J. Brouwer: Collected Works*, vol. 1, ed. Arend Heyting (Amsterdam and Oxford: North-Holland, 1975), 15–101 (p. 53).
34. Brouwer, 'On the Foundations of Mathematics', p. 72.
35. Hilbert qtd in Dirk van Dalen, *Mystic, Geometer, and Intuitionist II*, pp. 578–9.
36. 'Der Unterschied zwischen Moderne und Gegenmoderne spitzt sich auf die Frage zu: Wirklichkeit und ewige Wahrheit oder Gestaltungsfreiheit und Widerspruchslosigkeit?' (Mehrtens, *Moderne Sprache Mathematik*, p. 237).
37. Snapper, 'The Three Crises in Mathematics', p. 212.
38. Hilbert qtd in Dalen, *Mystic, Geometer, and Intuitionist II*, p. 491.

39. Dalen, *Mystic, Geometer, and Intuitionist II*, p. 639.
40. See Moritz Epple, 'Kulturen der Forschung: Mathematik und Modernität am Beginn des 20. Jahrhunderts', *Wissenskulturen: Über die Erzeugung und Weitergabe von Wissen*, ed. Johannes Fried and Michael Stolleis (Frankfurt am Main: Campus, 2009), 125–58 (p. 129).
41. Mehrtens, 'Modernism vs. Counter-Modernism', p. 521.
42. Jeremy J. Gray, 'Modernism in Mathematics', *The Oxford Handbook of the History of Mathematics*, ed. Eleanor Robson and Jacqueline Stedall (Oxford: Oxford University Press, 2009), 663–83 (p. 663); Jeremy J. Gray, 'Modern Mathematics as a Cultural Phenomenon', in *The Architecture of Mathematics*, ed. José Ferreirós and Jeremy Gray (Oxford: Oxford University Press, 2006), 371–96 (p. 374).
43. Mehrtens, 'Modernism vs. Counter-Modernism', p. 521.
44. Gray, *Plato's Ghost*, p. 14.
45. Gray, 'Modernism in Mathematics', p. 383.
46. Leo Corry, 'How Useful is the Term "Modernism" for Understanding the History of Early Twentieth-Century Mathematics?', in *Science as Cultural Practice: Modernism in the Sciences, ca. 1900–1940*, ed. Moritz Epple and Falk Mueller (Berlin: Akademie Verlag, forthcoming 2020).
47. José Ferreirós Domínguez, *Labyrinth of Thought: A History of Set Theory and its Role in Modern Mathematics* (Basel and Boston, MA: Birkhäuser, 2007), p. 7.
48. Ivor Grattan-Guinness, 'The British Isles', in *Writing the History of Mathematics: Its Historical Development*, ed. Joseph W. Dauben and Christoph J. Scriba (Basel: Birkhäuser, 2002), 161–78 (p. 176).
49. Moritz Epple, 'Styles of Argumentation in Late 19th Century Geometry and the Structure of Mathematical Modernity', in *Analysis and Synthesis in Mathematics: History and Philosophy*, ed. Michael Otte and Marco Panza (Dordrecht and Boston, MA: Kluwer, 1997), 177–98 (p. 191).
50. Moritz Epple, *Die Entstehung der Knotentheorie: Kontexte und Konstruktionen einer modernen mathematischen Theorie* (Braunschweig: Vieweg und Teubner, 1999), chap. 7.
51. Brian Rotman, 'Mathematics', in *The Routledge Companion to Literature and Science*, ed. Bruce Clarke and Manuela Rossini (London and New York: Routledge, 2011), 157–68 (p. 157).
52. G. H. Hardy, *A Mathematician's Apology* [1940] (Cambridge: Cambridge University Press, 1992), pp. 115 and 85.
53. Hardy, *A Mathematician's Apology*, pp. 135 and 139.
54. Poincaré, *Science and Hypothesis*, p. 3; Hermann Weyl, *Philosophy of Mathematics and Natural Science* (Princeton: Princeton University Press, 2009), p. 219.
55. Perron qtd in Jeremy J. Gray, 'Anxiety and Abstraction in Nineteenth-Century Mathematics', *Science in Context*, 17.1/2 (2004), 23–47 (p. 41).
56. Gray, 'Anxiety and Abstraction', p. 23.
57. William Mackintire Salter, 'Nietzsche and the War', *International Journal of Ethics*, 27.3 (1917), 357–79 (p. 357).
58. Friedrich Nietzsche, *Twilight of the Idols, or How to Philosophize with a Hammer* [1889], trans. Duncan Large (Oxford and New York: Oxford University Press, 1998), p. 3, and Friedrich Nietzsche, *The Gay Science* [1882], ed. Bernard Williams, trans. Josefine Nauckhoff (Cambridge: Cambridge University Press, 2001), p. 152.
59. Nietzsche, *The Gay Science*, p. 148.
60. Nietzsche, *The Gay Science*, p. 148.
61. Friedrich Nietzsche, *The Will to Power*, ed. Walter Kaufmann, trans. Walter Kaufmann and R. J. Hollingdale (London: Weidenfeld & Nicolson, 1968), p. 267.

62. Nietzsche, *The Will to Power*, p. 280.
63. 'Die arithmetischen Formeln sind ebenfalls nur regulative Fiktionen, mit denen wir uns das wirkliche Geschehen [...] vereinfachen und zurechtlegen' (Friedrich Nietzsche, 'Posthumous Fragments', NF 1885, Gruppe 38 [2], in *Nietzsche Source; Digital Critical Edition*, ed. Paolo D'Iorio (1885), Web, 30 May 2012, n. pag.).
64. Friedrich Nietzsche, *Beyond Good and Evil* [1886], trans. R. J. Hollingdale (London: Penguin, 2003), p. 35.
65. Oswald Spengler, *The Decline of the West: Form and Actuality*, trans. Charles Francis Atkinson (London: Allen & Unwin, 1922), p. 67.
66. Spengler, *The Decline of the West*, p. 59.
67. Spengler, *The Decline of the West*, pp. 59 and 46.
68. Spengler, *The Decline of the West*, pp. 47 and 56.
69. Spengler, *The Decline of the West*, p. 62.
70. Spengler, *The Decline of the West*, p. 67.
71. Ernst Cassirer, *Substance and Function and Einstein's Theory of Relativity* [1910], trans. William Curtis Swabey and Marie Collins Swabey (Chicago and London: Open Court, 1923), p. 3.
    Ernst Cassirer, *The Philosophy of Symbolic Forms 3: The Phenomenology of Knowledge* [1929], trans. Ralph Manheim (New Haven: Yale University Press and London: Oxford University Press, 1957), p. 357.
72. Cassirer, *Philosophy of Symbolic Forms*, pp. 383 and 384.
73. Cassirer, *Philosophy of Symbolic Forms*, p. 391.
74. Cassirer, *Substance*, p. 116.
75. Cassirer, *Substance*, p. 116.
76. Hans Vaihinger, *The Philosophy of 'As If': A System of the Theoretical, Practical, and Religious Fictions of Mankind* [1911], trans. C. K. Ogden (London: Routledge, 2000), pp. 57 and 51.
77. Vaihinger, *The Philosophy of 'As If'*, p. 148.
78. Vaihinger, *The Philosophy of 'As If'*, p. 44.
79. Hartry Field, *Realism, Mathematics and Modality* (Oxford: Blackwell, 1989), p. 3.
80. Eugene P. Wigner, 'The Unreasonable Effectiveness of Mathematics in the Natural Sciences', in *Symmetries and Reflections: Scientific Essays* (Cambridge, MA and London: MIT, 1970), 222–37 (p. 222).
81. Wigner, 'Unreasonable Effectiveness', p. 237; see Gerhard Vollmer, *Wieso können wir die Welt erkennen? Neue Beiträge zur Wissenschaftstheorie* (Stuttgart and Leipzig: Hirzel, 2003), pp. 121–42.
82. Alain Badiou, *Number and Numbers*, trans. Robin Mackay (Cambridge: Polity, 2008), p. 211.
83. Alain Badiou, 'Platonism and Mathematical Ontology', in *Briefings on Existence: A Short Treatise on Transitory Ontology*, ed. and trans. Norman Madarasz (New York: State University of New York Press, 2006), 89–100 (p. 95).
84. Alain Badiou, *Being and Event*, trans. Oliver Feltham (London and New York: Continuum, 2005), p. 4.
85. Max Tegmark, *Our Mathematical Universe: My Quest for the Ultimate Nature of Reality* (London: Penguin, 2015).
86. Badiou, *Being and Event*, p. 6.

I

MATHEMATICS AND POLITICS: THOMAS PYNCHON, *AGAINST THE DAY*

AGAINST THE DAY, MODERN MATHEMATICS, ANARCHISM

Thomas Pynchon's novel *Against the Day* (2006) is set in the period between the 1893 Chicago World's Fair and the aftermath of the First World War. Akin to the World's Fair itself, the novel takes stock of the world and its possible futures: it is, as Louis Menand put it in a review, 'a kind of inventory of the possibilities inherent in a particular moment in the history of the imagination. It is like a work of science fiction written in 1900.'[1] On closer examination, the statement only partly applies to *Against the Day*: while science fiction creates a future version of the world, Pynchon's text is clearly rooted in world history, exploring events such as the First World War, the decline of anarchism, and the foundational crisis in mathematics. But Pynchon's novel goes beyond historical events when also examining diverse paths the world could have taken, contrasting different worlds and multiple futures that were open at the turn of the century. With its combination of historical and exuberantly fictional elements, it looks at the 1880s to 1920s both with the eyes of the contemporary and of the historian, and this double temporality also informs *Against the Day*'s engagement with mathematics: Pynchon draws on its development in the decades around 1900 to explore political concerns in the twenty-first century and uses it as a metaphor for a new balance of the real and the imaginary in his postmodernist literary practice.

Pynchon's immense novel combines, interrelates and contrasts plotlines and different worlds over more than a thousand pages. It begins and ends with the Chums of Chance, a group of aeronauts who reside in a universe of boys' books adventures and inhabit the most fictional storyline of the novel: the conditions of the Chums' world differ from the earthly laws of other plotlines and their closer correspondence to historical reality. Lew, a character in a set of more realistic conditions, asks: '"But you boys – you're not storybook characters." He had a thought. "Are you?" "No more than Wyatt Earp or Nellie Bly," Randolph supposed' (AD 41). Since 'Nelly Bly' is the pen name of the journalist Elizabeth Jane Cochrane and Wyatt Earp better known as a novel hero than as his real-life model, Randolph's comparison underscores the Chums' higher degree of fictionality but nevertheless existing relation to the actual world. Combining aspects of the real and the imagined, the Chums take a look into the world's future: on their way to the World's Fair, they lose sight of the grounds and take a detour over the Chicago stockyards, where they observe herds of cattle that are being driven to the slaughterhouse: they see 'that unshaped freedom being rationalized into movement only in straight lines and at right angles and a progressive reduction of choices, until the final turn through the final gate that led to the killing-floor' (AD 11). When the Chums' route does not lead to the Fair's exhibition of the period's achievements and promises of a progressive future but to visions of slaughter, it foreshadows the path of the world in the novel and also in historical reality, mirroring a world that deprives itself of open routes until almost all possibilities collapse, the final turn leading to the First World War. 'The world came to an end in 1914', a character expresses the feeling that reverberates through Pynchon's novel and that echoes modernist reactions to a conflict that marks the end of a period of optimistic belief in progress and in the positive results of reason and scientific method (AD 1211). The opening of *Against the Day* introduces the role of mathematics in this revaluation of Enlightenment values, emphasising that the inevitable arrival at the slaughterhouse comes as a result of geometrical regulation in the 'straight lines and [. . .] right angles' of a mathematical coordinate system, a 'Cartesian grid' (AD 11).

If the opening passage points to mathematics as a means to rationalise and determine a one-way street towards future reality, in the course of *Against the Day* maths also emerges as part of an opposite movement towards uncertainty and openness. As the discipline enters a phase of modernisation in the nineteenth century, the questioning of fundamental concepts, including the notion of mathematical reality itself, results in a foundational crisis that is unsettling but also opens up formerly unthinkable possibilities. The growing sense of anxiety, so Yashmeen explains in a conversation with fellow mathematician Kit, mirrors the political situation:

> The political crisis in Europe maps into the crisis in mathematics. Weierstrass functions, Cantor's continuum, Russell's equally

inexhaustible capacity for mischief – once, among nations, as in chess, suicide was illegal. Once, among mathematicians, 'the infinite' was all but a conjuror's convenience. The connections lie there, Kit – hidden and poisonous. (AD 668)

The crises in maths and in politics respectively threaten established forms of existence, and the two domains further connect in *Against the Day* when both include movements that explore benefits of the resulting uncertainty. These are based on changed ideas about representation: as discussed in more detail below, Yashmeen lists concepts that are part of modern mathematics' departure from a direct representational relationship to the world, while, in the political domain, turn-of-the-century anarchism rejects representation and advocates self-organisation among equals. Anarchism and modern mathematics thus map into each other regarding an abandonment of *arche*, a term that is variously translated as 'origin', 'ground' or 'foundation'. With the added prefix, *anarche* denotes absence of rule or first principle. 'An-archistic' in terms of its loss of foundations, modern mathematics forms part of *Against the Day*'s exploration of anarchism across the twentieth century, from its failure as political movement to its transformations into cultural forms of resistance.

Anarchism is a consistent concern in Pynchon's writing, but the topic gains urgency in *Against the Day* when, in the double temporality typical of his work, the novel connects historical manifestations and the terrorist attacks of 9/11. The engagement with twenty-first-century affairs motivates a shift in Pynchon's postmodernist practice, which the novel reflects in its explorations of foundationalism and anarchism. In view of a modern transformation of mathematics, *Against the Day* develops possibilities of non-complicity with the establishment and explores a process encapsulated by David Weir's comment that 'anarchism succeeded culturally where it failed politically'.[2] Yet, at the same time as tracing the perpetuation of anarchist ideals into the cultural realm, *Against the Day* emphasises commitment to political action and responsibility to the real that, while present in Pynchon's previous novels, is unprecedented in degree and clarity. To newly calibrate the relation between the real and the imaginary in literature, *Against the Day* establishes the concept of complex numbers as a poetological model. Using maths to explore worrying developments of rationalisation as well as positive potential inherent in the absence of foundations, and employing it in an effort to adapt literary fiction to the demands of the twenty-first century, *Against the Day* is indeed aptly described as the 'most mathematical' of Pynchon's novels.[3]

Examining *Against the Day*'s engagement with modern mathematics in view of the novel's reappraisal of anti-foundational movements and its negotiations of the possibilities and responsibilities of literary fiction, the discussion to follow takes account of intricate links between the mathematical and the political. Interrelations of the two domains have only a short history of being acknowledged, since Western culture has been dominated by a Platonic understanding of maths as a realm of absolute truths that is independent of worldly concerns. Growing attention to its political dimension begins only with the questioning of received views during the foundational debate around 1900 and forms part of the argument that modern mathematics has to be considered in view of modernist culture. In Pynchon's work, connections between seemingly remote fields are characteristic and afford much of the texts' interpretative potential. Studies exclusively focused on any one area, while contributing important insights, at times fail to discuss their wider implications, so that research on Pynchon's use of science can seem irrelevant to examining his political concerns or, indeed, detrimental to it. In *Pynchon and the Political* Samuel Thomas laments:

> [I]nnovative and unsettling discussions of freedom, war, labor, poverty, community, democracy, totalitarianism and so on are often passed over in favor of constrictive scientific metaphors and theoretical play. Much of the urgency and force of Pynchon's writing [. . .] is nullified by this 'thermodynamical gloom' (*SL* 14).[4]

Yet, as Yashmeen's belief in a connection between the crises in these fields suggests, discussing science does not 'nullify' the urgency of Pynchon's writing but is integral to appreciating his vision of the political. In *Against the Day*, the political cannot be separated from the mathematical – the novel's negotiations of developments and possibilities in the early twentieth and twenty-first centuries require viewing the two together.

Foundational Crises

In its most sustained mathematical passage, *Against the Day* introduces the foundational crisis that, as Yashmeen suggests, mirrors the impasse in European politics, and it displays the disorientation that developments in maths provoke in and beyond the professional sphere. The section illustrates the shattering of the mathematical world and its implications by framing the passage with non-scientific instances of losing a reality thought secure, for example connecting the situation in maths to a drastic change in Yashmeen's personal life: having to leave Göttingen for an uncertain journey through Europe, she feels 'expelled from the garden' of this centre of research and also from what she considered to be mathematical reality:

> [W]e must discard everything, not only the objects we possess but everything we have taken to be 'real,' all we have learned, all the work we have put in, the theorems, the proofs, the questioning, the breath-taken trembling before the beauty of an intractable problem, all of which was perhaps illusion. (AD 746)

27

Yashmeen and Kit's visit to the 'Museum der Monstrositäten' – German for 'Museum of Monstrosities' – then details the loss of paradisiac certainty in maths and its implications for rational thought and our sense of reality.

The museum of mathematical monstrosities points back to the novel's beginning at the Chicago World's Fair and the dissolution of its promises in a vision of slaughter, when it constitutes 'a sort of nocturnal equivalent of Professor Klein's huge collection of mathematical models on the third floor of the Auditorienhaus' (AD 710). Felix Klein's models made up the main part of the mathematical exhibition at the World's Fair; an important step towards recognition of the discipline, which not only in Klein's eyes suffered from 'the custom to regard modern mathematical speculation as something having no general interest or importance'.[5] As the historians Karen Parshall and David Rowe explain, the presence of Klein's exhibition at the Fair signalled a change: it 'implicitly conveyed an assumption that mathematics and mathematical research were embedded at least as deeply in culture as architecture or literature or any other human intellectual endeavor'.[6] The World's Fair also saw a first international congress of mathematics, where Klein celebrated the state of his field in a speech: 'I wish on the present occasion to state and to emphasise that in the last two decades a marked improvement from within has asserted itself in our science, with constantly increasing success.'[7] In *Against the Day*'s embedding maths in its encyclopaedic show of the world and its possibilities, the German museum figures as a dark equivalent to Klein's presentation when the exhibited 'monstrosities' put into question the nature of mathematics and its linear development: it is 'a strange underground temple, or counter-temple, dedicated to the current "Crisis" in European mathematics' (AD 710–11).

The museum building and surrounding landscape indicate its place outside the en-lightened rational world: seemingly constructed from a 'black substance' left over 'after light [. . .] had been removed', the museum is set in the 'witchlike' brushland near the Brocken, a hill famously associated with the supernatural (AD 711, 710). The architecture also points to the fact that only insiders can appreciate the crisis: the subterranean museum 'could not be read from any exterior, because there was none, beyond an entranceway framing a flight of coal-black steps sloping downward in a fathomless tunnel to crypts unknown' (AD 711). Although the text then indeed turns to insider knowledge of the history of maths, a connection between 'the great Crisis that continued to preoccupy mathematics even to the present' and cracks in the fictional world of *Against the Day* ensures that even readers without mathematical expertise can appreciate the wider relevance of the foundational crisis and Günther's exclamation: 'How could anyone's nerves here remain unafflicted?' (AD 713, 711). The exhibit *'Discovery of the Weierstrass Functions'* points to the mathematically and emotionally upsetting developments that motivate the name of the Museum der Monstrositäten: the functions discovered by Karl Weierstrass in 1872 behave counter-intuitively so that practitioners referred to them as 'Weierstrass's monster' and responded with shock. 'I recoil with dismay and horror at this lamentable plague of functions which do not have derivatives [namely the Weierstrass function]', Charles Hermite professed.[8] Exhibiting discoveries that violated traditional understandings, introduced objects formerly thought impossible, or point to paradoxes, the museum displays a modern mathematical world that requires reconsidering what is possible and real. The passage set at the museum then suggests that the developments in maths also have implications for views on literary fiction and its relation to the world: the mural '*Professor Frege at Jena upon Receiving Russell's Letter Concerning the Set of All Sets That Are Not Members of Themselves*' points to dramatic consequences of self-referentiality in maths, and an immediately following metafictional episode reveals similar hazards in literature. Given its importance to the vision of literary fiction, it is worth looking at the concept of the 'set of all sets' in more detail.

A set is a basic concept in set theory, which was crucially developed by Georg Cantor in 1874 and promised to be a foundational theory, meaning that all of mathematics 'could be recast in the language of set theory and derived from its principles'.[9] Many professionals agreed with David Hilbert that this would put maths on a secure basis and prove the certainty it had always been believed to exemplify: 'No one shall drive us out of the paradise which Cantor has created for us.'[10] Based on this confidence, Hilbert could celebrate mathematics as a model for 'the continuity of the development of science' at the International Congress in 1900 and ended his introduction with a flourish:

> This conviction of the solvability of every mathematical problem is a powerful incentive to the worker. We hear within us the perpetual call: There is the problem. Seek its solution. You can find it by pure reason, for in mathematics there is no *ignorabimus*.[11]

In *Against the Day*, a character echoes Hilbert's statement that set theory had put maths on secure foundations, remarking of Cantor that 'he may have led us to [. . .] paradise, as Dr. Hilbert has famously described it' (AD 702). In the Museum der Monstrositäten, however, the installation that shows Hilbert at the International Congress is already overshadowed by 'the precipitously darkening sky of an approaching storm' (AD 712). Frege's mural illustrates the reasons for the dark prospects, showing the moment of his receiving a letter from Bertrand Russell that dealt serious blows to Hilbert's positive evaluation of the situation of maths. Frege had built on Cantor's work to further develop modern symbolic logic as a foundational theory, but when he was just about to publish his major oeuvre Russell noted an unsolvable problem that meant the failure of the project. Namely, in set theory, the question whether the 'set of all sets that are not members of themselves' is a member of itself reveals a paradox: if it is a member of itself then it is by definition not one of the sets that are not members of themselves; at the same time, if the 'set of all sets that are not members of themselves' is not a member of itself then it logically is to be counted towards the sets that are not members of themselves. This, and further antinomies that similarly emerge when applying a concept to itself, meant that set theory could not solve the problem of foundations, and it thus had devastating effects on the mathematical community. Frege himself stated that Russell's paradox had 'shattered one of the foundations of his [Frege referring to himself] construction', and the unsolved foundational questions changed Hilbert's optimism to despair: 'If mathematical thinking is defective, where are we to find truth and certitude?'[12] When in *Against the Day* a psychiatrist complains that 'Cantor, the *Beast of Halle*, who seeks to demolish the very foundations of mathematics, bring[s] these Göttingen people paranoid and screaming to my door', the novel draws attention to the personal and social ramifications of the loss of belief in the certainty of maths and any knowledge built on it (AD 702).

Against the Day establishes a connection between unsettling developments in maths and in literature when it introduces readers to a literary equivalent of the self-referential turn in modern maths; namely, a metafictional awareness of the novel's own fictionality. The mathematical excursion is set at the conclusion of a chapter, and the passage reveals a crack in the foundations of the novelistic world, before the chapter break further disturbs the flow of reading. In a direct address, maybe to the reader, a disembodied voice explains:

> The next time you visit, it might not be exactly where it stands today. [...] Because the cornerstone of the building is not a cube but its four-dimensional analogy, a tesseract. Certain of these corridors lead to other times, times, moreover, you might wish too strongly to reclaim, and become lost in the perplexity of the attempt. (AD 715)

If the cornerstone of the museum is four-dimensional, it escapes the framework of reality, and so does the warning voice when breaking the fourth wall that veils the fictional nature of the novel world. With its knowledge of different spaces and times, the voice might be an authorial one, a notion further suggested by its calling its creations 'Children' and claiming: 'You know who I am' (AD 715). Proposing that certain ways lead to other times, the voice acknowledges that readers at the end of the chapter, exhausted after a tour de force through events in the history of mathematics, might be tempted to close the book at this convenient incision and reclaim their own time. But it also suggests that the insights into the foundational crisis are likely to affect readers and leave them struggling to retrieve their previous state of believing maths uncomplicatedly certain and true. And even if not every reader might appreciate the just-witnessed ground-breaking events in maths, the metafictional rupturing of the novel world conveys their impact on questions of reality and certainty. Apart from illustrating the consequences of self-referential and other monstrous developments, *Against the Day* here also suggests the need to reconsider the foundations of literary fiction: if self-referentiality destroys the certainty of maths, it also challenges the truth of the fictional world and opens up questions about its relation to readers' reality. Based on their similarly world-shattering self-referential turns, *Against the Day* then explores parallels between maths and literary fiction regarding their potentials not to undo worlds but to build alternative ones. When constructing these without recourse to stable foundations, modern maths and literature support anti-foundationalist movements that in the political domain are associated with anarchism.

If the metafictional ending of the chapter conveys even to mathematically uninterested readers a sense of shaking grounds and clashing worlds, Yashmeen's personal fate relates the situation to political developments. At the same time as learning that all she has taken to be real in the mathematical world might have been an illusion, she becomes aware of the similarly crumbling landscape of European politics and discovers anarchism as a movement that takes account of the absence of a common foundation or *arché* (AD 746). For Yashmeen, mathematics, politics and the sense of crisis described in a terminology of foundational architecture come together at the grave of Bernhard Riemann, one of the initiators of the modern transformation in maths: when paying respect to Riemann, Yashmeen remembers stories about the *stranniki*, anarchistic Russian pilgrims who are also called 'underground men'. The subterranean existence of the *stranniki* signals their detachment from the world: 'they were no longer responsible to the world, let alone the Tsar [. . .]. The Government feared them more than it feared Social Democrats, more than bomb-throwers', Yashmeen explains (AD 745). While direct opposition still acknowledges the existence of official structures, the *stranniki* pose a threat to the very foundation of politics when ignoring any form of power and responsibility to the world. Their spatial location underlines the ground-breaking consequences of creating their own set of conditions. Hiding 'down under the house', the underground men open up new spaces and thus compromise former certainties: 'Floors that had once been solid and simple became veils over another world. It was not the day we knew that provided the *stranniki* their light' (AD 745). The use of architectural vocabulary connects the description of the *stranniki*'s anarchism to the earlier passage on the foundational crisis in mathematics, and Yashmeen's musings at Riemann's grave tightens the relation in view of their comparable opening up of alternative states. Where the underground men shape a subterranean world, Riemann revealed new spaces in geometry: he constructed non-Euclidean geometries, that is, curved spaces whose properties differ from the Euclidean space formerly taken for granted. With geometry literally being the measurement of the earth – from ancient Greek *gê-* ('earth') and *-metría* ('measurement') – his work can be seen to describe other worlds. Riemann geometry, foundational questions in mathematics, and the anarchistic *stranniki* thus all reveal cracks in what is perceived as real.

When *Against the Day* connects political and mathematical developments towards anti-foundationalist views, it reflects the historical situation in the early twentieth century where shared vocabulary underlined relations between crises in these fields. Hermann Weyl, a protagonist in the foundational discussion, fanned the flames with his 1921 paper 'On the New Foundational Crisis of Mathematics', choosing political terms to proclaim: 'Brouwer – that is the revolution!'[13] With this, Weyl, who had been a student of Hilbert and his formalist programme, signalled a drastic switch in allegiance when supporting L. E. J. Brouwer, the founder of rivalling intuitionism. In his counter-attack, Hilbert continued the use of political terminology:

> Brouwer is not, as Weyl thinks, the revolution, but only the repetition of an attempted coup (Putsch) by old means [. . .] which now, where the power of the state is so well armed and strengthened by Frege, Dedekind and Cantor, is all the more from the beginning doomed to failure.[14]

Taking up Hilbert's term, intuitionists began to call themselves 'Putschists', a further indication, so Dirk van Dalen argues, that mathematicians connected the crisis in their field to the pressing political situation in Germany with its various coups. The marked interest of a non-specialist audience further suggests that mathematical questions about truth and certainty fed into concerns with the unstable situation in 1920s Germany:

> The actual appearance of the great revolutionary [Brouwer] in the lecture halls in Berlin caused a furore. [. . .] The lecture hall was filled till the last seat – intuitionism and foundations became the talk of the town. Even the newspapers followed the events with interest. [. . .] The lectures were attended by a mixed audience, consisting of students, professional mathematicians and interested laymen.[15]

Weyl confirmed that more was at stake than mathematical questions alone. With hindsight, he argued that decisions in the foundational crisis were not made on purely rational grounds but in view of wider concerns: mathematicians 'are not indifferent to what their scientific endeavors mean in the context of man's whole caring and knowing, suffering and creative existence in the world', he explained.[16] Not least, questioning mathematics means threatening the 'paragon of truth and certitude', as Hilbert phrased it, and can reinforce anxieties about socially and politically unstable situations.[17]

The use of political terms, the interest in and beyond the professional community, and the reflections of practitioners suggest that the political instability in Germany gave an urgency to debates about the foundations of mathematics. Van Dalen goes so far as to conjecture that, in a politically stable atmosphere, the mathematical conflict would not have escalated: 'without the First World War, there would not have been a conflict [. . .] without the political complications there would not have been the fateful act' – the fateful act being Hilbert dismissing Brouwer from the editorial team of the journal *Mathematische Annalen*, thus forcing mathematicians to take sides in the conflict between formalism and intuitionism.[18] In a similar vein, Herbert Mehrtens aligns the subsiding of the foundational debate with political stabilisation in Germany:

> Beginning in the mid-1920s, the public and sometimes emotional debate around the crisis transformed into a specialist discourse among basic researchers. With the consolidation of the Weimar Republic, this crisis passed too. The question of meaning, which had become public as a political concern, dissolved into private interpretation.[19]

Interrelations between the mathematical and the political crises in 1920s Germany and the more politically stable situation of the Weimar Republic thus also help explain why the foundational crisis could abate without a solution or winner.

As is typical of Pynchon's fiction, *Against the Day* literalises and exaggerates historical connections, here between the crises in maths and politics. Indeed, the novel suggests that maths is part of the First World War and accordingly responsible for the world coming to an end. Contradicting G. H. Hardy's famous assertion that '[r]eal mathematics has no effects on war. No one has yet discovered any warlike purpose to be served by the theory of numbers', in Pynchon's novel a weapon draws its dangerous power directly from a mathematical expression: the 'Quaternionic Weapon [is] a means to unloose upon the world energies hitherto unimagined' (AD 609).[20] When an element of Quaternions seems to cause a massive explosion that may constitute the First World War 'collapsed into a single event', *Against the Day* sets mathematics at the very core of the political conflict and the annihilation of reality (AD 895).

The Modernist Transformation of Mathematics and the Anarchism of the Imaginary

Quaternions, used to create the Quaternionic Weapon and upset the world in the First World War, are also crucial to *Against the Day*'s vision of modern mathematics as a domain of imaginative possibilities and model for cultural anarchism. They are set at a particularly deep level of the Museum der Monstrositäten: following the sign 'ZU DEN QUATERNIONEN' – 'Towards Quaternions' – Kit descends dark stairways to an installation that shows William Rowan Hamilton formulating the concept in 1843 (AD 712). The discovery of Quaternions is not usually treated as part of the foundational crisis of mathematics, yet the inclusion in the Museum and the earlier description of Hamilton as a forerunner of 'the real maniacs [who] have gone into foundations work' mark Pynchon's intention to use it in this way (AD 601). Since *Against the Day* presents Quaternions as the deepest tier of the crisis and employs them in its discussion of anarchism and as an image of the nature of literature in the twenty-first century, it will be useful to look at the concept in some detail. *Against the Day* itself humorously acknowledges that some kind of mathematical knowledge is needed to understand the unfolding of the novel and that readers might not possess or be particularly inclined to acquire it. Reef's reaction to Yashmeen explaining the mathematics of roulette is demonstrative boredom: 'She was interrupted by the thud of Reef's head on the table, where it remained. "I don't think he's been following this," she muttered' (AD 967). Reef seems to absorb the lessons during his sleep, however, and begins to win at the game – instilling hope, maybe, that laypersons might also somehow profit from the mathematical material in the text. Indeed, as we shall see, *Against the Day* showcases the real benefits of attending to fanciful mathematical concepts.

The Quaternion formula reads: $a+bi+cj+dk$; with a, b, c and d being variables that can take on any real number, and i, j and k denoting imaginary numbers. The imaginary unit i is defined as $i=\sqrt{-1}$, which is equal to $i^2=-1$. This contradicts the rule in the real number system that a square cannot be negative: $1^2=1$ and $(-1)^2=1$. Mathematicians therefore felt uneasy about the nature and existence of imaginary numbers, claiming that such numbers had to be assumed instead of being found by observation of nature. The seventeenth-century mathematician and philosopher Gottfried Wilhelm Leibniz illustrates the problem: 'I did not understand how [...] a quantity could be real, when imaginary or impossible numbers were used to express it.'[21] Complex numbers, which combine the real number a and the imaginary element bi into the complex number $a+bi$, similarly disconcerted Leibniz: he saw them as 'amphibian[s] between being and not-being', and mathematicians shared his scepticism regarding their reality and existence well into the nineteenth century.[22] For instance, George Airy declared: 'I have not the smallest confidence in any result which is essentially obtained by the use of imaginary symbols'; George Boole spoke of 'the uninterpretable symbol $\sqrt{-1}$', and Augustus De Morgan concluded his proof of the nonexistence of imaginary numbers with the words: 'We have shown the symbol $\sqrt{-1}$ to be void of meaning, or rather self-contradictory and absurd.'[23] However, mathematicians who questioned the existence of imaginary numbers did not necessarily contest the usefulness of the symbol. Carl Friedrich Gauss even suggested that the tendency to view imaginary numbers as problematic could be traced back not to inherent characteristics but to the unfortunate labelling: the term 'imaginary number' highlights questions of existence, whereas the alternative he proposed

– 'lateral number' – does not. Gauss's renaming did not come to general recognition, but the geometrical representation of complex numbers aided the imagination and somewhat reconciled mathematicians to imaginary numbers: a complex number $(a+ib)$ can be depicted as a point on a two-dimensional coordinate plan – with the x-axis showing the real part (a) and the y-axis the imaginary part (ib).[24]

Against the Day places complex numbers at the beginning of the mathematical crisis when, in the Museum der Monstrositäten, the exhibit showing Hamilton carve the Quaternion formula into Brougham Bridge in Dublin includes a 'pocket-knife part real and part imaginary, a "complex" knife one might say' (AD 713).[25] The non-mathematical meanings of the terms 'real' and 'imaginary' are present throughout the novel, not least when, shortly before the description of Hamilton's complex knife, the imaginary is cautiously connected to fiction: the museum displays combine painted murals with real objects that are set in front of them, and when items at the intersection are partly three-dimensional and partly painted, they 'could not strictly be termed *entirely* real, rather part "real" and part "pictorial," or let us say "fictional"' (AD 712). The further explorations of the real and imaginary elements of Quaternions thus also have implications for related questions of representation in art, not least regarding *Against the Day* itself.

Given that Quaternions employ three imaginary elements, John Graves wrote to Hamilton that there was 'something in the system that gravels me. I have not yet any clear views as to the extent to which we are at liberty arbitrarily to create imaginaries, and to endow them with supernatural properties.'[26] Hamilton and other mathematicians indeed fiercely discussed the nature of Quaternions, and the debate both reflected and contributed to the development of a modern understanding of maths as a self-referential domain that does not represent the given world but is independent of physical reality. Pynchon's novel considers such concerns in view of identifying spaces for freedom and alternatives in maths. If Graves worried about the reality of Quaternions, in *Against the Day* Pléiade raises a related question when asking: '"but what is a Quaternion?" Hilarity at the table was general and prolonged. "What *'is'* a Quaternion? Ha, hahahaha!"' (AD 604–5). The answer illustrates what Graves called the 'supernatural properties' of imaginary numbers and suggests that, understood as independent of physical reality, maths opens up spaces of possibility. Namely, in a practical demonstration, Dr Rao shows that Quaternions can be used in calculations of a vector's lengthening and rotation in space: he conducts a Quaternion-Yoga-movement that becomes 'contrary-to-fact' and has him reappear in a different place and as a slightly different person; he is taller, for example, or has changed the colour of his skin or hair (AD 605). He explains that the potential for altering his appearance resides in the imaginary element:

> [Quaternions work] among axes whose unit vector is not the familiar and comforting 'one' but the altogether disquieting *square root of minus one*. If *you* were a vector, mademoiselle, you would begin in the 'real' world, change your length, enter an 'imaginary' reference system, rotate up to three different ways, and return to 'reality' a new person. (AD 605)

Dr Rao thus demonstrates a Quaternion to be a concept that combines real and imaginary elements in order to arrive at altered states of reality.

Quaternions can be understood as 'plotting complex numbers along three axes instead of two', as Barry Nebulay explains in *Against the Day*; that is, they are an extension of complex numbers to the third dimension, used to describe points in space (AD 605). But Hamilton disliked this geometrical interpretation. In the 1853 preface to his *Lectures on Quaternions*, he states to have 'felt dissatisfied with any view which should not give to [imaginaries], from the outset, a clear interpretation and *meaning*; and wished that this should be done, for square roots of negatives, without introducing considerations *so expressly geometrical*'.[27] Hamilton therefore devised a new notation which replaced the complex number $a+ib$ with a couple (a, b):

> [I]n the theory of couples, the same symbol $\sqrt{-1}$ is *significant*, and denotes a possible extraction, or a real couple, namely [. . .] the *principal square-root of the couple* $(-1, 0)$. In the latter theory, therefore, though not in the former, this sign $\sqrt{-1}$ may properly be employed.[28]

Hamilton thus circumvented the 'disquieting' nature of $\sqrt{-1}$ by taking it to represent an unproblematic operation on a 'real couple'. But having dispensed with the geometrical interpretations of Quaternions, Hamilton considered it necessary to identify a link between algebra and physical reality in order to guarantee the interpretation and meaning of algebraic symbols. Given that geometry was seen as the science of space, Hamilton's solution was to treat algebra as the science of time, arguing that seemingly symbolical and uninterpretable expressions 'may pass into the world of thoughts, and acquire reality and significance, if Algebra be viewed as not a mere Art or Language, but as the Science of Pure Time'.[29] More precisely, Hamilton saw the temporal element as 'ORDER IN PROGRESSION'.[30] Quaternions illustrate this idea particularly clearly: unlike in the real number system where the order of multiplication has no effect ($a*b=b*a$), in the case of the non-commutative Quaternions it bears information as it changes the algebraic sign: $i*j=-j*i$. Here, the time of calculating with an element in relation to the next element is crucial. In the case of Quaternions, Hamilton attributed the three imaginary elements to the three dimensions of space and the real element to time. Thus, he argued, the Quaternion 'may be said to be "time plus space", or "space plus time": and in this sense it has, or at least involves a reference to, four dimensions'.[31] *Against* *the Day* draws on Hamilton's interpretation when Barry Nebulay considers 'the three vector terms as dimensions in space, and the scalar term as Time' and when the Quaternionic Weapon gains its dangerous power from the scalar term and is therefore described as '[a] weapon based on Time' (AD 626). As we shall examine in more detail below, not least with reference to Hamilton's allocation of meaning, Quaternions form part of the novel's various scientific, pseudo-scientific and non-scientific ways of reconsidering space and time.

Having found a way to argue for the significance and meaning of the symbol $\sqrt{-1}$, Hamilton maintained that Quaternions represented reality better than any other mathematical system. His colleague Peter Guthrie Tait seconded that they eluded the artificiality of other mathematical systems and constituted an absolutely natural one: 'To me Quaternions are primarily a Mode of Representation [. . .]. They *are*, virtually, the thing represented [. . .]. Quaternions, in a word, *exist* in space, and we have only to recognize them.'[32] Tait stressed the relevance of Quaternions as basic parameters of experience, namely as representing, or indeed being, the three dimensions of space and the additional dimension of time:

> I have always considered (after perfect inartificiality) their chief merit: – viz. that they are *'uniquely adapted to Euclidean space*, and therefore specially useful in some of the most important branches of physical science.' What have students of physics, as such, to do with space of more than three dimensions?[33]

Pynchon found Tait's argument ingenious enough to quote it in *Against the Day* – having Heino Vanderjuice add: 'I invite your attention to "as such"' (AD 365). However, the novel follows the historical development in which Hamilton's attribution of algebra to time did not become widely accepted and Tait's belief that Quaternions exist in space was superseded by the modern understanding of the independence of mathematics from physical reality. Even Hamilton ultimately admitted that 'there is a sort of symbolical science, or *science of language*, which well deserves to be studied, abstraction being made for a while of *meaning*, or interpretation; and *forms of expression* being treated as themselves the subject-matter to be studied'.[34] Hamilton's reluctance to abandon his claims for a representational relationship between Quaternions and physical reality is rooted in his concern about truth: regarding 'Algebra as an *Art*, or as a *Language*: as a System of Rules, or else as a System of Expressions, but not as a System of *Truths*' merely asks about its usefulness and replaces the weightier question: 'Is a Theorem of Algebra *true?*'[35] If algebra is understood not as a system of truths but as comprising diverse structures with different rules, the existence of imaginary numbers ceases to be problematical. The explanation for the curious nature of $\sqrt{-1}$ then is that negative square roots are not part of and therefore do not exist in the real number system but are defined and thus real in the system of complex numbers. But Hamilton lamented the loss of certainty: when working from the assumption that numbers are not true but 'that numbers, called *imaginary*, can be found or conceived or determined, [. . .] [i]t must be hard to found a S CIENCE on such grounds as these'.[36]

As Quaternions relinquished claims of representation and existence in space, abandoned the rule of commutativity, and sported not only one but three imaginary elements, they 'broke bonds set by centuries of mathematical thought', so Michael Crowe explains in *A History of Vector Analysis*, a likely source of Pynchon's.[37] In *Against the Day*, a character's question whether 'beyond the third [. . .] do dimensions exist as something more than algebraists' whimsy?' echoes Hamilton's concern regarding the actual existence of the four dimensions Quaternions were thought to represent (AD 677). But when the novel employs Quaternions to explore nineteenth-century developments towards a break with mathematical orthodoxy, it does not only give voice to laments concerning lost truth and meaning but also renders fruitful the transformation in maths for the rejection of political representation in anarchism. Fittingly, the passage introducing Quaternions as part of foundational work also develops their role for notions of anarchism:

> They found Root's quarters, which like Kit he seemed to be sharing with a dozen or so others of the Hamiltonian persuasion. Clothing in a wide selection of colors, sizes, and degrees of formality littered the available floor space. 'Take your pick I guess. Closest we'll see to Anarchism in our lifetime.' Back down in the Salon, the noise and centrifugal jollification had picked up markedly. 'Maniacs,' cried Root, 'every one of us! Fifty years ago of course more than today, the real maniacs have gone into foundations work, set theory, all abstract as possible, like it's a race to see who can venture out furthest into the borderlands of the nonexistent. [. . .] Grassmann was German and hence automatically among the possessed, Hamilton was burdened with early genius and in the grip of a first love [namely Quaternions] he could never get beyond.' (AD 601)

In the novel, Quaternionists of the 'Hamiltonian faith' indeed describe themselves as anarchists who work in independent and self-organised local groups: 'Anarchists always lose out [. . .]. We were only [. . .] drifters who set up their working tents for as long as the problem might demand, then struck camp again and moved on, always ad hoc and local' (AD 147, 599). The anarchist minority fights the 'Quaternion Wars' against the Vectorists, who use a different mathematical language to calculate similar problems (AD 590).[38] The Vectorists are described as 'Bolsheviks', not only because they are the majority but because they adhere to a centralised order when vectors always refer to the origin of a coordinate system with the axes x, y and z: they 'grimly pursued their aims, protected inside their belief that they are the inevitable future, the *xyz* people, the party of a single Established Coördinate System, present everywhere in the Universe, governing absolutely' (AD 599). Unlike vectors, for which the origin of a coordinate system provides a stable point of reference, Quaternions do not lead to one unified governing viewpoint. Not referring to the origin (*arche*) of a reference frame, Quaternions are an-archistic and afford multiple viewpoints by working spontaneously and locally.

In *Against the Day*, the anarchism that Quaternionists claim for their subject and externalise in their maniacal World Convention fails – in mathematics as in politics a unified viewpoint defined by a governing frame of reference is more easily manageable. In a phrase that echoes Josiah Willard Gibbs's prediction of a rivalry between Hamilton's methods and those of other mathematicians, the Quaternionists in Pynchon's novel connect the loss of a representational relationship in their anarchist mathematics to forfeiting their own reality: '"Face it. The *Kampf ums Dasein* is over, and we have lost." "Does that mean we only imagine now that we exist?" "Imaginary axes, imaginary existence"' (AD 598–9).[39] Relating mathematics to questions of existence, *Against the Day* locates in it a potential to create new forms of being and, as we shall see below, to open up alternative worlds. Based on the examination of the anarchist and imaginary existence of Quaternions and their supporters, the next sections further explore the ontological implications of modern maths and examine these in relation to anarchist possibilities in other imaginary domains, not least in the literary fiction *Against the Day* itself.

Mathematical Worlds

Against the Day illustrates the contested reality of imaginary numbers and the notion of modern mathematics' independence of physical givens with the concept of an '"imaginary" mirror-world' (AD 558). The novel thus treats science not only as a way to know the world but to create new ones, adding to the epistemological concern a commitment to ontological questions that becomes prominent in the later twentieth century.[40] At the same time as celebrating the world-building potential of maths, however, *Against the Day* also emphasises its restrictions, and, taken together, the possibilities and limits of mathematical creations provide a mirror to the novel's revaluation of the powers and responsibilities of art in the twenty-first century.

Clearly committed to plurality, *Against the Day* features various ways of doubling perspectives, people and worlds: characters possess the ability to be in two places at once; the crystalline structure of Iceland spar causes double-refraction by splitting light rays, while the magical instrument *La Doppiatrice* uses the same process to divide a person into two; and a ship separates into the civilian *Stupendica* and its secret counterpart, the dreadnought *Emperor Maximilian*. A librarian identifies such doubling as the 'sub-structure of reality' and relates the effect of Iceland spar and the reflection of essential duality in mathematics:

> [Iceland spar brings about the] doubling of Creation, each image clear and believable. ... And you being mathematical gentlemen, it can hardly have escaped your attention that its curious advent into the world occurred within only a few years of the discovery of Imaginary Numbers, which also provided a doubling of the mathematical Creation. (AD 149)

If Iceland spar provides 'that all-important ninety-degree twist' to light that renders invisible the subterranean world of the 'Hidden People', imaginary numbers similarly displace their '"imaginary" mirror-world' along the vertical: in a coordinate system, the greater the imaginary element, the higher it is set on the vertical y-axis, which is therefore also called the imaginary axis (AD 149, 558). Maths thus visualises what the leader of the mathematical-spiritual order T.W.I.T. describes in more general terms: the '[l]ateral world-sets, other parts of the Creation, [that] lie all around us' can be found '"somewhere not *on* the surface of the Earth so much as–" "Perpendicular"' (AD 248, 1163). The perpendicular axis accordingly denotes distance from the surface as well as imaginary value, and the Chums of Chance further relate these two aspects to the literary imagination: soaring above the earth in their airship and living in a storybook world with its own conditions, they lead a highly fictional existence. As the novel links the mathematical imaginary and the literary fictional, the nature and use of the mathematical mirror-world in *Against the Day* illuminate the potential of fictional literature to double existence without escaping the demands of the real.

Against the Day introduces the traditional belief that mathematics constitutes universal truth and is independent of historical and cultural contexts. Supporting this notion, Quaternions unite a 'band of varying ages and nationalities, whose only common language [. . . was] that of the Quaternions', and the Chums of Chance experience maths as an international language:

> 'The Italian number that looks like a zero, is the same as our own American "zero." The one that looks like a one, is "one." The one that looks like a two–' 'Enough, cretin!' snarled Darby, 'we "get the picture"!' (AD 589, 273–4)

Next to trusting in its universality, several characters start out with a belief in a separate mathematical world, a Platonic realm of absolute truth where mathematical objects exist and of which the physical world is only an imperfect shadow. Yashmeen describes her initial conviction in such terms: 'Mathematics once seemed the way – the internal life of numbers came as a revelation to me, [. . .] – a reflection of some less-accessible reality, through close study of which one might perhaps learn to pass beyond the difficult given world' (AD 841). Similarly, Kit finds in Vectorism glimpses of 'transcendence, a coexisting world of imaginaries, the "spirit realm"' and hopes to discover an alternative to earthly reality where the powerful capitalist Scarsdale Vibe threatens his family (AD 759). Upon Kit's retreat into maths, Professor Vanderjuice observes that '[w]hen human tragedies happen, it always seems as if scientists and mathematicians can meet the situation more calmly than others' (AD 366), echoing G. H. Hardy's famous conviction that '[w]hen the world is mad, a mathematician may find in mathematics an incomparable anodyne'.[41] Yet, if the Quaternionic Weapon invalidates Hardy's belief in the irrelevance of mathematics to war, the developments in *Against the Day* also reveal flaws in his strategy to evade reality. In the course of the novel, Kit learns that trying to access the Platonic realm of abstract mathematical truths is futile: the promises of transcendence 'had not shown Kit, after all, a way to escape the world governed by real numbers. His father had been murdered by men whose allegiance [. . .] was to that real axis and nothing beyond it' (AD 759). The emphasis on real numbers and the real axis suggest that maths is not a separate realm but implicated in the world that it is hoped to transcend, and Yashmeen's experience similarly stresses its relevance to the real. Her highly abstract work is a 'refuge' from reality, but it finds unexpected applications and helps her manage the given world, for example by winning at roulette and using Riemann's work on multiply connected spaces to walk through walls (AD 558). Like Kit, she is expelled from the safety of her studies, and their visit to the Museum der Monstrositäten details why any belief in a perfect realm of mathematical existence and truth has to fail: as experts discover modern maths to itself be fundamentally disturbed by unknowability, uncertainty and paradox, it becomes futile to seek refuge there and mathematicians instead approach psychiatrists for help in the real world. The metafictional shaking of fictional reality points to a comparable situation concerning literature: escapist retreat into fiction is impossible since, sooner or later, the end of a chapter upsets the novelistic world.

If modern developments shake belief in an ideal mathematical realm, they also lead to greater acknowledgement of the cultural dimension of maths. In *Against the Day*, the idea of a transcendent mathematical realm animates hope to find in Quaternions a means to pass beyond time and thus death, and the failure to do so points to the fact that mathematical concepts themselves are not outside time but that their existence depends on specific historical conditions. In accordance with Hamilton's view that Quaternions refer to 'time plus space', in the novel the so-called scalar or real part of a Quaternion is related to time: 'any energy encountered inside that term might be taken as due to Time, an intensified form of Time itself', Barry Nebulay explains, and Dr Rao details that it signifies 'the merciless clock-beat we all seek to escape, into the pulselessness of salvation' (AD 626). Quaternions inspire hope for transcendence when their scalar part promises ways to manipulate time. Considering that its movement is linear from past to future, a reversal of direction seems to many characters the one way of change. Mathematically, this means turning the arrow of time by 180 degrees, so that time flows from future to past. Yet, Quaternions do not work with a one-dimensional axis but with four dimensions, and even in the two-dimensional system of complex numbers, the possibilities of turning proliferate: next to the x-axis that can be viewed as the one-dimensional arrow of time, there is an '*additional axis* whose unit is $\sqrt{-1}$' and enables rotations by any angle in a two-dimensional plane (AD 147). As Dr Rao explains in dazzling mathematical diction:

> [M]appings in which a linear axis becomes curvilinear – functions of a complex variable such as $w = e^z$, where a straight line in the z-plane maps to a circle in the w-plane, [...] do suggest the possibility of linear time becoming circular, and so achieving eternal return. (AD 147)

Converting linear input in the z-plane to curvilinear output in the w-plane, Quaternions can bend time, encouraging hope for immortality in a circular recurrence. Yet, ultimately, the aim of transcendence is to arrive at a timeless condition, and characters in *Against the Day* do attain forms of timelessness: at Candlebrow U. the Chums 'would find exactly the mixture of nostalgia and amnesia to provide them a reasonable counterfeit of the Timeless', books may be '[o]utside of time', and Cyprian reflects on a '"convergence" to a kind of stillness, not merely in space but in Time as well' (AD 457, 149, 1076). Mathematics is not a means to such timelessness in *Against the Day*; the temporal element of Quaternions might be used in the Quaternionic Weapon to bring about the end of time as we know it, but instead of transcendence Quaternions promise only circular recurrence.

As characters become disillusioned with the promises of an ideal mathematical world and the ability of Quaternions to transcend time, the novel shows the concept to itself be dependent on a specific time period for its existence: developed by Hamilton in 1843, contended during the Quaternion Wars, and passing into imaginary existence, Quaternions are a product of a specific historical moment and its social and cultural contexts. Seeming universality gives way to different beliefs in the 'Quaternion Wars' where experts of the 'Hamiltonian faith' oppose specialists of a 'semi-religious attachment' to Vector calculation (AD 147, 177). As the religious terminology suggests, the war between the factions does not primarily concern mathematical truth but originates in pre-formed beliefs about how the world ought to be:

> Quaternions failed because they perverted what the Vectorists thought they know of God's intention – that space be simple, three-dimensional, and real, and if there must be a fourth term, an imaginary, that it be

assigned to Time. But Quaternions came in and turned that all end for end, defining the axes of space as imaginary and leaving Time to be the *real* term [. . .]. Of course the Vectorists went to war. (AD 599)

The social and cultural motivations directly affect mathematical existence when, on the losing side, Quaternions and their supporters cease to exist outside the imaginary. The mirror-world built in maths thus should not be understood as an ideal Platonic realm but as a world that provides refuge for aspects of maths that are no less correct than other concepts but do not fit the dominant political, social and cultural views. In other words, *Against the Day* uses Quaternions to show that a system of seeming universality and absolute truth is at least partly constructed by social factors.

Quaternions hold an important place in discussions on the social aspects of scientific knowledge not only in *Against the Day* but in the history of science studies, too. When Pynchon's novel employs a concept that features prominently in the debate about scientific knowledge and the ontological status of mathematical objects, it calls up the context of the 1990s 'Science Wars' where supporters of scientific realism clashed with postmodern scholars advocating understanding scientific concepts as social and cultural constructs. Mathematical examples are sparse in the sociology of science, since the dominant view of maths as universal and true long precluded investigation. In one of the first studies on the sociology of maths in 1976, David Bloor complained about the 'enormous amount of work [that] is devoted to maintaining a perspective which forbids a sociological standpoint'.[42] Aiming to remedy this state of affairs, Bloor examines Hamilton's work on algebra in view of the social, political and philosophical contexts of his time and argues that it depended significantly on these factors.[43] Other studies use Hamilton's construction of Quaternions to illuminate the production of knowledge in theoretical practice as opposed to the better-explored experimental sciences, and Andrew Pickering more generally establishes Quaternions as an example of the culture of science – that is, as one of 'the "made things" of science [. . . such as] scientific facts and theories'.[44] Viewed not as being found in nature or pre-existing in a Platonic realm but as 'made' in specific historical and cultural circumstances, Quaternions feature as one of the most prominent mathematical examples in postmodern accounts of scientific knowledge. As we have seen, *Against the Day* employs the concept in a comparable way, presenting it as undermining the notion of the universality of mathematical knowledge, and not only as made but as itself making (imaginary) worlds. Yet, the presentation of the social embeddedness of maths in Pynchon's novel does not embrace arbitrary constructions of concepts and is not subject to accusations of freewheeling relativism that were levelled against science studies in the 1990s. *Against the Day*'s cautious approach to notions of maths as a social and cultural construction becomes particularly apparent when comparing it to Pynchon's treatment of the idea in his earlier novel *Mason & Dixon*. We shall therefore take a brief look at this novel published during the 'Science Wars' in 1997, before further examining the world-building potential of maths in *Against the Day*.

Mason & Dixon calls into question the universal nature of mathematics much more drastically than *Against the Day* when even the basic geometrical element of the circle is open to cultural and religious construction: 'It was five and a Quarter Degrees that the Jesuits remov'd from the Chinese Circle, in reducing it to three hundred sixty'.[45] This alternative geometry, which might have arrived from another planet together with China, indeed measures a different world: the 365,25-degree circle opens up additional space that is not available when measuring in standard Enlightenment geometry but that, in Pynchon's novel, really exists. Similarly, adhering to the outdated time measurement after the 1752 calendar reform releases a different reality: while in the new calendar September 2 is followed by September 14, some characters live through the eleven missing days. Alternative mathematical concepts and measurement systems thus open up other spaces and times, ultimately creating different worlds.[46] In *Mason & Dixon*, the cultural specificity of mathematics includes even its most basic elements such as the circle and numbers, which have to be 'transnumerated' outside their culture of origin.[47] This aspect is far less pronounced in *Against the Day*, where even the Chums in their higher imaginary existence note the international nature of number. When only more complex concepts depend on mathematical faiths based on preformed assumptions about the world, the socio-cultural constructedness and world-building potential of maths emerges as subject to stricter conditions, and, as we shall see, the twenty-first-century novel explores the possibilities of alternative maths and worlds built from these with a new emphasis on their rootedness in the real.

In *Against the Day*, the Axiom of Choice works as an illustration of the necessary connectedness of mathematics to earthly conditions, showing that its constructions are not arbitrary departures from the world but remain tied to the real:

> [Kit] was presented with a startling implication of Zermelo's Axiom of Choice. It was possible in theory, he was shown beyond a doubt, to take a sphere the size of a pea, cut it apart into several very precisely shaped pieces, and reassemble it into another sphere the size of the sun. (AD 1212)

What appears as strikingly counterintuitive and initially provoked strong criticism by professionals is now widely accepted as the Banach–Tarski paradox. The example in *Against the Day* is commonly used in the philosophy of science to illustrate the strange implications of the paradox:

One of the amazing results in the Banach–Tarski paper implies that a solid ball of any size can be cut up – in theory – into a finite number of pieces that can be reassembled to make a ball of any other size. In other words, 'a pea can be cut up to make the sun'![48]

Unlike other antinomies, for example those discovered in set theory, the Banach–Tarski paradox does not question accepted assumptions of modern maths, and no mathematical inconsistency compromises Professor Vanderjuice's far-reaching conclusion from Zermelo's Axiom of Choice in *Against the Day*: 'you see what this means don't you? [. . .] the world we think we know can be dissected and reassembled into any number of worlds, each as real as "this" one' (AD 1212). Supporting the notion that mathematics does not transcend the real or build arbitrary imaginary worlds but that it remains rooted in the world and creates alternative states of it, the Axiom of Choice exemplifies what several characters realise over the course of the novel: maths always comes back to the real, even if a sojourn into mathematical realms can change reality in the process. Yashmeen employs mathematical insights to solve problems in her real life, Dr Rao uses the '"imaginary" reference system' of Quaternions to reappear in a different place and as a different person, and Kit learns that a reassembled and counterintuitively changed world can be as real as the one taken for granted (AD 605). Recreating what is thought to be 'the' world, mathematics incorporates possibilities of plurality and freedom, but without stable foundations and not completely independent of reality, it is neither a tool for transcendence nor for random construction.

Against the Day very carefully presents modern mathematics as constructed in specific contexts and lacking the certainty and universality that might seem to define it. Although precisely not embracing a notion of complete social constructedness that is associated with the postmodern faction in the 'Science Wars', maths in its modern notion does become comparable to other fields of knowledge in Pynchon's novel. Given that in *Against the Day* the mathematical and the political map into each other in view of shared crises and movements towards *an-arche*, the opportunities and limits of world-making in modern maths lend themselves to examining politically relevant strategies of tapping into imaginary existence to break the world into pieces and recreate it.

The Modernist Transformation of Anarchism into the Imaginary Domain

This section turns to the more immediately political implications of the interrelations of maths and politics and aims to show that the mathematical discussion does not 'nullif[y]' the urgency of Pynchon's writing but is integral to *Against the Day*'s vision of the political.[49] More specifically, it examines the crisis and failure of political anarchism and its transformation, considers these developments in view of the mathematical discussion, and argues that both can be understood in the terms of David Weir's thesis of modernism's 'aesthetic realization of anarchist politics'.[50] In light of the modernist transformation of anarchism into the realms of maths and art and its implications for Pynchon's political engagement, I then consider in what ways *Against the Day* marks a shift in Pynchon's postmodernist practice.

In *Against the Day*, anti-foundationalist movements do not only find expression in mathematics, but anarchism develops into different forms after its political failure, which a character predicts to come about with the First World War: 'A general European war [. . .] would be just the ticket to wipe Anarchism off the political map' (AD 1053). Webb Traverse, a miner using explosives to protest against big corporations, is the most active anarchist in the novel, and his aims appear in a positive light, as a laudable protest against unfair power distribution, suppression, systemic violence and the tycoon Scarsdale Vibe as the embodiment of capitalist evil. Robert McLaughlin explains that by pitting Webb's terrorist activities against a repulsive system of inequality and evil, *Against the Day* 'sets something of a trap for readers, inviting us to sympathize with, even root for, acts of violence'.[51] Kathryn Hume even goes so far as to argue that Pynchon himself condones violence by showing again and again that '[d]ynamiting capitalist structures is worthy of a particular kind of saint in *Against the Day*'s spiritual economy'.[52] It does, at least, not require much of a stretch to detect a certain sympathy with anarchist views when a character counters the challenge 'how can anyone set off a bomb that will take innocent lives?' with the question: 'If you are not devoting every breath of every day waking and sleeping to destroying those who slaughter the innocent as easy as signing a check, then how innocent are you willing to call yourself?' (AD 97). Webb's death by the hands of arch-capitalist Vibe signals the decline of political anarchism: his children do not step into his shoes, and *Against the Day* then traces the – successful and unsuccessful – transformation of anarchism into other forms.

Outside mathematics where Quaternionists work in small-scale groupings against systems that 'govern[] absolutely', the family unit is Pynchon's primary example of an anarchist, that is, small and self-organised, community (AD 599). Characterised as likely to unselfishly forgo profit in order to provide others with unconditional help, family is not restricted to biological kinship here, but committing totally to another person's welfare creates a family-tie of some sort. Moreover, where the non-representational nature of Quaternions questions foundations and leads to their imaginary existence, anarchism finds new imaginary expressions in literature, music and painting. Gratuitous aid is, so Fleetwood points out, not a frequent occurrence on earth but more prevalent in literary fiction: 'I used to read Dickens as a child. The cruelty didn't surprise me, but I did wonder at the moments of uncompensated kindness, which

I had never observed outside the pages of fiction' (AD 187). Next to literature, a character proposes music as a form in which a functioning anarchistic society is possible. With its emphasis on improvisation, the early twentieth-century phenomenon of 'Jass' shows 'the most amazing social coherence, as if you all shared the same brain' and thus constitutes a realisation of anarchistic ideas in music (AD 417).

Together with the examples in mathematics, literature and music, the painter Tancredi's artistic anarchism forms part of a transformation from the violent political to the cultural plane. Tancredi shares the Futurists' demand for a new form of art that responds to the changed conditions of the modern world, and he directly refers to the Futurist programme that celebrates engaging with science and technology and exalts 'aggressive action'.[53] Importantly however, Tancredi implicitly distances himself from the praise of violent means: 'He sympathized with Marinetti and those around him who were beginning to describe themselves as "Futurists," but failed to share their attraction to the varieties of American brutalism' (AD 657). Instead of using brutal methods, understood in its double meaning as artistic movement and violent quality, Tancredi hopes to change and redeem the world through peaceable modernist art. Unlike Webb's violent anarchist attacks then, he does not try to kill Scarsdale Vibe with bomb explosions but commits a purely artistic attack with paintings which are 'like explosions. He favored the palette of fire and explosion. [. . .] "He's a sort of infernal-machine specialist"' (AD 658). More precisely, Tancredi's paintings reveal a counter-side of reality by rearranging 'dot[s] of color which become the basic unit of reality' and thus create what Dally thinks of as 'a contra-Venezia, the almost previsual reality behind what everyone else was agreeing to define as "Venice"' (AD 660). In his anarchist attack, the reorganisation of foundational elements of reality is supposed to show Vibe the unfoundedness of his power: 'Some define Hell as the absence of God, and that is the least we may expect of the infernal machine – that the bourgeoisie be deprived of what most sustains them', Tancredi explains (AD 659). However, the an-archist vision does not change Vibe's views of the world; Tancredi is shot and maimed before he gets the picture to him, and Vibe only revels in his 'victory over Anarchist terror' (AD 834).

When Tancredi identifies with modernist artistic programmes and objects to violent action, his attack provides a literal exposition of Weir's thesis that 'anarchism succeeded culturally where it failed politically'.[54] Weir examines how modernist art begins to exhibit elements of aesthetic anarchism, for example in its tendency towards fragmentation. This transformation becomes concrete with Tancredi's transfer of Webb's bombings to the sphere of art where paintings are 'like explosions': the violent detonations of Webb's bombs literally turn into Tancredi's 'palette of fire and explosion' (AD 658). However, Tancredi's modernist aesthetic form of anarchism is an ambiguous successor of Webb's morally difficult use of violence. On the one hand, the non-violent examining of the world's foundational elements and the reimagining of Venice as a contra-city shows alternatives to taken-for-granted reality. On the other hand, Tancredi might be 'a virtuous kid, like all these fucking artists', but his attack on Vibe remains unsuccessful and, showing 'a curious reluctance to speak of what the design might actually do', not even Tancredi himself seems able to pin down the expected effects of his art (AD 836, 659). Unlike Webb's terrorist actions that also harm innocent people, virtuous artistic anarchism does not entail such ethical difficulties, but the lack of effectiveness puts into question the transformation to the aesthetic plane as a way to realise anarchist ideals. Tancredi's painted announcement of the absence of God and shattering of reality into the basic unit of dots – the artistic revelation of the lack of foundations and consequent fragmentation – might evade the ethical quandary of violent action but comes with its own problems of ineffectiveness.

The contrast between Webb's violent actions and Tancredi's ineffective anarchism by art, and the only imaginary existence of Quaternions and their questioning of mathematical representation, have implications for the political potential of literature. The failure of non-violent means to initiate change also applies to language, which at the turn of the century is subject to a pervading scepticism or *Sprachkrise* (see also Chapter 2). Seeing the ineffectiveness of voicing his discontent through language, Webb turns to the more direct expression of explosives, which, so the leader of the mathematical-spiritual order T.W.I.T. holds, 'may easily open, now and then, passages to elsewhere' (AD 248). Webb thus 'always expressed himself more by way of dynamite', and his son understands 'that in each explosion, regardless of outcome, had spoken the voice Webb could not speak with in the daily world' (AD 356, 528). *Against the Day* also reflects the impossibility of verbalising ungraspable reality when it does not represent the First World War but marks its arrival through the explosion of the Tunguska Event: 'the explosion arrived, the voice of a world announcing that it would never go back to what it had been' (AD 878). The basic sound structure or *signifiant* communicates the death of former reality, and the war, condensed into one explosion, changes the world drastically. With the contrast of verbal and, on the other hand, explosive means of communication and change, *Against the Day* questions the reliability of literary language and raises concerns about the effectiveness of its own medium as well as about its stance on expression by way of dynamite. Significantly, *Against the Day* does not end with a palette of fire and explosion – it differs from Tancredi's artistic expression and also from Pynchon's earlier novel *Gravity's Rainbow* where, in a formulation including readers in the imminent destruction, a rocket is about to fall on 'us' (see Chapter 4). Instead, *Against the Day* closes with a vision of the Chums of Chance preparing to fly towards grace. To appreciate this ending, we have to examine how it relates to anarchist issues in *Against the Day*, to the freedom identified in imaginary realms of modern maths, and to questions about the effectiveness of political engagement through art.

Against the Day draws attention to its own fictionality when it begins and ends with the storyline of the Chums of Chance and highlights their ambiguous ontological status. The Chums' flight on the first page – and with it the novel's setting off – is marked as a disconnection from the everyday world and as an ascent into the imaginary, into fictional realms. The first pages also introduce the topic of anarchism, doing so with explicit reference to fiction. *Against the Day* thus immediately calls attention to literature as a domain of anarchist expression and emphasises the fictional nature of the presentation that is to follow. Indeed, Lindsay's comment on the destination of the Chums of Chance also applies to the readers' trajectory through the novel: 'the inexorably rising tide of World Anarchism, [is] to be found particularly rampant, in fact, at our current destination' (AD 6). Following this warning is the reassurance that encounters with anarchism will occur only in the realm of fiction: the dog Pugnax reads Henry James's novel about anarchism, *The Princess Casamassima*, whereupon Lindsay describes anarchism as:

> 'a sinister affliction to which I pray we shall suffer no occasion for exposure more immediate than that to be experienced, as with Pugnax at this moment, safely within the fictional leaves of some book.' Placing upon the word 'book' an emphasis whose level of contempt can be approached perhaps only by Executive Officers. (AD 6)

The emphasis on the literary nature of the encounter with anarchism continues outside Lindsay's speech when Pugnax, the reading dog clearly signalling the fictional nature of the entire episode, fails to identify a human smell in Lindsay and thus underlines the fact that the Chums of Chance are of ambiguous ontological status even in the reality of the book *Against the Day*. And when a couple of sentences later an authorial voice explains that the airship is powered by an 'anemometer' that violates scientific laws but that 'my young readers may recall from the boys' earlier adventure (*The Chums of Chance at Krakatoa*, *The Chums of Chance Search for Atlantis*)', the episode further stresses the fictional side of the Chums' existence (AD 7). Thus, the introduction of anarchism is twice removed: the first encounter takes place in a novel that itself occurs as part of a markedly fictional adventure series. The box-structure then draws attention to the fact that *Against the Day* itself is a novel and that any anarchism about to occur does so in the realm of fiction.

The Chums' destination is indeed a state of rampant anarchism and is, as we are assured in the beginning, met with only in fiction. The Chums become anarchists themselves in the sense of giving uncompensated help to any population in need. Ignoring national boundaries and politics altogether, they are 'declared enemies of whatever is in power now' and do not expect recognition or reward for their 'supranational' commitment: 'Their motto was "There, but Invisible"' (AD 1152, 1217). The reassurance that anarchism remains safe 'within the fictional leaves of some book' turns to disappointment when the Chums' conversion to anarchism leads to the most hopeful ending of any Pynchon novel: 'They will put on smoked goggles for the glory of what is coming to part the sky. They fly toward grace' (AD 6, 1220). The stereotypical happy ending in a mass wedding of all the Chums, the simultaneous births of children to all couples, and the hopeful flight towards a bright future might be appropriate to the serial adventures of storybook characters, but it is not a likely destination outside of fiction. The close relationship between anarchism and fiction that is highlighted at the beginning and ending of *Against the Day*, then, suggests that the novel's anarchism has to be thought of in light of its emphatically imaginary existence. So, when Seán Molloy claims that the novel advocates transcending politics altogether and bases his view on the, as he claims, apolitical status of the Chums' flight towards grace, his interpretation has to be reconsidered to take account of the tight connection between anarchism and imaginary heights.[55] Greater attention to the expressly fictional nature of the presentation of anarchism also eases Hume's malaise regarding what she claims to be Pynchon's call to violent action. When she deplores the explicitness of 'this anarchist and Catholic Pynchon' who presents only the two alternatives of 'entering a convent and becoming a dynamiter', she loses sight of the overt fictionality with which the topic of anarchism is introduced.[56] Just as mathematics in *Against the Day* cannot be thought without considering both its real and its imaginary components, discussions of politics gain complexity when attending more closely to the transformation of political action into artistic forms of anarchism. At the same time, the contrast between violent action and ineffectual art means that the anarchism of *Against the Day* cannot be seen *only* in the light of its emphatically imaginary existence but has to be considered in view of its complex relation to the real and the responsibilities that come with it. This is the topic of the next section.

Complexity in *Against the Day*

Anarchism and political questions around it gain new urgency in the wake of the terrorist attacks of 9/11, and critics have viewed Pynchon's more decidedly political stance in *Against the Day* as part of a more general shift towards the real. This new emphasis informs Sascha Pöhlmann's suggestion: 'We may have to stop calling Thomas Pynchon a postmodern writer.'[57] Pöhlmann stresses that Pynchon's texts are still postmodern but that *Against the Day* with its determinedly political tone forcefully goes beyond the limitations of postmodernism: 'this is not to claim that Pynchon's writing is not postmodern, but that it is also other things, and that it seems more and more inappropriate to limit one's view of these texts to a postmodern framework'.[58] Taking a closer look at the relation between the real, the imaginary and the fictional through the lens of the novel's engagement with mathematics elucidates the shift in Pynchon's practice: it clarifies his stance on the modernist transformation of anarchism into aesthetic and imaginary realms, and illuminates his concern with the possibilities and responsibilities of art in the twenty-first century.

Against the Day employs mathematics to illustrate the necessary interrelation of the real and the imaginary and draws on it as a poetological metaphor – that is, as an image of the principles of literature in the twenty-first century. In the novel, Yashmeen notices the indispensability of a constitutional real element even in her arcane research into Riemann's zeta-function and the 'whole "imaginary" mirror-world' of which this complex function takes account (AD 558). The zeta-function is part of the still unsolved Riemann hypothesis – a famous conjecture about the location of the function's zeros: it states that the zeta-function has so-called trivial zeros at the negative even integers (−2, −4, −6, etc.) and so-called non-trivial zeros at complex numbers with the real part ½. Geometrically, this means that, in a complex coordinate system, all non-trivial zeros lie on a line that is parallel to the perpendicular y-axis and goes through the value ½. Yashmeen sees this vertical line as the backbone of the complex realm and its combination of real and imaginary values: '"There is also this ... spine of reality." Afterward she would remember she actually said "*Rückgrad von Wirklichkeit*"' (AD 679). Yashmeen's imagery suggests that the spine holds up and connects different imaginary values and relates these to earthly reality. Metaphorically, the common real part ½ links sets of conditions with higher or lower imaginary components to the real, for example connecting the Chums' storybook universe and the earthly world engaged in war. Any world with an imaginary value is thus necessarily complex in the sense of combining real and imaginary elements. When in *Against the Day* Hilbert takes up Yashmeen's idea of the spine of reality and formulates it into the 'celebrated Hilbert-Pólya-Conjecture', the concept constitutes part of the spine of reality of the novel itself: Hilbert and the Hilbert–Pólya conjecture are part of the history of mathematics and act as a bridge between the novel world and readers' reality (AD 679). More generally speaking, the novel's excursions into mathematics and multiple imaginary domains are all rooted in historical actuality, making *Against the Day* a 'complex' text.

A connection to the real is not in itself a laudable characteristic; it is open to facilitate acts of kindness as well as abuse. It is the real rather than the long-questioned imaginary element of Quaternions that is used in a weapon to destroy the known world and its seemingly self-evident conditions, and the Chums of Chance recognise the perpendicular dimension 'as a means for delivering explosives' (AD 1218). At first sight, Lindsay only comments on the ambiguity of access to the third dimension, but the suggestion that a higher setting on the perpendicular imaginary axis may be used for anarchistic action also points to the danger of dismissing the imaginary as inconsequential. In the paragraph preceding its happy ending, *Against the Day* illustrates the potential of the imaginary and its relevance to the real in relation to the mathematics of complex numbers. When estranged Kit and Dally are about to meet after long separation and get another chance of happiness, the paragraph ends: 'May we imagine for them a vector, passing through the invisible, the "imaginary," the unimaginable, carrying them safely into this postwar Paris [...]. A vector through the night into a morning' (AD 1217). The implied answer is affirmative: of course, we may *imagine* a happy ending for them, not least as we follow the Chums' approach to grace immediately afterwards. The mathematical terminology of imaginaries and vectors further supports the suggested answer: if imaginary elements are usefully employed in mathematics then, so the implication, other forms of working with the imaginary – and not least literary fiction – might similarly be of real consequence. Indeed, the mathematics of complex numbers provides a proof for Yashmeen's conviction that '[w]e can do whatever we can imagine' when the imaginary is a realm of productive transitioning between two real states (AD 987). Where Dr Rao uses the Quaternionic '"imaginary" reference system' and Yashmeen draws on 'something that would allow access to a different ... I don't know, "set of conditions"? [...] Unreal, but not compellingly so' (AD 605, 694) to travel to different places, stepping into the imaginary constitutes productive routes in non-mathematical contexts, too. The Chums of Chance draw on the power of the imaginary to secure their escape when they 'chose lateral solutions, sidestepping the crisis by passing into metaphorical identities' (AD 471). Kit similarly benefits from access to imaginary domains when travelling through the real and imaginary territories of mystical Shambhala and, after a process that is 'like the convergence of a complex function', emerges into a state that might see him and Dally as a happy couple once again (AD 1214).

The phrase that describes the end of Kit's journey as a merging of real and imaginary realms identifies the characters' problem-solving as equivalent to a mathematical strategy formulated by Jacques Hadamard: 'the shortest and best way between two truths of the real domain often passes through the imaginary one'.[59] With the metaphor of complex numbers, *Against the Day* emphasises connections of the imaginary with the real, and the mathematical relevance of the imaginary puts into perspective the questioned effectiveness of literary fiction. While the potential of art to change reality remains ambiguous in the novel, Yashmeen's opinion that after exploring other sets of conditions we 'return to the bourgeois day and its mass delusions of safety, to report on what we've seen' and her mathematically inspired conviction that '[w]e can do whatever we can imagine' provide a fairly good brief for readers, who, putting down the book with its happy ending in imaginary heights, step back into their day with a vision of what the world might be (AD 1058, 987). The novel's mathematical explorations and questioning of the value of art thus do not advocate connecting to the real by abandoning the imaginary. Rather, *Against the Day* challenges and renegotiates the place of fiction in a changed world, using concepts and imagery from maths to suggest that the imaginary remains a necessary and powerful part of literature but that a core connection to the real is needed to save it from excesses of self-referentiality which, as the passage at the Museum der Monstrositäten shows, threaten to destroy worlds.

In view of the importance of anarchism for *Against the Day*'s turn to the real and the repositioning of Pynchon's postmodernism, it is worth reiterating that the fragmented, plural style of Pynchon's novels constitutes a form of narrative anarchism. Graham Benton summarises: 'Pynchon's formal techniques – which favor heterogeneity over uniformity, spontaneity over conformity, and fragmentation over consolidation – align with an anarchist aesthetic that reflects a sustained skepticism toward all typologies and classifications of genre.'[60] The postmodernist form of *Against the Day* also illustrates Weir's thesis of the translation of anarchism from the political to the cultural domain when it exhibits 'all the variety, multiplicity, and freedom of human expression that anarchism encouraged in the past'.[61] Yet, while *Against the Day* with its various plotlines, styles and genres constitutes such an aesthetic way of perpetuating the anarchist agenda, Pynchon goes a step further than the modernist writers Weir examines: he does not practice anarchism by describing fragments of the given world but sets multiple possible and coexisting worlds side by side. Importantly, these worlds always remain related to the one understood as real and indeed are the world, reassembled into different but nevertheless real forms. Thus, on the one hand, *Against the Day* illustrates a further development of Weir's thesis of the transformation of anarchism into art; on the other hand, the juxtaposition of worlds and attention to the interrelatedness but distinctiveness of the real and the imaginary communicate the insufficiency of aesthetic anarchism and the need for real political action. Significantly, the Chums of Chance's flight to grace in imaginary heights is possible only after they acknowledge their responsibility to the earthly world. They are in danger of losing touch with it and are not even aware of the First World War, as if 'in soaring free from enfoldment by the indicative world below, they had paid with a waiver of allegiance to it' (AD 1149). Only after the Chums reduce wartime suffering by providing anarchist help do they find a balance between journeys into imaginary heights and return to earthly reality, and only then do they approach grace. McLaughlin's statement that fiction after 9/11 concerns itself with 'the *complex* role of fiction in a culture where literature of any kind, but especially serious literature, seems less and less relevant' (my emphasis) thus appropriately describes *Against the Day* in more than one sense: the novel asks about the value of fiction in a time of real urgency, and, drawing on the metaphor of complex numbers, illustrates the connection between the real and the imaginary and the need for both to account for a complex world.[62]

The complex relations of the real, the imaginary and the fictional in mathematics, politics and literature demonstrate that there is more to *Against the Day* than the all-pervasive polarity between light and dark at first suggests. Reminiscent of Pythagoras's Table of Opposites, *Against the Day* presents contrasted pairs: day and night, light and 'counter-light', the 'Anti-Stone' that brings death but at the same time freedom which is 'counter-Death', cities as well as a 'counter-City', and, next to Earth, a 'counter-Earth' (AD 653, 89, 419, 279, 658, 1147). The 'unyielding doubleness of everything' not least shows in the both good and bad aspects of anarchism (AD 1074). Yet, as the novel develops in view of mathematics, the contrast of basic elements cannot be considered outside the context of the fictional. It does not stop at setting elements against each other or conflating them, but the one-dimensional opposition of positive and negative, of presence and absence, is complemented by another dimension: the perpendicular imaginary.[63] Neither positive nor negative themselves, imaginary numbers indicate a further dimension where the opposition does not apply. The imaginary does not merge or alleviate the contrast of presence and absence on the real axis, but it provides a domain that can connect and change real magnitudes. The mathematical model thus shows in unprecedented clarity the complexity of worlds in Pynchon's writing: what is $(+1)$ and what is not (-1) is completed by what could be, by lateral, imaginary worlds $(\pm\sqrt{-1})$.

Modern mathematics is central to *Against the Day*'s negotiation of political questions around foundations and anarchism and its invitation to 'rethink what the political actually is': using concepts and metaphors of maths, *Against the Day* urges us to view the imaginary as part and a further dimension of the political and to account for both components of the complex world – the real *and* the imaginary, always interrelating, influencing and changing each other.[64] Maths itself gains political significance when on the smaller level Quaternions constitute an anarchist alternative to centrally governing systems, and, more generally, modern maths in its foundational crisis is in a state of *an-arche* that occasions a sense of uncertainty but also allows for creative new constructions. Reconsidering modernist movements towards anarchist absence of foundations in light of limitations that become obvious in a later political landscape, *Against the Day* combines concerns from the early twentieth and the early twenty-first centuries. The novel's double temporality and its interrelation of historical and fictional elements signal that only by considering issues with adequate complexity can anti-foundationalist movements save themselves from self-referentiality and serve as constructive ways to rebuild the world. The concept of complex numbers becomes a metaphor for political and literary approaches to the world, and the relevance of maths to literary developments also shows when it shares with it modernist features such as a loss of traditional foundations, questioning notions of representation, a self-referential turn, and focus on the possibilities of imaginary domains. Presenting maths as part of modernist movements and metaphorically encompassing a later reappraisal of the complex nature of anarchism, *Against the Day* illustrates the continued relevance of the history of maths around 1900. The next chapters focus on texts from the first half of the twentieth century to examine the beginnings of viewing maths in terms of modernist culture and, vice versa, of framing modernist literature in terms of mathematics.

NOTES

1. Louis Menand, 'Do the Math: Thomas Pynchon Returns', review of *Against the Day* by Thomas Pynchon, *The New Yorker*, 27 Nov. 2006.
2. David Weir, *Anarchy and Culture: The Aesthetic Politics of Modernism* (Amherst: University of Massachusetts Press, 1997), p. 5.
3. Menand, 'Do the Math', n. pag.
4. Samuel Thomas, *Pynchon and the Political* (New York: Routledge, 2007), p. 12. Quotation from Pynchon's introduction to his short-story collection *Slow Learner*.
5. Felix Klein, 'The Present State of Mathematics', in *Mathematical Papers Read at the International Mathematical Congress held in Connection with the World's Columbian Exposition Chicago 1893*, ed. Eliakim Hastings Moore, Oskar Bolza, Heinrich Maschke and Henry White (New York: Macmillan, 1896), 133–5 (pp. 133–4).
6. Karen V. H. Parshall and David E. Rowe, 'Embedded in the Culture: Mathematics at the World's Columbian Exposition of 1893', *The Mathematical Intelligencer*, 15.2 (1993), 40–5 (p. 45).
7. Klein, 'The Present State of Mathematics', p. 134.
8. Letter to Stieltjes, qtd in Joseph L. Doob, 'The Development of Rigor in Mathematical Probability (1900–1950)', *The American Mathematical Monthly*, 103.7 (1996), 586–95 (p. 586).
9. Marcus Giaquinto, *The Search for Certainty: A Philosophical Account of Foundations of Mathematics* (Oxford: Clarendon, 2002), pp. 136–7.
10. David Hilbert, 'On the Infinite' [1925], in *Philosophy of Mathematics: Selected Readings*, ed. Paul Benacerraf and Hilary Putnam (Oxford: Blackwell, 1964), 134–51 (p. 141).
11. David Hilbert, 'Mathematical Problems', trans. Mary Winston Newson, *Bulletin of the American Mathematical Society*, 8.10 (1902), 437–79 (pp. 437 and 445).
12. Friedrich Ludwig Gottlob Frege, *Grundgesetze der Arithmetik* (Jena: Pohle, 1903), p. 253. 'eine der Grundlagen seines Baues erschüttert' (Hilbert, 'On the Infinite', p. 141).
13. Hermann Weyl, 'On the New Foundational Crisis of Mathematics' [1921], in *From Brouwer to Hilbert: The Debate on the Foundations of Mathematics in the 1920s*, ed. Paolo Mancosu (New York and Oxford: Oxford University Press, 1998), 86–118 (p. 99).
14. Hilbert qtd in Dirk van Dalen, *Mystic, Geometer, and Intuitionist: The Life of L.E.J. Brouwer; vol. 2: Hope and Disillusion* (Oxford: Clarendon, 2005), p. 486.
15. Dalen, *Mystic, Geometer, and Intuitionist II*, pp. 544–5.
16. Hermann Weyl, 'Mathematics and Logic', *The American Mathematical Monthly*, 53.1 (1946), 2–13 (p. 13).

17. Hilbert, 'On the Infinite', p. 141.
18. Dalen, *Mystic, Geometer, and Intuitionist II*, p. vii.
19. 'Die öffentliche, zum Teil leidenschaftlich geführte Debatte um die Krise verwandelte sich seit Mitte der zwanziger Jahre in einen Fachdiskurs unter Grundlagenforschern. Mit der Konsolidierung der Weimarer Republik ging auch diese Krise vorüber. Die Sinnfrage war als politische öffentlich geworden, löste sich in private Sinngebung auf' (Herbert Mehrtens, *Moderne Sprache Mathematik. Eine Geschichte des Streits um die Grundlagen der Disziplin und des Subjekts formaler Systeme* (Frankfurt am Main: Suhrkamp, 1990), p. 294).
20. G. H. Hardy, *A Mathematician's Apology* [1940] (Cambridge: Cambridge University Press, 1992), p. 140.
21. Leibniz qtd in Paul J. Nahin, *An Imaginary Tale: The Story of $\sqrt{-1}$* (Princeton: Princeton University Press, 1998), p. 26.
22. Leibniz qtd in Adrian Rice, 'Inexplicable? The Status of Complex Numbers in Britain, 1750–1850', in *Around Caspar Wessel and the Geometric Representation of Complex Numbers*, ed. Jesper Lützen (Copenhagen: Reitzels, 2001), 147–80 (p. 150).
23. George Airy, 'Supplement to a Proof of the Theorem that every Algebraic Equation has a Root', *Transactions Cambridge Philosophical Society*, 10 (1858), 327–30 (p. 327). George Boole, *An Investigation of The Laws of Thought on Which are Founded the Mathematical Theories of Logic and Probabilities* [1854] (New York: Dover, 1958), p. 69. Augustus De Morgan, *On the Study and Difficulties of Mathematics* (Chicago and London: Open Court and Kegan Paul, 1910), p. 152.
24. The changing sense of a number's reality can be illustrated more clearly with the case of irrational numbers. The Pythagoreans feared deadly consequences when talking about irrationals since these are not part of the system of rational numbers: irrationals cannot be expressed by fractions or be written down, as their decimals go on indefinitely without repeating themselves. From a contemporary viewpoint, irrational numbers are comparatively unproblematic: for example, the irrational number $\sqrt{2}$ can be drawn as the diagonal of a square with side length 1, or π be described as the ratio of a circle's circumference to its diameter. The case of irrational numbers demonstrates that the understanding of a number's reality is changeable and that it can be said to be real only in relation to a mathematical reference system while a match with physical reality is irrelevant. The explanation for the imaginary nature of imaginary numbers, then, is that negative square roots are not part of and therefore do not exist in the real number system but are defined and thus real in the system of complex numbers. In other words, a number's existence depends on the number system in use and, in effect, all numbers are equally real or unreal. The fact that the relevance of imaginary numbers to the physical world is not intuitive made their acceptance more difficult.
25. The description closely follows Hamilton's own account of his discovery of Quaternions (see Hamilton's letter to his son, dated 5 August 1865; see also Thomas L. Hankins, *Sir William Rowan Hamilton* (Baltimore and London: Johns Hopkins University Press, 1980), pp. 293–4).
26. Graves qtd in John C. Baez, 'The Octonions', *Bulletin of the American Mathematical Society*, 39.2 (2002), 145–205 (p. 146).
27. William Rowan Hamilton, *Lectures on Quaternions* (Dublin: Hodges and Smith, 1853), p. 2.
28. William Rowan Hamilton, 'Theory of Conjugate Functions, or Algebraic Couples; with a Preliminary and Elementary Essay on Algebra as the Science of Pure Time', *The Transactions of the Royal Irish Academy*, 17 (1831), 293–422 (pp. 417–18).
29. Hamilton, 'Theory of Conjugate Functions', p. 422.

30. Hamilton, 'Theory of Conjugate Functions', p. 297.
31. William Rowan Hamilton, 'Elementary Sketch of the Nature of that Conception of Mathematical Quaternions, which is Developed more in Detail by Sir W. R. Hamilton, in his recently published Volume on Lectures on that Subject', in *Life of Sir William Rowan Hamilton* III, ed. Robert Perceval Graves (Dublin: Hodges, Figgis & Co., 1889), 635–7 (p. 635).
32. Peter Guthrie Tait, 'On the Intrinsic Nature of the Quaternion Method' [1894], in *Scientific Papers* II (London: Forgotten Books, 2013), 392–3 (p. 393).
33. Tait qtd in American Association for the Advancement of Science, *Proceedings of the American Association for the Advancement of Science*, 40 (1891), p. 80.
34. Letter to Graves, 30 April 1846, qtd in Robert Perceval Graves, *Life of Sir William Rowan Hamilton II*, 3 vols (Dublin: Hodges, Figgis & Co, 1882–9), pp. 521–2.
35. Hamilton, 'Theory of Conjugate Functions', p. 295.
36. Hamilton, 'Theory of Conjugate Functions', p. 294.
37. Michael J. Crowe, *A History of Vector Analysis: The Evolution of the Idea of a Vectorial System* (New York: Dover, 1994), p. 31.
38. For a historical account of the Quaternion Wars, see Hankins, *Sir William Rowan Hamilton*, p. 319.
39. Gibbs wrote to Thomas Craig in 1888: 'I believe that a Kampf ums Dasein is just commencing between the different methods and notations of multiple algebra, especially between the ideas of Grassmann & of Hamilton' (qtd in Crowe, *A History of Vector Analysis*, p. 161).
40. See Chapter 4 for Brian McHale's work that uses Pynchon's writing to develop a distinction between modernism and postmodernism: where modernist novels pose epistemological questions and negotiate the knowability of the world but are less concerned with the ontological stability of reality, postmodernism focuses on ontological issues.
41. Hardy, *A Mathematician's Apology*, p. 143.
42. David Bloor, *Knowledge and Social Imagery* (Chicago and London, University of Chicago Press, 1991), p. 84.
43. David Bloor, 'Hamilton and Peacock on the Essence of Algebra', in *Social History of Nineteenth Century Mathematics*, ed. Herbert Mehrtens, Henk Bos and Ivo Schneider (Boston, MA: Birkhäuser, 1981), 202–32.
44. Andrew Pickering and Adam Stephanides, 'Constructing Quaternions: On the Analysis of Conceptual Practice', in *Science as Practice and Culture*, ed. Andrew Pickering (Chicago: University of Chicago Press, 1992), 139–67.
    Andrew Pickering, *The Mangle of Practice: Time, Agency, and Science* (Chicago: University of Chicago Press, 1995), p. 3.
45. Thomas Pynchon, *Mason & Dixon* (New York: Picador, 1997), p. 629.
46. For a further discussion of mathematics in *Mason & Dixon* and its role in questioning the truth claims of history and science, see Nina Engelhardt, 'Scientific Metafiction and Historiographic Metafiction: Measuring Nature and the Past', in *Twentieth-Century Rhetorics: Metahistorical Narratives and Scientific Metafictions*, ed. Giuseppe Episcopo (Naples: Cronopio, 2014), 145–72, and Nina Engelhardt, 'Scientific Metafiction and Postmodernism', *Zeitschrift für Anglistik und Amerikanistik: A Quarterly of Language, Literature and Culture*, 64.2 (2016), 189–205.
47. Pynchon, *Mason & Dixon*, p. 142.
48. Anita Burdman Feferman and Solomon Feferman, *Alfred Tarski: Life and Logic* (Cambridge: Cambridge University Press, 2004), p. 43.
49. Thomas, *Pynchon and the Political*, p. 12.
50. Weir, *Anarchy and Culture*, p. 169.

51. Robert McLaughlin, 'After the Revolution: US Postmodernism in the Twenty-First Century', *Narrative*, 21.3 (2013), 284–95 (p. 292).
52. Kathryn Hume, 'The Religious and Political Vision of Pynchon's *Against the Day*', *Philological Quarterly*, 86.1–2 (2007), 163–87 (p. 180).
53. Filippo Tommaso Marinetti, 'The Founding and Manifesto of Futurism' [1909], in *Manifesto: A Century of Isms*, ed. Mary Ann Caws (Lincoln, NE and London: University of Nebraska Press, 2001), 187–9 (p. 187).
54. Weir, *Anarchy and Culture*, p. 5.
55. Seán Molloy, 'Escaping the Politics of the Irredeemable Earth-Anarchy and Transcendence in the Novels of Thomas Pynchon', *Theory & Event*, 13:3 (2010), n. pag. *Literature Online*, Web, 14 Apr. 2014.
56. Hume, 'The Religious and Political Vision of Pynchon's *Against the Day*', p. 164 and p. 165.
57. Sascha Pöhlmann, 'Introduction: The Complex Text', in *Against the Grain: Reading Pynchon's Counternarratives*, ed. Sascha Pöhlmann (Amsterdam and New York: Rodopi, 2010), 9–34 (p. 33).
58. Pöhlmann, 'Introduction: The Complex Text', pp. 9–10.
59. Jacques Hadamard, *The Mathematician's Mind: The Psychology of Invention in the Mathematical Field* (Princeton: Princeton University Press, 1996), p. 123.
60. Graham Benton, 'Daydreams and Dynamite: Anarchist Strategies of Resistance and Paths for Transformation in *Against the Day*', in *Pynchon's* Against the Day: *A Corrupted Pilgrim's Guide*, ed. Jeffrey Severs and Christopher Leise (Newark: University of Delaware Press, 2011), 191–213 (p. 191).
61. Weir, *Anarchy and Culture*, p. 259. Weir argues that the characteristics of fragmentation and autonomy consolidate in culture only when their survival in the political domain is threatened. On the other hand, it could be argued that a unidirectional national politics allows for more easily accommodating uncertainty in other domains; an explanation employed by van Dalen in his account of the acceptance of contradictory mathematical philosophies during the politically stable Weimar Republic.
62. McLaughlin, 'After the Revolution', p. 294.
63. In *The Crying of Lot 49* Oedipa notes the repressed possibilities in between the certainties of 0 and 1 with a metaphor from mathematics: 'She had heard all about excluded middles; they were bad shit, to be avoided.' In *Against the Day*, the emphasis is not on the space between poles but on the role of the imaginary, which goes beyond oppositions (Thomas Pynchon, *The Crying of Lot 49* (London: Picador, 1979), p. 125).
64. Thomas, *Pynchon and the Political*, p. 152.

2

MATHEMATICS, LANGUAGE, STRUCTURE: HERMANN BROCH, *THE SLEEPWALKERS*

Like Thomas Pynchon's *Against the Day*, Hermann Broch's trilogy *The Sleepwalkers*, published in German from 1930 to 1932, brings together modern mathematics and the First World War in its search for a literature that could respond to the pressures of its time. While *Against the Day* has a focus on political implications, *The Sleepwalkers* primarily draws on maths in terms of structure: it employs maths as a formal language and structural science to frame the experience of a period of crisis, and, more subtly but importantly, a competition of methodologies in modern maths informs the innovative form of the trilogy. This chapter is accordingly concerned with ways in which the foundational debate in mathematics connects with ideas of literary style and form. Its focus on structure does not involve the use of number as an organising element – a strategy that is, for example, explored by Oulipo, a group of mathematicians and poets founded in the 1960s, but that plays no role in *The Sleepwalkers*. Instead, as part of its modernist attentiveness to matters of form, Broch's work engages with research on the relations of maths and language and with the new approaches that emerge with it: the formalised language of analytic philosophy and literary formalism's concentration on language as the basic building block of texts and its aim for a scientific method of studying literature. An orientation towards the methodology of the modern sciences is evident both in Broch's fictional and his extensive non-fictional work, and *The Sleepwalkers* illustrates his central claim that 'literature has to submit to the spirit of the epoch, to its scientificity, [. . .] and it does so by becoming polyhistoric'.[1]

In his demand to integrate various fields of knowledge in an encyclopaedic approach to the period, Broch stresses the leading role of modern science, which he takes to be exemplary in its methodological and structural advances. As a consequence of this focus, it is irrelevant for Broch whether a literary text addresses scientific topics directly, as long as it is suffused with what he calls the 'spirit of scientific thinking'. With *The Sleepwalkers*, where direct references to science are relatively sparse even though contemporary mathematical debates permeate its structure, Broch attempts to distance himself from writers who lack this 'real sense of science': in his view, authors such as André Gide, Thomas Mann and Robert Musil 'take science to be a crystalline block from which they break off some piece or other to garnish their narratives, mostly in improper places, or to equip a scientist-character with it'.[2] H. G. Wells, a proponent of science as the subject of fiction, openly acknowledged his need to convey science-related information in an artificial manner: 'I had very many things to say. [. . .] I began therefore to make my characters indulge in impossibly explicit monologues and duologues.'[3] As we shall see below, James Joyce is a writer who escapes Broch's censure and whose *Ulysses* is profoundly influential for Broch's concept of a modernist literature in the spirit of scientific thinking, and Chapter 3 shows that Broch shares a more similar approach with, and holds more admiration for, Musil than this remark might seem to suggest. Yet Broch's view that his approach is different from that of other writers highlights his aim to integrate science in the structure of narrative. As a science of structure, mathematics can offer a particularly advantageous approach here, as well as providing a means to examine the underlying patterns of the period and the relations between different forms of knowledge. While contending that other avenues are possible, Broch claims that maths has particular explanatory power and stresses that for himself, 'probably because of my mathematical-constructivist disposition, a different way is hardly practicable'.[4]

As a consequence of Broch's aversion to characters presenting ready-made discourses on science, *The Sleepwalkers* does not feature scientists (although Broch is not against employing scientist-characters per se; he does so in *The Unknown Quantity* and *A Methodological Novella*, for example). Instead, the last book of the trilogy contains an essay that offers abstract analyses of topics also addressed in the fictional strands of the novels and proposes that mathematics occupies a crucial role in coming to terms with changes in the early twentieth century. The essay first diagnoses a widespread transformation in the 'logical structure of thought' and then continues: 'We have before our own eyes the clearest example of such a process in the research into first principles of modern mathematics' (SWIII 481).[5] It is a commonplace in Broch scholarship, yet bears repeating, that the integrated essay does not constitute an exclusive interpretative key to the trilogy: it cannot comment on it from the outside but is itself part of the novels and implicated in what it might seem to analyse. Nevertheless, the essay usefully puts into words the 'great question' that *The Sleepwalkers* pursues across its three novels and for which it suggests mathematics as an example and model for possible responses: 'The great question remains: how can an individual whose ideas have been genuinely directed towards other aims understand and accommodate himself to the implications and the reality of dying?' (SWIII 374). The First World War features as only one expression of a 'sweeping revolution in the style of thinking' that the trilogy explores across political, social and psychological developments (SWIII 481). The essay clarifies the claim that examining modern maths, rather than any other approach, offers the best chance to understand the period and its changes. It explicitly sets out what is also evident from *The Sleepwalkers* as a whole, namely the view that a period is characterised by a specific style. As the underlying structure of thinking is understood to 'uniformly permeate[] all the living expressions of the epoch', a change in the style of thinking similarly affects all areas (SWIII 397). Accordingly, it is possible to follow a development in any one area of thought and apply its structure to other fields by way of analogy, so that when research into its foundations brings about a change in the style of mathematics, a similar transformation should be detectable in all other areas of expression, be it in architecture, politics, ethics or literature.

Since mathematics is a structural science that abstracts from empirical reality to describe general relations, it is, in the terms of *The Sleepwalkers*, the field in which change can best be observed and lends itself to understanding the course of modern reality and its crisis in the First World War. The integrated essay thus presents maths as an example of wider developments, almost as a condensation of the epoch. Fittingly, the notion of a central expression of a time is described in mathematical terms: according to the theory, each style of a period has a unique 'ornament' which 'becomes the formula of style itself, and with that the formula of the entire epoch and its life' (III 398). With the suggestion that mathematics does not present itself as eternal truth but changes across periods, *The Sleepwalkers* echoes Oswald Spengler's contention in *The Decline of the West* that each epoch has a definitive style that also shows in a historically specific mathematics. In contrast to Spengler's cyclical model, Broch's trilogy presents the turn-of-the-century period not as a regress into a former state but as a disintegration into nothingness, an endpoint never reached before. Characterising the wartime-style as having lost its ornament and thus expressing only the absence of a common point of reference, Broch's trilogy proposes maths as a model of a state of absolute dissolution for which it might then also work as a guide to regeneration.

The Sleepwalkers spans the period from 1888 to the 1920s, presenting the time as approaching complete rationality while simultaneously tracing a development of mathematics, a primary expression of reason, from a classical realist to a contradictory modern notion. In the first part of the trilogy,

Pasenow or The Romantic – 1888, maths plays virtually no role; this absence emerges as significant in the context of the other novels, as it indicates the still-unproblematic character of this tool of rational investigation. In *Esch or The Anarchist – 1903* August Esch's attempt to respond to the chaos of the new century with numerical means fails, and the disintegration of ordering systems reaches its end in *Huguenau or The Realist – 1918*: Wilhelm Huguenau works his way through wartime without regard to any supra-individual meaning, and the theoretical essay questions the very foundations of mathematics. Unlike the approach of a number of recent studies, what follows here is not intended to develop in detail the cultural context of *The Sleepwalkers* so as to situate the text, and similarly this is not an exercise in tracking down Broch's scientific sources and reading material. Rather, I examine Broch's trilogy in view of scientific and philosophical discourses that are relevant to the interpretation of the novels and affect our ability to understand the trilogy, its engagement with mathematical material, and its negotiation of relations between maths, modernism and literature. With a main focus on ways in which mathematics features as a structural model in *The Sleepwalkers*, this chapter shows how the trilogy presents maths as deeply implicated in the cultural development and, secondly, explores the role of its modern transformation for the form of the trilogy and Broch's conception of modernist literature. In other words, this chapter examines modernist innovation in novelistic form through the trilogy's recourse to foundational research in mathematics as the 'clearest example' of a general development (SWIII 481).

MODERN MATHEMATISATION AND DISINTEGRATION OF VALUES

Broch's trilogy covers a time span comparable to Pynchon's *Against the Day* in closing its main plot with the German revolution at the end of the war and pursues one of its plotlines to 1926 in the epilogue. But, published from 1930 to 1932, *The Sleepwalkers* is written from the perspective of a time when the legacies of the war were still felt and the foundational crisis of mathematics just drew to a close. Exploring the period's disorientation and sense of need for renewal and reflecting these through its form, the trilogy is considered one of the most important modernist works in literature in German. Yet, though often mentioned in the same breath as Robert Musil's *The Man without Qualities* and Thomas Mann's *The Magic Mountain*, which similarly include up-to-date scientific knowledge in an encyclopaedic compilation of contemporary discourses, Broch's trilogy has not received the same general recognition; a fact that might be explained with the comparatively conventional first book of the trilogy and the less readily approachable abstract discussion in the last novel. However, it is precisely the essayistic chapters and the relationship between the three novels that is crucial to the questioning of the foundations of the period, which also features in Musil's and Mann's modernism. As part of their self-reflective views to the epoch, the texts by Broch, Musil and Mann address epistemological considerations that dominate scientific and philosophical research in the early twentieth century. It will therefore be useful to situate Broch in the discussion of his time, while we shall take a closer look at the place of mathematics and literature in epistemological debates in Chapter 3.

Broch engaged extensively with epistemological debates in the years before writing *The Sleepwalkers*. He enrolled at the University of Vienna aged forty to follow his lifelong interest in mathematics and philosophy and during his studies from 1925 to 1930 took courses with members of the Vienna Circle, thus coming into contact with a major movement in the contemporary debate on epistemology and philosophy of science. The Vienna Circle, which included the mathematicians Hans Hahn and Karl Menger and the philosophers Moritz Schlick and Rudolf Carnap with whom Broch studied, discussed foundational questions of mathematics as well as philosophical implications of modern scientific developments.[6] United in their aim to make philosophy scientific by placing it on a basis of modern logic, members of the circle excluded as non-scientific the transcendental and the spiritual. In an emphatic statement on the exclusion of metaphysical questions, tellingly entitled 'The Elimination of Metaphysics through Logical Analysis of Language', Carnap complained that the metaphysician 'produces a structure which achieves nothing for knowledge and something inadequate for the expression of attitude'.[7]

Broch criticised the anti-metaphysical approach of the Vienna Circle's logical positivism and in a series of essays denounced the sole concentration on logic and scientific philosophy. In one of these papers, which he might have developed towards a doctoral dissertation in the philosophy of mathematics, Broch presents mathematicians' perspectives on the foundations of their field and compares these with philosophical positions, which he describes as predominantly positivist in their occupation with correspondence between thought and reality.[8] The historical survey of maths that the essay provides, and its focus on foundational problems and epistemological concerns, are typical of Broch's mathematical studies. While early scholarship viewed Broch as a polymath and offered his education at the University of Vienna and the numerous references to scientific topics in his essays and letters as evidence of his mastery of the material, the recognition of his predominantly historical and philosophical interests has led to a more critical view of his scientific expertise. It acknowledges that Broch's essays at times demonstrate remarkable mathematical knowledge but stresses that the non-technical writings do not enable us to determine the exact level of his command of the theories.[9] Accounting for Broch's mathematical expertise is of more than biographical interest. It suggests that *The Sleepwalkers* is part of a culture of notable engagement with mathematical questions in which Broch, extraordinarily well informed about certain scientific topics but not a professional mathematician, felt in a position to participate. With the trilogy his engagement takes a new form: profoundly inspired by the questions discussed in the Vienna Circle, but dissatisfied with their reduction of knowledge to its logical and scientific foundations, literature seemed to him a way to address the excluded mystical-ethical domain and to reformulate the role of mathematics in the period.

'Disintegration of Values', the title of the essayistic chapters in the final part of *The Sleepwalkers*, points to the ultimately ethical concern that animates the theoretical analysis and its turn to foundational research in mathematics as the most promising way to understand the period. Where parts one and two present Pasenow's and Esch's struggles through an increasingly anarchical world, the breakdown of value-systems is complete in the last novel and the consequences of losing their ordering function manifest in a loss of community, meaning and, ultimately, reality. Failing to adapt to a value-free post-war world, Pasenow and Esch, the representatives of past worldviews, die. The 'unchivalrous' war erodes the military value-system to which Major Pasenow clings, and, without its guidance, he is incapable of action, finally becoming a 'living and motionless puppet' and being taken advantage of by Huguenau, the personification of a period without values (SWIII 618). Similarly, a belief in self-sacrifice that is associated with Esch breaks down in wartime, and his attempt to save the injured Pasenow results in their falling into the hands of Huguenau who uses the latter for his own plans and murders Esch. In a society of Huguenaus, where people are entirely 'free of human obligations' and take themselves as the only points of reference, the world disintegrates into a multitude of disconnected personal realities (SWIII 350). The theoretical essay sums up the situation of wartime with the questions: 'Can this age be said still to have reality? Does it possess any real value in which the meaning of its existence is preserved?' (SWIII 559).

The Sleepwalkers also traces the increasing disintegration through its style and thus implicates literary fiction in the general process of fragmentation. The first part adheres to a conventional realist style and develops so predictably that, to echo Broch's statement about the prostitute Ruzena who drops from the narrative after Pasenow abandons her, the central character's 'fate is [. . .] calculated with almost mathematical exactitude'.[10] Equally predictable is the conventional love plot, so that the novel can end: 'How this came about need not be told here. Besides, after the material for character construction already provided, the reader can imagine it for himself' (SWI 158).[11] In the second part, the focus on Esch's inner life and a subjectively distorted diction reflect a turn away from the outside world and shared value systems, and the absence of any common organising principle then shows in *Huguenau* with its multiple, disintegrated plotlines that are only partly linked and stylistically diverse. As the language and structure of the novels act as an immediate indication of disintegration, when the essay suggests the 'clearest example' of mathematics to illuminate the modern crisis, the foundational debate in maths promises to also shed light on changes in the period's literature.

MATHEMATICS AND LANGUAGE: KEEPING BOOK OF THE MODERN WORLD

The Sleepwalkers introduces mathematics as one of two 'great rational vehicles of understanding in the modern world, the language of science in mathematics and the language of money in book-keeping' (SWIII 484). The triad of maths, language and bookkeeping evokes Galileo Galilei's celebration of maths as the language of the Book of Nature, and *The Sleepwalkers* takes up this notion of realist recording and traces it to a modern reconsideration of the rational vehicles' relations to language and physical reality. As Broch's trilogy reflects, the modernisation of maths and language go hand in hand: both research in maths and turn-of-the-century attempts to rationalise spoken language follow agendas of formalisation and grounding in logical foundations. The dream of an unambiguous language that could ensure perfect communication manifests in a large number of artificial languages, with over forty systems proposed in the years between 1880 and 1907.[12] Several of these share personnel with foundational research in mathematics: in 1903 Giuseppe Peano created 'Latino sine flexione', a simplified version of Latin, and Louis Couturat refined Esperanto – first introduced in 1887 and the probably best-known artificial language today – to 'Ido' in 1907. The crossover between maths and ideal language goes back to work by Gottlob Frege, who suggested logic as the basis of both fields. He thus founded the mathematical school of logicism and laid the groundwork for a modern philosophy of language. With his so-called 'concept-script' or 'concept notation', Frege developed an ideal language based on the model of mathematics and its definite rules, and published it as *Concept Notation: A Formula Language of Pure Thought, modelled upon that of Arithmetic* in 1879. Frege's aim was to strip language of its ambiguities and rhetorical embellishments and to then use this ideal system of expression for foundational research into maths:

> I started out from mathematics. The most pressing need, it seemed to me, was to provide this science with a better foundation. [...] The logical imperfections of language stood in the way of such investigations. I tried to overcome these obstacles with my concept-script. In this way I was led from mathematics to logic.[13]

Frege's repeated turns to spoken language in his research encouraged philosophers to draw on logic not only to examine mathematical objects but also to analyse knowledge about the world that is expressed in everyday language. Frege's 'linguistic turn' thus eventually led to the establishment of philosophy of language as a new discipline and to the rise of analytic philosophy with its aim to clarify discourse by explicitly setting out the assumptions and structure of an argument. As part of their examination of the logical structure of talk about the world, Bertrand Russell and G. E. Moore developed the mathematical symbolism that distinguishes analytic philosophy from earlier philosophical writing. In its highly technical style and symbolic language, analytic philosophy combines the formalism of maths with research into everyday language as the basis of understanding and representing the world. Although Broch was critical of analytic philosophy's restriction to matters of logic and science, mathematics in *The Sleepwalkers* does not feature as a straightforward tool of deplorable rationalisation. Rather, when the trilogy puts a focus on modern maths itself, it brings into view questions about its scope of application, its relation to language and reality, and possible entanglements with the non-rational.

Before the last part of the trilogy turns to mathematics in a more abstract discussion, *The Sleepwalkers* introduces changes in the rational means of gaining knowledge of the world in relation to the system of bookkeeping. In the middle part, Esch is a bookkeeper dedicated to the realist notion that reverberates in Galileo's phrase; like the early modern natural philosopher, he is convinced of the direct representational relation between the numbers and calculations in his books and reality: 'disorderly accounts meant a disorderly world' (SWII 216). He believes correct bookkeeping to be essential to ascertain order in reality, but the system of accounting is in confusion even at the opening of the novel, and Esch grows convinced that the world in the new century has become too incomprehensible to be described with his perfect bookkeeping. Since the books and anarchical reality no longer comply with each other, Esch sets out to instil order and balance entries in the Book of Nature according to the 'upright book-keeping of his soul' (SWII 236). Doing so, he expects to arrive at right – correct as well as morally good – solutions to worldly problems. For instance, Esch believes that he has to save the assistant of a knife-thrower who is, so he feels, wrongly put in danger during the performances. He aims to free Ilona from the hazardous acts as well as from any sexual exploitation, and even renounces having a relationship with her himself. But he is appalled when this sacrifice is not balanced by a corresponding gain:

> [H]e was conscious of some discrepancy in his calculations. He had given up Ilona, yet he was supposed to look on while Erna turned away from him [. . .]. It was against all the laws of book-keeping, which demanded that every debit entry should be balanced by a credit one. (SWII 215)

Esch thus experiences that the new century's lawless disorder renders all attempts of traditional bookkeeping futile: there always remains an ineradicable error, a 'contradiction so colossal and so terrible that it cannot even be put down to a book-keeping error' (SWII 314). The straightforward accounting Esch encounters at work therefore falsifies the more complicated Book of

Nature that just cannot be contained in the rational system. Coming to see his job as a 'prison of hypocritical ciphers and columns', he leaves his employment and renounces the realist attempt to keep the books of the world as inadequate (SWII 217). Up to this point, Esch's development falls into the pattern of modernist scepticism of rational systems, which is based on their inability to account for inner, emotional or, in other words, human aspects of life. *The Sleepwalkers* shares its critical attitude towards an exclusive rule of reason with many other modernist works, but here numerical and calculatory systems emerge not as the cause of the disintegration in the early twentieth century but as part of it. Instead of dismissing his system as too limited, Esch clings to and modifies it, and thereby reflects a historical development in mathematics that the last novel then explores as a model for the period at large.

Esch reacts to the failing of traditional bookkeeping by developing a new understanding of the relation between number and nature. As he loses his naively realist faith in the direct correspondence between the characters in his books and reality, he feels obliged to achieve the balance by introducing an element outside of rational accounting, maintaining that the 'glaring error in the books [. . .] could only be put right by a wonderful new entry' (SWII 190). Since the ineradicable error in the books is always to one party's disadvantage, Esch understands that willingly taking on the consequences of the error and thus ensuring the balance constitutes the 'wonderful new entry' and leads to the correct solution. Repeatedly in novels two and three, Esch proclaims his insight: 'that's the only thing left to do, to sacrifice oneself [. . .]; a decent man must sacrifice himself or else there's no order in the world' (SWII 290). He sacrifices himself by committing to the wrestling business that replaces the knife-throwing and in this way saves Ilona from the daggers, by accepting that Erna is not a compensating credit entry to his loss of Ilona, and by abandoning his plans to emigrate to America, which he imagines to be a well-ordered new world. When Esch gives himself in marriage to the old and infertile widow Mother Hentjen, this greatest sacrifice balances the account. The wonderful entry in this calculation is essential: 'the sacrifice had to be, had to grow even greater along with his devotion to this ageing woman, so that the world might be put in order and Ilona might be shielded from the daggers' (SWII 273). His life correctly balanced with help of a non-rational and individual deed of sacrifice, Esch reaches some kind of personal stability in a reality no longer graspable by numerical means.

In the context of the first part of the trilogy, Esch's mathematical bookkeeping appears as a surrogate for Pasenow's nineteenth-century faith in social and religious order. Yet, the use of religious imagery in the second novel suggests that the figure of Esch does not stand for the modern narrative of reason replacing traditional beliefs. Ultimately, Esch does not hold a disinterested view or support the ideal of rational order, but, driven by what he considers to be morally correct and putting sacrifice at the core of his personal system, he could be said to 'shape his own religion'.[14] Esch does not aim for the extreme rationality of a 'mathematically perfect life', then, as do, for example, the citizens in Evgeny Zamyatin's novel *We*. This dystopian text, written in 1920 and published in English in 1924, illustrates the modernist concern about a growing rationalisation of life that threatens to curtail inner freedom and to take over even moral considerations: 'Only the four rules of arithmetic are unalterable and everlasting. And only that moral system built on the four rules will prevail', the narrator-protagonist explains the order governing totalitarian OneState.[15] In contrast to such dystopian visions of a mathematisation of ethics, Esch's moral demands triumph over calculations and alter the system of accounting. If the classical view of numerical languages stresses their infallibility, either celebrating or deploring it, *The Sleepwalkers* introduces the possibility that they might be imperfect and part of modern disintegration. Esch's conviction of the moral obligation to supplement a rational system with the personal, human element of self-sacrifice then prefigures the presentation of mathematics in the final part of the trilogy, which develops implications of its modern crisis for the understanding of reality and literature.

In the fifteen years between the events depicted in *Esch* and the wartime setting in *Huguenau*, the shifts in accounting have reached their conclusion and severed any relation to the actual world. Knowing 'that in the store, as in life, that perfect order can never be achieved which he maintains in his books', the bookkeeper no longer concerns himself with calculating numbers as representations of real counterparts but restricts his view to the system of bookkeeping itself (SWIII 368). His reaction to discrepancies between the accounts and the Book of Nature is to turn away from reality: if an 'error has occurred not in the books but in the stocktaking in the storeroom, then the head bookkeeper simply shrugs his shoulders, and his lips wear a pitying or sarcastic smile, for the stocktaking lies outside his province' (SWIII 368). The world of bookkeeping holds particular appeal in its order and regularity as well as in its meaning – all entries and calculations work together to the final result, the balance at the end of term: 'this intricate maze of established connections between account and account [...] in which not a single knot is missing, is symbolized at last in a single figure' (SWIII 368). The orderly world of the books thus culminates in the unity of the final result that comprises all other figures and expresses the whole in a single number. As the calculations assume aspects of divinely granted unity and certainty, the generalised character of the accountant in *Huguenau* prefers his books to confusing reality. When the bookkeeper then attempts to make reality comply with the rational, ordered world of accounting, the assumed relation between books and nature reverses that in the previous novel: where Esch expects his books to mirror reality, is disappointed and adjusts his system, the accountant in *Huguenau* gives precedence to the order of the books and aims to make reality conform to it. Here, the rational vehicle of understanding is also one of domination and a symptom of the changed conditions in wartime, which is 'so rational that it must continually take to its heels' (SWIII 541).

While bookkeeping is the main source of imagery in *Esch*, the second novel also begins to put into question the rational domain of mathematics. Increasingly disillusioned by the injustice he perceives, Esch loses his trust in the logic of the world's order, and he begins to doubt the last stronghold of rationality and systematisation: mathematics itself. Questioning even basic forms of calculation and grappling with the suddenly unstable meaning and relation of numbers, he concludes 'that it was mere chance if the addition of the columns balanced' (II 339). Not only is the balance of debit and credit fortuitous, but uncertainty spreads to the calculations themselves; like Esch, the Voyager, a personification of the wish to escape the anarchy of the world, 'believes no longer in the correctness of addition sums' and 'doubts that two and two make four' (SWII 224–5, 295). Yet, like bookkeeping which is challenged and transformed, mathematics becomes questionable but is not abolished: the narrator's assertion that 'they do not dare [. . .] to invoke that terrible revolution of knowledge in which two and two will no longer be capable of addition' does not claim that the system of mathematics is wrong but suggests that inherent paradoxes render it unfit for application to the world (SWII 295). Thus, even before introducing mathematics directly in its third part, the trilogy shows the questions and uncertainties raised in the foundational crisis to filter through to number-based disciplines and to result in the impossibility of rationally accounting for the world. In the second part of *The Sleepwalkers* calculation is not invalidated, then, but *Esch* begins to trace a development at whose end the language of maths no longer constitutes truth.

In the war setting of *Huguenau*, the decline of mathematical certainty manifests in questions concerning its foundations: 'the research into first principles of modern mathematics [. . .] achieved a revolution of mathematical method whose extent cannot yet be estimated' (SWIII 481). Like bookkeeping, maths emerges as an entirely self-referential system that is independent of physical reality, when it is described in the essay as arising 'from that single and exclusive concentration on its own value-system and from that esoteric of expression' (III 484).[16] And if, in the eyes of the accountant, reality has to adjust to the perfect order of the books, the essay develops the precedence of structure over reality in theoretical terms: 'reality submits to the erection of the most impossible theoretic structures, – and so long as the theory does not itself declare its bankruptcy it will be supported with confidence, and reality will take a subordinate role' (SWIII 482–3).[17] In other words: the structure constructs reality. A revolutionary change in the structure of thinking, and consequently in conceptualisations of reality, takes place when the logic of thought turns towards itself and 'is compelled to revise its own basic principles' (SWIII 481). If a structure breaks down for structural reasons and not due to changed conditions in the world, it is appropriate that the essay turns to foundational concerns in mathematics to answer its question about the cause of the First World War: according to its theory, this drastic change cannot be explained by concrete political, historical or social processes, but it derives from a logical revision of the basic principles of thought. The theoretical reflections in the essayistic chapters thus establish that the developments initiated by foundational research in mathematics provide a model for understanding change in the modern structure of thinking and the reality it con-structs.

The last book of *The Sleepwalkers* links rational and literary 'vehicles of understanding' when Esch turns from his work with numbers and accounts to relating to the world as editor of a newspaper. In accordance with his initially realist notion of bookkeeping, Esch expects newspapers to report real events that render the world understandable; as editor, he consequently leads a 'fight for precise evidence of the world's doings, and against the false or falsified book-keeping entries which people tried to fob off on him' (SWIII 370–1). When in the chaos of war keeping track of events is impossible, the newspaper performs a similar self-referential shift as mathematics and accounting, and turns into a means to create its own 'patriotic reality' dictated by the Censor's office (SWIII 369). Pasenow's doubt that his leading newspaper article has any effect illustrates the questionable connection of literature to the world, and readers of the novel are bound to agree with him since only fragments of Pasenow's article appear in the text and his argument necessarily remains sketchy. Rational keeping book of the world is impossible, then, in accounting and mathematics, as well as in factual journalistic writing. But, if maths is presented as the model of the period's disintegration and crisis of representation, its not yet determinable revolution in method might also lead the way towards a solution. Indeed, as we shall see below, *The Sleepwalkers* proposes mathematics as an example for formal innovation and reflects this in the structure of the trilogy.

Language: The Structure of Crisis and Renewal

To draw nearer to *The Sleepwalkers*'s vision of mathematics as a model for renewal through form, we have to come back to the interconnected developments of its foundational questions and research into language. Bertrand Russell rediscovered Frege's work on mathematical logicism and language in the early 1900s, bringing it to the attention of a wider audience and further developing formal logic in the *Principia Mathematica*, written together with Alfred North Whitehead. Published from 1910 to 1913, the *Principia* was immediately noted for its philosophical relevance – so much so that it left the authors disappointed with the lack of attention to their innovative mathematical techniques – and it introduced modern mathematical logic to an audience that included artists and literary writers.[18] With a focus on the cultural history of mathematics and the visual arts, Lynn Gamwell examines ways in which logic found its way into British art via the reception of Russell's work, and she points to the Bloomsbury Group as a fertile ground for his ideas. Although none of its members was trained in the symbolic notation used in the *Principia Mathematica*, the circle around Virginia Woolf, the art critic Roger Fry and the painter Vanessa Bell accessed the ideas via Russell's introduction and reviews of the book, some of which were very prominently placed, for example on the front page of the *Times Literary Supplement*.[19] Through these channels mathematical logic and philosophical questions attached to it inspired various projects in the Bloomsbury Group, from Fry's art criticism with its emphasis on a work's formal properties to Woolf's engagement with Russell's logical atomism, that is, the theory that truths depend on irreducible atomic facts and analysis should start from simpler notions to reconstructing more complex ones. But the reach of logicism goes far beyond the Bloomsbury Group. In 1920s literary criticism, I. A. Richards developed the formalist technique of breaking down objects of study into small units into the method of literary close reading, which came to prominence with New Criticism in the middle decades of the twentieth century. And, regarding Russell's work towards perfect mathematical logic in particular, T. S. Eliot claimed that it also inspired greater attention to clarity in everyday language: 'the work of logicians has done [much] to make of English a language in which it is possible to think clearly and exactly on any subject. The *Principia Mathematica* are perhaps a greater contribution to our language than they are to mathematics.'[20]

Broch, aware of Russell's work and its profound influence on the Vienna Circle, discusses it in his essay on the foundations of maths, and he reflects on the interrelations between mathematical and linguistic questions in 'Hugo von Hofmannsthal and his Time' (1947). This long essay is far more about the intellectual climate of Europe in the decades around 1900 than about the Austrian writer himself, and it expresses Broch's conviction that Frege stands at the beginning of a transformation that extends beyond mathematics and defines the period: 'Who [. . .] was aware at the time of the revolution in scientific axiomatics being prepared in the work of Gottlob Frege and Georg Cantor – not to mention the fact that work of this kind penetrates a wider circle of knowledge.'[21] By tracing Hofmannsthal's time to roots in mathematical logicism, Broch also stresses connections of maths and language, given that Hofmannsthal's 'Lord Chandos Letter' is almost synonymous with the turn-of-the-century crisis in language: published in 1902, the fictional author of the letter gives voice to modernist distrust of language when deploring that he 'grew by degrees incapable of discussing a loftier or more general subject in terms of which everyone, fluently and without hesitation, is wont to avail himself'.[22] He identifies a loss of unity as the reason for his inability to express himself and notices that going back to the smallest units results in a disintegration of meaning: 'My mind compelled me to view all things occurring in such conversations from an uncanny closeness. [...] For me everything disintegrated into parts; no longer would anything let itself be encompassed by one idea.'[23] Analytical attention to language here leads to a sense of disintegration, even if the eloquent formulation of the problem already points to the possibility of reframing the fragmentation in positive terms.

As in the Chandos Letter, which claims that language and ideas break down together, in *The Sleepwalkers* mistrust in mathematical and spoken language goes hand in hand with the disintegration of order and value systems. While, in *Pasenow*, characters notice obstacles to comprehending each other but also enjoy a nevertheless existing feeling of community and mutual comprehension, for Esch everyday language disintegrates at the same rate as the ordering system of bookkeeping and he resolves to replace his native German with unblemished English. The phrasing that describes Esch's future wife's unease regarding the missing connection of language to reality echoes the famous phrase from the Chandos Letter that words 'crumbled in my mouth like mouldy fungi': 'She had expressed her point of view, but her last words had fallen from her lips, like tattered feathers, so that she herself scarcely recognized them' (SWII 250).[24] In the final part, scepticism of everyday language intensifies to the point that Esch despairs of communication and, in fragmentary sentences that mirror the disintegration he deplores, berates Huguenau for still believing in the accuracy of language: 'Express myself precisely, express myself precisely, it's very easy to talk like that ... as if a man can give a name to everything ... [...] until you know that all names are false you know nothing' (SWIII 360). Over the course of the novels, then, the loss of certainty in language questions the possibility to communicate and to grasp reality, order it and imbue it with meaning, and various plotlines illustrate what Dr Flurschütz, a doctor in a war hospital, explicitly expresses: 'all that is written and said has become completely deaf and dumb' (SWIII 586).[25]

Language scepticism in the trilogy includes mathematics, the 'sole unambiguous language': it has become a 'dumb language' as it no longer allows for elucidating nature; it is 'not a means to an end' but, only referring to itself, solely follows the logic of its own system (SWIII 484). Self-referentiality and intra-systemic coherence also are issues in early twentieth-century research on non-mathematical language: if inquiry into mathematical signs is known by the name of formalism, structuralism is its counterpart in everyday language, originating with Ferdinand de Saussure's linguistic method of examining the system of language without regard to its referent in the real word. In Saussure's theory, a sign has two aspects: the *signifiant* or sound structure, and the *signifié*, the mental concept this sound evokes. The referent does not figure in the system, and, as the relation to reality is not considered a part of language, it does not occasion the meaning of a sign. Instead, meaning depends on the relation to other signs in the system of language itself: the word 'cat' names the animal not because it has a natural connection to it, but because the signifier 'cat' is different from other signifiers such as 'hat' or 'mat'. *The Sleepwalkers* presents a corresponding picture of 'dumb' mathematics, depicting both maths and everyday language as self-referential and having no meaning and value in the world. Precisely because of this consequence, L. E. J. Brouwer deplored the self-referentiality that David Hilbert's influential approach had established in maths: 'Formalism [is a] meaningless series of relations to which mathematics are reduced.'[26] Tracing the historical interconnections of language and foundational research in mathematics to the 1920s will introduce attempts to recover the properties of meaning and value and illuminate how *The Sleepwalkers* employs maths as a model not only for the loss but also for the possible restoration of meaning.

The relation between mathematics and language received increasing attention in the 1920s and is, as Herbert Mehrtens argues in his influential study, at the very core of the foundational debate and the opposed positions for which he coined the terms 'modernist' and 'counter-modernist' mathematics.[27] Broch had an already well-developed interest in the foundational debate by the 1920s and further engaged with its questions at the University of Vienna, where the Vienna Circle was profoundly influenced by Russell's thought and by his student and collaborator Ludwig Wittgenstein's work on the limits of language. In *Tractatus Logico-Philosophicus* (1921), Wittgenstein contrasts what can be said and what cannot be expressed in language. In his view, sentences of logic and mathematics are always tautologies and therefore 'senseless' (*sinnlos*). Broch, who at the time of writing his trilogy encouraged fellow author Franz Blei to study Wittgenstein's work, similarly notes that maths is an independent, tautological field of knowledge. Terming it a 'dumb language' that carries no meaning, *The Sleepwalkers* mirrors Wittgenstein's proposition 6.124: 'The propositions of logic describe the scaffolding of the world, or rather they represent it. They have no "subject-matter".'[28] In contrast to senseless propositions, 'non-sense' for Wittgenstein is that which cannot be put into words and remains outside of language. Since the mystical is inexpressible, he ends the *Tractatus Logico-Philosophicus* with the proposition: 'What we cannot speak about we must pass over in silence.'[29] As he believed that he had solved all philosophical questions, Wittgenstein abandoned his work in the early 1920s and his infrequent contributions to debates in the Vienna Circle took the form of turning his back and reciting poetry. But L. E. J. Brouwer's 1928 lecture 'Mathematics, Science and Language' at the University of Vienna might have inspired Wittgenstein to return to philosophy. As the founder of the school of intuitionism, Brouwer stands for an alternative to logicist and formalist positions, and he introduced a view of mathematics, science and language that differed profoundly from that proposed by Frege, Russell and the logical positivists. As Brouwer's criticism also applied to Wittgenstein's work, it is not unlikely that it encouraged his return to philosophy, and the questions and solutions raised by intuitionism certainly interested Broch and inform the presentation of language scepticism in his trilogy.

Crucially, Brouwer and the intuitionist school he founded contest the very notion of mathematics as language. In his Vienna talk, Brouwer turns against 'a false belief in the magical character of language', a criticism levelled against the equation of mathematics with its symbolic representation: in formalism, maths 'is' its language – anything that can be constructed in mathematical language without contradicting the rules of the system 'magically' exists.[30] That is to say, for the formalists mathematical existence and meaning depend only on the position of signs in a system that is self-contained and internally consistent. Against this belief, Brouwer holds maths to be a thought-construction outside of language. He does not dispute that it is expressed and communicated in a kind of language, but claims that this language is already removed from its true, prelinguistic nature. The intuitionist school defines itself in view of this notion of maths as prelinguistic thought-construction: '*Intuitionism* [. . .] highlights the existence of pure mathematics independent of language.'[31] If not creating existence with its language, maths has to originate elsewhere, outside of its formal structure. Brouwer locates this origin in the individual human mind and holds that pure mathematics can be intuited, for example in meditation where numbers reveal themselves directly: 'Mathematics is a free creation, independent of experience; it develops from one single a priori Primordial Intuition.'[32] Since the human consciousness that brings about mathematics is part of reality, it relates its product, namely mathematical language, to the world. This connection to reality then ensures that maths can be applied to scientific explanations and guarantees its value. The turn to intuition thus connects mathematics to the world and rescues it from the loss of truth and meaning that it experiences in the formalist school.

Brouwer's attempt to liberate real mathematics from its expression is part of his more general scepticism of language. He was engaged in the Dutch Signific Movement, which propagated linguistic reform and, as Brouwer remembers, first came together in 1915 'under the startling impression of the false slogans with which this war was waged'.[33] Viewing language as an instrument of conflict that creates divisions and misunderstandings, the group stated its first aim as: 'To coin words of spiritual value for the languages of western nations and thus make those spiritual values enter into their mutual understanding.'[34] Members of the movement here assume a direct relation between words and values and treat language as a way to instil Europe with common spiritual concepts that the war has put under pressure or eradicated. But Brouwer took a more negative attitude, regarded language as a mere means to transmit will from one person to another, and was convinced of the impossibility of direct communication between people.[35] He consequently aimed to redefine the most basic units of thought with 'intuitive significs': similar to his work on numbers as the foundational parts of mathematics, intuitive significs is 'concerned with the creation of *new words*, which form a code of elementary means of communication for the systematic activity of a new and holier society'.[36] Tracing maths and everyday language to intuition liberates them from problematical aspects and ensures a value and meaning that is lost in formalist conceptions. Brouwer's intuitionism thus counters the modern language crisis and fears of disintegrating meaning with what historians of mathematics call a 'counter-modernist' recovery of the properties that formalists give up as lost. Or, viewed from a purely mathematical perspective, intuition as the originating and legitimating source of mathematics saves it from being part of the modern crisis of language in the first place.

Since *The Sleepwalkers* presents mathematics as mirroring a loss of everyday communicative means, the introduction of an intuitionist position in the theoretical essay holds implications for language at large: 'research into mathematical first principles, pursuing the questions "what is number?" and "what is unity?" has reached a point at which it has found itself compelled to accept intuition as the only way out of its difficulties' (SWIII 563–4). And, indeed, the epilogue presents a vision in which a similar move to intuition might save the value of everyday communication and, through it, community and value. This last part of the theoretical essay proposes that the irrational element of intuition is common to everything: the 'irreducible residue of the irrational' is the 'zero-point' that is part of any order, even of the supposedly most rational systems of bookkeeping and mathematics (SWIII 626, 645). And as intuition is a human trait shared by all people, it ensures a connection between them and 'provides in the unity of thought a common denominator for all human speech' (SWIII 564). The trilogy can therefore end with the vision of a common voice that expresses shared experience, namely that of complete disintegration: 'from our bitterest and profoundest darkness [. . .] there sounds the voice that binds all that has been to all that is to come, that binds our loneliness to all other lonelinesses' (SWIII 648). When it is a voice that announces hope, disintegration ends in a vision of community- and value-building language that, like intuitionist mathematics, originates in the common element of intuition.

Although the final voice might be taken to signal a hopeful future, the tentative phrasing in which the trilogy presents intuitionist solutions suggests that the turn to intuition does not constitute a model solution but is, rather, a troubleshooting move: maths is described as 'compelled' to 'accept' intuition as the 'only way out' of its crisis, and the novel's final turn to language can similarly appear as a wished-for stopgap rather than a credible solution to the time's disintegration. Indeed, resorting to intuition seems to go contrary to the 'logical structure of thought' that the essay presents as exemplary of the period's development; it appears as an intervention from the outside, motivated not by intra-systemic developments but by non-mathematical anxieties about meaning and value. The saving recourse to intuition thus echoes Esch's concept of the bookkeeper's non-rational, individual sacrifice that guarantees the order and correctness of the system. And, as the trilogy establishes with Esch's case, the introduction of an individual element into the rational system originates primarily from a wish for its continued use and value in the world.

The shift to an intuitionist notion of mathematics in *The Sleepwalkers* might not be obvious to all readers, but the contrast between the pessimistic ending of the main plot that is in concert with the disintegration depicted over the course of the three novels, and the optimistic vision announced by a common voice based on intuition has left many readers puzzled and unsatisfied. Some hold, as Erich Herd does, that the ending does not develop from what comes before and thus destroys the trilogy's choreographic symmetry, or feel, like Jürgen Heizmann, that the reconciliatory conclusion cannot balance the sense of disintegration.[37] Other scholars, in the tradition of pioneering works by Leo Kreutzer and Hartmut Reinhardt, contend that the hopeful ending is in concert with the rest of the trilogy – not emerging from its content but coherent with its overall structure.[38] As the foundational debate of mathematics is immediately concerned with form and content, and the trilogy engages with formalist and intuitionist positions on relations between language (structure) and meaning (content), maths provides a way into analysing the contrasted endings and the form of *The Sleepwalkers* as a whole.

Structure: Bringing the Self into Form

Hofmannsthal's 'Lord Chandos Letter' is an example of a text that expresses language scepticism but does so in such eloquent style that it reaffirms the power of language while questioning it. Although Lord Chandos claims to have lost the ability to recognise a 'deep, true, inner form' that goes beyond organising subject-matter and is itself a source of meaning and as such 'as marvellous as music or algebra', the clearly structured letter does not formally reflect the disintegration it portrays.[39] Other modernist texts similarly mourn a loss of unity and, in their nostalgic look back to what cannot be recovered, integrate disparate elements into a new whole. We will take a closer look at the dynamics between fragmentation and reintegration in the discussion on Musil's *The Man without Qualities* in Chapter 3, and focus here on a narrative intuitionist turn in *The Sleepwalkers* that has received much scholarly attention but is rarely considered in view of mathematics. Doing so will give a more nuanced picture of how maths functions as a way to both model and question literary structure in Broch's trilogy and thus points towards a new novelistic form.

As we have seen, *The Sleepwalkers* presents the turn to the human being and their intuition as a response to disintegration even in maths, and the integrated essay explains it as part of a general principle: the principle of the 'product of products' that 'provides intuition with its logical legitimation' (SWIII 564). The 'product of products' is an epistemological concept reminiscent of Friedrich Nietzsche's perspectivism, which, as discussed in the introductory chapter, is based on the view that the world has no intrinsic truth but takes on different meanings depending on the perspective from which it is observed. *The Sleepwalkers*, in its essayistic chapters and across its various plotlines, similarly suggests that human beings cannot conceive the world directly but that it is always mediated: reality is shaped and produced by ordering structures such as religion, bookkeeping, mathematics or language. Even more, reality is always several steps removed: it is '"a product of products," "a product of products of products," and so on in infinite iteration' (SWIII 563). Accordingly, reality can only be grasped, or rather, as the essay develops, reality only *exists* as a product of a 'value-positing subject' that acts as a point of reference (SWIII 561). This principle 'probably extends right into mathematics', or, to be more precise, to intuitionist maths, where the human mind is taken to 'produce' mathematical language (SWIII 563). Unusual for its overall focus on mathematical ideas, the essay also illustrates the principle with an example from modern physics:

> [M]ethodologically regarded, to define a thing as the 'product of a product' is nothing else than to introduce the ideal observer into the field of observation, as has been already done long since by the empirical sciences (by physics, for example, in the Theory of Relativity). (SWIII 563)

The Sleepwalkers only addresses in passing the analogy between the world as a product of a specific perspective and the way modern physics accounts for the observer in the process of measurement, but a preoccupation with the theory of relativity in Broch's letters and particularly in his essay 'James Joyce and the Present Age' (1936) has received much attention and is recognised as central to his vision of modernist literature. Yet, as we shall see, even if Broch's views on literature and relativity might 'be regarded as one of the most important theoretical statements of the aims and methods of the Modernist novel', *The Sleepwalkers* with its use of mathematics draws a distinct picture of modern science and its relation to literature.[40]

In his essay on Joyce, Broch explicitly connects the discovery in physics to literary fiction, explaining that it 'can give no offence to the theory of relativity if we draw a parallel with literature'.[41] He compares classical measuring to the realisation in modern physics that the act of observation can affect the result. For example, in Albert Einstein's theory of relativity, the result of an observation depends on the frame of reference in which the observer is based. In Broch's words:

> But the theory of relativity has revealed that in addition to this, there exists a basic source of error, namely, the act of seeing in itself, the act of observing *per se*, so that, consequently, in order to avoid this source of error, both the observer and his act of seeing – an ideal observer and an ideal act of seeing – must be drawn into the field of observation; in short, that for this, theoretical unity of the physical object and the physical act of seeing must be established.[42]

Broch translates this situation in physics to the literary domain, explaining that the classical novel employs language as an unproblematic instrument and implies it to objectively 'measure' and realistically represent the world. He then positions himself against literary naturalism and particularly its founder, Émile Zola, and explains why, in his view, modern physics demonstrates the misguidedness of this approach:

> [I]t is not permissible simply to place the object under observation and do nothing other than describe it; but that representation of the subject, in other words 'the narrator as idea', and not the least the language with which he describes the representational object, belong to it in the role of representational media. What he [Joyce but also referring to Broch himself] seeks to create is a unity of representational object and representational means.[43]

It is no secret that, with his praise of Joyce's method, Broch also intended to set out his own ideas, and scholars have examined the intricate narrative structure of *The Sleepwalkers* in light of his discussion of modernist representation in Joyce's work and the key concept of 'the narrator as idea'.

'Broch has succeeded in translating the theory of relativity into fictional terms by making the reader *experience* the relativization of the world.'[44] Theodore Ziolkowski arrives at this evaluation based on a connection that arises between two of the multiple, disintegrated strands in the last book of Broch's trilogy. In the course of *Huguenau*, a link emerges between the theoretical essay and the 'Story of the Salvation Army Girl', which addresses the ultimate non-rational topic of love in a first-person narration and lyrical style. The narrator of the latter chapters, Dr Bertrand Müller, states to be working on a thesis on the disintegration of values and is thus suggested to be the author of the essay 'Disintegration of Values'. Chapters across the two dissimilar episodes share common topics and at one point begin almost identically: the opening question 'Can this age be said still to have reality?' echoes the beginning of a section in the other strand – 'Can this age, this disintegrating life, be said still to have reality?' (SWIII 559, 557). While identical phrases appear across all plotlines and novels, the close proximity and prominent place of the repetition strengthens the suggestion that Müller composes the essay.

In a second step, it is understood that, if Bertrand Müller is to be seen as the author of the essay, he also composes the trilogy at large: since 'Disintegration of Values' refers to events in the main plot, it 'becomes clear that Bertrand Müller has to be pictured as the narrating I of the whole trilogy'.[45] If readers accept that Müller composes the essay, the reading process reveals that they do not get directly at the reality presented but that the novels depend on Müller's subjective perspective and are products of his consciousness. Through the stepwise disclosure of Müller's function in the trilogy, *The Sleepwalkers* showcases its theory of a necessarily mediated reality and of the impossibility to separate the subject and the object of observation. At the same time, it draws attention to the relation between the narrative content and the form of the trilogy.

Broch does not illuminate details of his notion of the 'narrator as idea' or of its possible significance for his own fictional writing. Ernestine Schlant, among others, therefore criticises its place in the interpretation of relativity and the function of Bertrand Müller in *The Sleepwalkers*. Arguing that the innovative nature of the concept is lost if the 'narrator as idea' is taken to be a concrete character, she instead proposes that it shows in strategies indicating that the novel is a construct and defined by a specific style and perspective: it 'is present in any device which draws attention to the fact that the novel is a deliberate, "scientific" construct, expressing not only narrative content but cognizance of stylistic and technical limitations as well as those of perspective'.[46] Schlant also questions that Broch meant to refer to relativity theory and suggests that his descriptions make more sense in view of quantum mechanics and the indeterminacy principle, where the act of observation is of central importance and the unity of object and subject more immediately relevant.[47] To refute this view, Ruth Bendels compares Broch's writing to contemporary texts on relativity theory and its epistemological consequences and persuasively argues that he referred to Einstein's theory deliberately and informedly.[48] What this debate shows is that the concept of the 'narrator as idea' does not derive organically from concepts in relativity theory and even less so from the isolated allusion to relativity in *The Sleepwalkers*. Moreover, a focus on Broch's engagement with literary relativity runs the risk of overlooking the role of mathematics in favour of the better-known, if in the trilogy less prominent, concept of physics. So, if, as Ziolkowski argues, the theoretical chapters of Broch's trilogy set out what is at the 'structural heart of his fiction', we have to look not to relativity theory but to the more sustained engagement with mathematics, and this leads us to a revaluation of the very notions of structure and its 'heart'.[49]

Broch points to shared features of modern physics and mathematics that also motivate the reference to relativity theory in the trilogy:

> [T]he present shock of the total world, on the one hand the almost earthquake-like one in all exterior events, on the other hand the, as it

were, precise revolution in the central field of cognition, in physics and the fundamental research in mathematics, almost unequivocally points to a common root: [...] the deposition of previous absoluteness.[50]

Hilbert similarly compares the methodologies of maths and physics to explain his formalist programme: 'we must, I am persuaded, make the concept of specifically mathematical proof itself an object of investigation, just as the astronomer considers the movement of his position, the physicist studies the theory of his apparatus, and the philosopher criticizes reason itself'.[51] Here, and similarly in Broch's essay and *The Sleepwalkers*, a questioning of basic certainties is closely associated with concern about the absoluteness of knowledge as it is understood to depend on the knowledge-gaining process. To explain the role of the observer, Broch uses the image of the theatrical 'stage of cognition': knowledge is not just presented on stage but requires active participation of the audience, and this turns the spectator into a 'mathematical person' in maths, into a 'physical person' in the sciences, and into a 'linguistic person' in language-based processes of cognition.[52] As Broch specifies, the 'mathematical person' is radically abstract, and similarly the 'physical person' points to a conceptual entity: 'It is, of course, not a matter of an empirical observer but of an abstract one, the "observer as such"'.[53] The participation of the audience as an entity producing knowledge is therefore necessary in all forms of knowledge, if formulated in mathematical symbols or everyday language. Yet, maths inhabits a particular position when there is only one step in the 'production line': in maths, there is no 'product of a product of a product'.[54] In other words, understanding maths as produced by an abstract mathematical person and translated into language from intuition, it constitutes the simplest example of a process common to all forms of knowledge.

As Ziolkowski emphasises, *The Sleepwalkers* can make readers '*experience* the relativization of the world' – if by picking up and accepting the indications that Müller composes the essay and the trilogy, readers have to reconsider what they have read and view it as the product of a subjective perspective.[55] This productive readerly participation exemplifies an understanding of form as process. As Raymond Williams explains, next to the idea of form as static and superficial 'outward shape', form can be viewed as 'an essential shaping principle', and this motivates the participatory role of the audience as necessary to realise the formative process.[56] Henry S. Turner accordingly proposes that form 'should be understood as a verb rather than a noun, as an active relation among significant parts that are apprehended through a transaction between that artefact and its readers, viewers, listeners or speakers'.[57] Taking up Turner's argument in her study on science and literary form, Janine Rogers elaborates for the case of literature: 'Form, I contend, should be understood as an experience and an action, which means that it should be recognized as both a *writerly* and a *readerly* activity.'[58] *The Sleepwalkers* illustrates readers' involvement in actualising form when they are crucial to viewing the trilogy as a unified whole, and it also supports Rogers's notion of form as a 'connective value' between science and literature: if the process of identifying a forming consciousness links readers and Müller as the fictional author of the trilogy, it also connects the trilogy and mathematics in a shared intuitionist turn.

However, as suggested above, in Broch's trilogy intuitionist mathematics and the related processes of unification in human consciousness are presented as possibilities but not as givens: Bertrand Müller emerges as the author and origin of the trilogy only in concert with the reader's participating interpretation, and it is possible not to pick up the clues that he composes the essay or to deem them not convincing enough. Thus, while identifying Müller as the unifying consciousness constitutes an option that readers wishing for an overall unity might feel tempted to embrace, it does not need to be realised. That the unifying move does not appear as obvious or necessary is consistent with the reluctant introduction of intuitionist solutions in the text. Mathematics is 'compelled' to turn to intuition as a way out, the principle of a product of products only 'probably' extends to maths, and moreover the saving powers of intuition are ambiguous when they are introduced in the theoretical chapters but do not translate into practice (SWIII 563). For example, the ninth part of the essay concludes with the hopeful picture of the 'continuing unity of the world, a unity of man, illuminating all things, still surviving and imperishable through all eternities of space and time', but the beginning of the next chapter at least questions the unity of man: 'Dr Flurschütz was helping Jaretzki to fit on his artificial arm' (SWIII 565).[59]

The possibility of 'bringing oneself into form', of the reader actualising a whole by participating in the forming process and acknowledging Müller's producing consciousness as an origin, recreates on the level of form what the trilogy introduces with the models of bookkeeping, mathematics and language: an intuitionist turn to the inner self, tied not to a physical person but to abstract underlying intuition. The incorporation of the reader into textual form might share with relativity theory a focus on the role of the observer, yet, considered in the light of the trilogy's more sustained view to mathematics, it does not appear as inevitable. Rather, if in maths the intuitionist interpretation triggered opposition from the formalists, so its markedly tentative introduction in *The Sleepwalkers* renders it ambiguous. The next section therefore takes a closer look at the alternative, namely formalist ideas of structure, and shows how the trilogy considers form not only as a carrier of meaning that is ultimately activated by human consciousness but as meaningful in itself.

Structure: The Value of Pure Form

In a letter written shortly after completing the last part of *The Sleepwalkers*, Broch professes to seek insights through writing in new forms even though running the risk of alienating his readers: 'Writing means aiming to win knowledge through form, and new knowledge can only be created through new form.'[60] The formal innovations in his trilogy, such as the turn to human consciousness that mirrors the structure of intuitionist movements in mathematics, are testament to this practice. But, if a shift to intuition can reaffirm content, meaning and value, the competing model of formalism suggests another way of using form to confront the modern absence of foundations. *The Sleepwalkers* illustrates the potentialities of concentrating on structure itself with the character Gödicke who, as a bricklayer turned soldier, dies in the First World War, is resurrected and then concerns himself with recreating his soul, life and identity. Gödicke's disintegration is an analogy of the world falling apart in war and also of stylistic fragmentation in the novel *Huguenau*. His resurrection then suggests renewal and can be seen as a self-interpretation and self-justification of the trilogy, setting out the value of literature in a period of crisis. Viewing the character of Gödicke in the light of formalist maths and its contrast to intuitionist notions clarifies the trilogy's competing drives towards complete disintegration and, on the other hand, promise of a reinstitution of unity. This contrast then illuminates how *The Sleepwalkers* reflects the split into modernist and counter-modernist mathematics in its own structure and puts into question the very idea of stable form.

Gödicke, having died on the battlefield and then risen from the dead, personifies the disintegrated post-war period where disparate self-centred realities do not form into a unity. Having lost connection to his former existence, he is deprived of the basis of his life and unable to build up his identity; all he can do is erect a structure that might encourage future constructions: 'Ludwig Gödicke the bricklayer had, so to speak, built a scaffolding for the house of his soul, and as he hobbled about on his sticks he felt himself to be merely a scaffolding with supports and stresses on all sides' (SWIII 382). Gödicke erects only the supporting framework, the form and possibility of a future building, while the actual content of his life remains impossible to construct. The substance of his past even threatens to destabilise the new framework: when his former life returns as an 'intruder' in the form of a postcard from his wife, the past recurs as 'bricks' of content that cannot be used for building the scaffolding (SWIII 437). Since he cannot integrate the past, Gödicke blocks it out, together with any input from outside reality: 'the man Gödicke must see nothing, hear nothing, eat nothing' (SWIII 438). Isolated from the world and uninhibited by any real content, Gödicke solely concentrates on the construction of the framework, and the scaffolding exists autonomously, 'in itself and by itself' (SWIII 382).

The Gödicke-strand is saturated with architectural terminology and shares this vocabulary with the foundational debate in mathematics, particularly with formalist formulations of maths as a self-contained structure that, as a language referring only to itself, is pure form. But, more importantly, it shares with formalist maths and other formalist movements an emphasis on the value of concentrating on structure to the exclusion of content. Indeed, with his championing of mathematical form independent of its relations to meaning or reality, Hilbert turned the work on form into the very subject matter – the content – of maths. Given its independence from the real world, Hilbert and his colleagues understood formalist mathematics as a structure of pure possibility and work on it as extending this framework of potentiality to increase its reach and power.[61] Paul Bernays, Hilbert's closest collaborator in the 1920s, explains that possibility, rather than reality, is crucial in a mathematical system: 'the axiom system itself does not express something factual; rather, it presents only a possible form of a system of connections'.[62] Hilbert similarly emphasised the need to extend the system beyond the immediately applicable: 'The mathematician will have also to take account not only of those theories coming near to reality, but also [...] of all logically possible theories.'[63] Work on the language of maths thus is geared towards finding descriptions and theories that develop new possibilities of mathematical expression, regardless of their applicability to the world. In an essay from 1934 Broch takes up this line of argumentation and stresses the creative potential of maths, contending that it 'includes every conceivable logical structure that could exist [...], or more correctly, every new discovery in mathematics expands its range but defines a new possible logical structure for the real world as well'.[64] In Broch's view, then, maths might even open up new avenues in reality; so not only does he reject the understanding of maths as a representation of the world, but he suggests that its generation of possibilities has part in creating reality.

The notion of extending possibilities for the real world through formalist manipulation of an autonomous structure informs the presentation of Gödicke's scaffolding and his attempts to regain reality and the unity of his self. As the turn away from the world liberates modern mathematics and widens its possibilities, so Gödicke's scaffolding can grow precisely by disregarding its surroundings. Moreover, as he embodies disintegrated wartime reality, his work on a structure for the possibility of prospective content inspires hopes of similarly constructing the framework for a future of the world. In the eyes of Esch's Bible group, Gödicke accordingly stands for the promise of regeneration and personifies the divine new entry that Esch deems indispensable for future development: he answers Esch's demand 'for the son who shall build the house anew ... only then will the mists thin away and the new life will come' (SWIII 500). While, at the end of the trilogy, the German revolution overthrows the old world order and Huguenau's generation manages to exist only in their respective egoistical realities, Gödicke might finally achieve reintegration into the world. His ability of foresight grows with the height of his scaffolding, and he comments on the events of the revolution from the elevated viewpoint of his construction and moreover gaining distance when 'standing on the hillside, which he had chosen as a coign of vantage' (SWIII 607). While Gödicke does not take in any input from the outside when he sets out to rebuild himself – he 'must see nothing, hear nothing, eat nothing' – having elevated himself over the war events, he obeys the call 'Ludwig, it's the dinner-hour, come down from the scaffolding' (SWIII 438, 608). Abandoning the self-contained framework for the intake of nourishment, he might begin to build the content of his self, so that the concentration on the scaffolding as a creation of possibilities and the suppression of content promises the possibility of eventual renewal – even if it does not actually arrive there.

Even before the suggestion of Gödicke's potential reintegration into the world, his self-contained framework has value and meaning: it fulfils 'real purpose, since invisibly in the centre of the scaffolding, and yet also in every single supporting beam, the ego of Ludwig Gödicke was precariously suspended and had to be preserved from dizziness' (SWIII 382). In other words, Gödicke becomes the self-contained scaffolding itself, and the structure of the possibility of future content is itself existence. The epilogue arrives at a similar change in perspective, turning the focus from a solution to the possibility of solution when suggesting that 'the mere hope of wisdom from a Leader is wisdom for us, the mere divination of grace is grace, and [. . .] our goal remains approachable, [. . .] and the renascence of values is fated to recur' (SWIII 648).[65] The hope to conquer disintegration thus derives from the possibility of regeneration rather than renewal itself. With the notion that structure does not only order content but has creative potential, *The Sleepwalkers* intensifies the understanding of form as process rather than static shape: it is clear that 'form *does* things' when the framework constitutes identity for Gödicke and the formal possibility of a future becomes the solution to modern disintegration.[66] Therefore, as Turner clarifies, 'form is never simply a tool of knowledge: it is an attribute of being, a category of ontology'.[67] This is particularly evident in formalist mathematics, which exists and creates through pure form: a mathematical entity exists in its formal description, and absence of contradiction is being. In this sense, to repeat the quotation by Alain Badiou from the introductory chapter, (formalist) 'mathematics = ontology' and, in Broch's words, '[t]he possibility of mathematical being is purest ontological knowledge [. . .]: it brings the necessity of being and logical possibility to perfect identical evidence'.[68] In this way, literature and mathematics indeed meet in form or, to take up Rogers's term, form works as a connective value: in both, it is part of *poiesis* or making; both speaking poetically and mathematically is to create the thing one describes. And when, as Moritz Epple emphasises, the 'productive imagination' of mathematical acts receives considerable attention with its new style in the twentieth century, it is with the emergence of a modern mathematics in particular that the capacity for poetic creation connects maths and literature.[69]

Formalism, with its claim that form provides a privileged perspective to the study of mathematics, art or literature, has come to stand for an ahistorical position that is unconcerned with political and social issues. As Susan J. Wolfson emphasises in her re-evaluation of formalism and its reception, much of the criticism is not aimed at the focus on form itself but precisely levelled against considering form as 'the product of any historically disinterested, internally coherent aesthetics'.[70] *The Sleepwalkers*, engaging with the period and its turn towards maths and language that initiated formalist perspectives, gives a strong sense of the inevitability of logical development across all fields of knowledge. But it also draws attention to the historicity of form, suggesting, with a view to the 'clearest example' of mathematics, that even the structures of supposedly stable systems are open to revision and implicated in the period's grappling with the loss of unity, meaning and value. Indeed, maths appears as part of the modern crisis and its turn to intuition as motivated not by inner-mathematical logic but by general anxieties about loss of reality and value: depicting a mathematics 'compelled' to accept intuition as 'the only way out', *The Sleepwalkers* presents it as influenced by, and in turn changing, historically specific mindsets, aims and beliefs.

Contrasting formalist and intuitionist ideas in mathematics, language, value-systems, and regarding its own structure, *The Sleepwalkers* cannot be said to have a clear-cut 'structural heart' in relativity theory or elsewhere, but structure and form themselves are under reconsideration and open to diverse developments: complete disintegration, the promise of unification in intuition, or a focus on creatively enhancing formal possibilities. Regarding Broch's trilogy as a whole, the creative potential of the formalist approach that Gödicke personifies clarifies the unexpectedly reconciliatory ending: even if the counter-modernist prospect of regaining unity and value through intuition might remain unconvincing, theoretically envisioning it in the essayistic epilogue and introducing the possibility of viewing Bertrand Müller as a unifying consciousness correspond to building a framework that creates the prospect of future content and might thus advance the world on its way to an unattainable vision. As in the foundational debate of mathematics, then, *The Sleepwalkers* presents competing formalist and intuitionist views with advantages and disadvantages without offering a solution or winner. What is clear, however, is that ideas of reliable structure and form have to be abandoned in favour of acknowledging their being part of historical and cultural changes – in mathematics, in value-systems and in literature.

The Language and Structure of Modernism: Mathematics and Literature

As the above has shown, *The Sleepwalkers* suggests that modern maths and literature develop in parallel and relates characters' worldviews to competing notions of mathematical existence, truth and meaning. Pasenow's belief in value-systems that order and make sense of the world corresponds to the realist belief that the universe can be understood through mathematics as the language of the Book of Nature; Esch's adding a wonderful new entry into bookkeeping to ensure the system's usability in an anarchical world complies with the counter-modernist notion that the value of maths can be saved only by the introduction of the non-rational human element of intuition; and Huguenau's concentration on himself as his own value-system relates to the self-referentiality of formalist maths that does not lend itself to create outside value. Modern mathematical positions then also inform the two scenarios of the future introduced in the epilogue: a world stagnated in the unreality of countless egoistical realities bears traits of the formalist turn to the system itself, and the hopeful outlook based on the theory of unifying non-rational feelings mirrors counter-modernist mathematics' recourse to intuition. The stylistic characteristics of the novels – the realist style in *Pasenow*, the expressionist diction and concentration on the protagonist's inner life in *Esch*, and the focus on formal disintegration in *Huguenau* – and the simultaneously existing possibilities of putting hope in the openness of form or in the unifying force of a central narrative consciousness, implicate literature in the development exemplified by maths.

While establishing parallels between modern literature and maths, *The Sleepwalkers* also illuminates their specific functions in the comprehension and formation of reality. Even if maths can be understood as language, it differs from literature in the way it lends itself to examining the place of human beings. Mathematics might be employed as an example, even 'the clearest example', of the 'sweeping revolution in the style of thinking', but its symbolic expression is not suited to personal communication (SWIII 481): it is, as Broch stresses, 'largely detached from the mathematician; he cannot interpret subjectively with it, [. . .] it is a precise, mute, de-subjectified language'.[71] In Broch's experience with Viennese logical positivism, the increasingly mathematised sciences and philosophy suffer a similar fate, and, since they cannot address the individual and the irrational course of the world, no longer fulfil a communicative function: according to Broch, the sciences have become mute too.[72] Given what he calls the self-restriction of the scientific sphere, Broch claims that it is the role of literature to cover the areas no longer encompassed by science, namely the irrational aspects of life.[73] Literature can achieve this since, so he argues, it does not rely on language as the sciences do, but exists in the tension between words and lines. Like intuitionist maths that is understood to be expressed in language but to exist independently of it, literature is thus able to point to the dream-like, to that which Wittgenstein in his *Tractatus* excludes from philosophy and relegates to passing over in silence. When modern literature has to account for the irrational but also for the spirit of scientific thinking, it unities these opposed aspects and can satisfy human beings' 'desire for the totality of the worldview'.[74]

In Broch's fictional and non-fictional writings on language, literature and science that he develops over several decades and that include modifications and contradictions, it can be challenging to locate mathematics – a structural science that is part of many scientific endeavours but in its abstractness can also be close to the creative possibilities of literary fiction. That it takes an unstable position among the two cultures and moreover veers between formalist and intuitionist conceptions indicates that Broch uses maths not as a fixed model but as a field in which controversies crystallise and that therefore lends itself to exploring change in the early twentieth century. Nevertheless, when *The Sleepwalkers* employs foundational research in maths to address questions of structurality itself and relates these to developments in literary form, including its own, it suggests modern maths to model ways of finding new forms of cultural expression. More precisely, when Broch's trilogy presents the modern transformation of maths as an example of the period's style of thinking and its foundational debate as proposing possible future scenarios, it does so in ways that we could call modernist, counter-modernist or Romantic, and postmodernist. The term 'counter-modernist', introduced by Mehrtens, designates the recovery of meaning, values and relation to the world that is lost in formalist mathematics, and it includes a celebration of unity and totality that in literary studies is more commonly identified as characteristic of Romanticism. But more important to criticism is Broch's anticipation of postmodernist characteristics. Little is to be gained by labelling *The Sleepwalkers* 'through and through a modern work' or hailing it as postmodern, but the move from structuralism to post-structuralism provides a useful schema to grasp how modern mathematics works as a model for narrative innovation in *The Sleepwalkers*.[75]

In his seminal talk that introduced post-structuralism, Jacques Derrida sets out the consequences of thinking the 'structurality of structure'.[76] In *The Sleepwalkers* where maths exemplifies the 'structure of thought', research into its 'first principles' similarly concerns the structurality of structure and puts into question the 'fundamental ground' of (mathematical) reality (SWIII 481). As Derrida explains, when the structurality of structure begins to be thought, the centre of a structure becomes a problematical concept: the centre 'which is by definition unique, constituted that very thing within a structure which while governing the structure, escapes structurality'.[77] Derrida concludes that a centre does not exist and contrasts two reactions to the resulting openness of a post-structural situation: a negative or nostalgic position attempts but fails to regain stable truth and origin, while, on the other side, an affirmative view embraces the loss of foundations and the unstoppable proliferation of meanings. The nostalgic view designates a modernist perspective, while the joyful acceptance of unlimited play of meaning constitutes a postmodernist position. Derrida's exploration of structure can help clarify the partly contradictory ways in which modern mathematics works as a structural example and model for narrative. *The Sleepwalkers* proposes a counter-modernist or Romantic solution to the questioning of structure and the disintegration of meaning, value and reality when the possible readerly realisation of Bertrand Müller as unifying narrative consciousness introduces an extra-systemic entity that takes on the centralising function. Even this move does not recover Romantic unity, however, but opens up the textual structure to multiple meanings residing in multiple readers. In contrast, formalism can take the form of mourning the lost centre without replacing it, or of finding hope in creatively using the absence of an origin to build a framework of possibility. Not least, setting next to each other intuitionist and formalist possibilities, Broch's trilogy reflects the foundational split in modern mathematics with a formal indeterminacy that suggests a postmodern acceptance of pluralism.

The Sleepwalkers employs its 'clearest example' in its experimentation with narrative structure and literary form and presents the modern development of maths as relevant to the path literature takes to respond to pressures in the early twentieth century. While in Broch's eyes his trilogy is to compensate for a mathematisation of philosophy, its structure reflects the tensions between content and form that animates modern maths in its foundational opposition of formalism and intuitionism. Using maths not as an example of certainty but as a model of responding to a loss of unity, *The Sleepwalkers* employs it in a specifically modern notion and locates in it the very irrational and transcendental that the mathematised sciences and philosophy no longer encompass. Presenting maths as addressing the non-rational along with questions of representation, language and form that similarly animate modernist literature, the trilogy considers it as part of the crisis of the period and of determining possible futures. It thus establishes maths not only as modern but as modernist, that is, as part of culture and as sharing central concerns and features with modernist literature.

The Sleepwalkers addresses the challenges of reconstituting a world experienced as having become disintegrated and unreal in wartime with a view to tensions between increasing rationalisation and a resurgence of intuition, between form and content, and between language and meaning created in between words and lines. Following this chapter's focus on interrelations between language and mathematics and ways of employing maths as a model for novelistic form, the next chapter turns to Musil's *The Man without Qualities* to examine in more detail the role of mathematics in attempts at fusing rationalism and mysticism and thus respond to modern questions of epistemology and ethics.

NOTES

1. 'die Dichtung [... muß sich] dem Geist der Epoche, muß sich seiner Wissenschaftlichkeit unterordnen, [...] und sie besorgt dies, indem sie polyhistorisch wird' (Hermann Broch, *Das essayistische Werk und Briefe 1913–1951: Kommentierte Werkausgabe 9/1*, ed. Paul Michael Lützeler (Frankfurt am Main: Suhrkamp, 1986), p. 209).
2. 'die Wissenschaft ist ihnen wie ein kristallener Block, von dem sie das eine oder das andere Stück abbrechen, um damit ihre Erzählung an zumeist ungeeignetem Ort zu garnieren oder einen Wissenschaftler als Romanfigur damit auszustatten' (Broch, *Das essayistische Werk und Briefe*, p. 148).
3. Herbert George Wells, *Experiment in Autobiography: Discoveries and Conclusions of a Very Ordinary Brain (Since 1866)* (Philadelphia and New York: J. B. Lippincott, 1967), pp. 418–19.
4. 'aber für mich ist, wahrscheinlich infolge meiner mathematisch-konstruktivistischen Anlage, ein anderer Weg kaum gangbar' (Broch qtd in *Materialien zu Hermann Brochs 'Die Schlafwandler'*, ed. Gisela Brude-Firnau (Frankfurt am Main: Suhrkamp, 1972), p. 45).
5. 'the clearest example': 'am deutlichsten' (DSW 533). The pagination of the trilogy is continuous, but quotations will be identified as belonging to part I, II or III.
6. For a list of university courses taken by Broch, see Paul Michael Lützeler, *Hermann Broch: Eine Biographie* (Frankfurt am Main: Suhrkamp, 1985), pp. 96–8.
7. Rudolf Carnap, 'The Elimination of Metaphysics through Logical Analysis of Language' [1932], in *Logical Positivism*, ed. A. J. Ayer, trans. Arthur Pap (New York: The Free Press, 1959), 60–81 (p. 80).
8. Hermann Broch, 'Die sogenannten philosophischen Grundfragen einer empirischen Wissenschaft' [1928], *Philosophische Schriften 1: Kritik*, ed. Paul Michael Lützeler (Frankfurt am Main: Suhrkamp, 1977), pp. 131–46. About the status as doctoral dissertation, see Paul Michael Lützeler and Michael Kessler, eds, *Hermann Broch Handbuch* (Berlin and Boston, MA: De Gruyter, 2016), p. 99.
9. Carsten Könneker, 'Moderne Wissenschaft und moderne Dichtung. Hermann Brochs Beitrag zur Beilegung der "Grundlagenkrise" der Mathematik', *Deutsche Vierteljahrsschrift für Literaturwissenschaft und Geistesgeschichte*, 73 (1999), 319–51 (pp. 331–2). Ruth Bendels, *Erzählen zwischen Hilbert und Einstein: Naturwissenschaft und Literatur in Hermann Brochs 'Eine methodologische Novelle' und Robert Musils 'Drei Frauen'* (Würzburg: Königshausen & Neumann, 2008), pp. 67–8. For an account of Broch's mathematical knowledge, see Willy Riemer, 'Mathematik und Physik bei Hermann Broch', in *Hermann Broch*, ed. Paul Michael Lützeler (Frankfurt am Main.: Suhrkamp, 1986), 260–71.
10. Hermann Broch, *Briefe: Dokumente und Kommentare zu Leben und Werk*, ed. Paul Michael Lützeler (Frankfurt am Main: Suhrkamp, 1981), p. 89.
11. 'das Schicksal [...] ist ja schon [...] mit ziemlicher mathematischer Exaktheit errechnet'; 'need not be told here': 'muß nicht mehr erzählt werden' (DSW 149).
12. Herbert Mehrtens, *Moderne Sprache Mathematik: Eine Geschichte des Streits um die Grundlagen der Disziplin und des Subjekts formaler Systeme* (Frankfurt am Main: Suhrkamp, 1990), p. 527.
13. Gottlob Frege, 'Notes for Ludwig Darmstaedter' [1919], in *Posthumous Writings*, ed. Hans Hermes, Friedrich Kambartel and Friedrich Kaulbach, trans. Peter Long and Roger White (Chicago: University of Chicago Press, 1979), 253–7 (p. 253).

14. Ernestine Schlant, *Hermann Broch* (Boston, MA: Twayne, 1978), p. 46.
15. Evgeny Zamyatin, *We*, trans. Clarence Brown (New York: Penguin, 1993), p. 4 and p. 111. For a detailed discussion of mathematics in *We*, see Leighton Brett Cooke, 'Ancient and Modern Mathematics in Zamyatin's *We*', in *Zamyatin's We: A Collection of Critical Essays*, ed. Gary Kern (Ann Arbor: Ardis, 1988), 149–67; T. R. N. Edwards, *Three Russian Writers and the Irrational: Zamyatin, Pil'nyak, and Bulgakov* (Cambridge: Cambridge University Press, 1982); and Nina Engelhardt, 'Mathematics between Totalitarian Order and Revolution: Yevgeny Zamyatin's *We*', in *Imagine Maths 5: Between Culture and Mathematics*, ed. Michele Emmer et al. (Bologna: Monograf, 2016), 91–101.
16. 'eindeutigen Gerichtetheit auf das eigene Wertgebiet und aus einer Esoterik des Ausdrucks' (DSW 538).
17. 'reality will take a subordinate role': 'die Wirklichkeit ordnet sich ihr unter' (DSW 536).
18. Bertrand Russell, *My Philosophical Development* (London: Routledge, 1993), p. 86.
19. Lynn Gamwell, *Mathematics + Art: A Cultural History* (Princeton and Oxford: Princeton University Press, 2016), p. 212.
20. T. S. Eliot, 'A Commentary', *The Monthly Criterion*, 6.4 (1927), 289–91 (p. 291).
21. Hermann Broch, *Hofmannsthal and His Time: The European Imagination, 1860–1920*, trans. Michael P. Steinberg (Chicago: University of Chicago Press, 1984), p. 53.
22. Hugo von Hofmannsthal, *Selected Prose*, trans. Mary Hottinger (New York: Pantheon Books, 1952), pp. 133–4.
23. Hofmannsthal, *Selected Prose*, p. 134.
24. 'Sie hatte ihre Meinung gesagt, aber schon die letzten Worte waren ihr vom Munde zerflattert, wie zerschlissene Federn, so daß sie selber kaum sie erkannte' (DSW 281). Hofmannsthal, *Selected Prose*, p. 134.
25. 'has become completely deaf and dumb': 'taub und stumm geworden' (DSW 647).
26. L. E. J. Brouwer, 'Intuitionism and Formalism' [1912], *Bulletin of the American Mathematical Society*, 20.2 (1913), 81–96 (p. 83).
27. See Herbert Mehrtens, *Moderne Sprache Mathematik: Eine Geschichte des Streits um die Grundlagen der Disziplin und des Subjekts formaler Systeme* (Frankfurt am Main: Suhrkamp, 1990).
28. Broch, letter to Franz Blei, 1931, qtd in Paul Michael Lützeler, *Hermann Broch und die Moderne: Roman, Menschenrecht, Biografie* (Munich: Fink, 2011), p. 29. Ludwig Wittgenstein, *Tractatus Logico-Philosophicus*, trans. D. F. Pears and B. F. McGuinness (London and New York: Routledge, 2014), p. 76.
29. Wittgenstein, *Tractatus Logico-Philosophicus*, p. 89.
30. L. E. J. Brouwer, 'Mathematics, Science, and Language' [1928], in *From Brouwer to Hilbert: The Debate on the Foundations of Mathematics in the 1920s*, ed. Paolo Mancosu (New York and Oxford: Oxford University Press, 1998), 45–52 (p. 49).
31. Brouwer, 'Mathematics, Science, and Language', p. 50.
32. E. L. J. Brouwer, 'On the Foundations of Mathematics' [1907], in *L. E. J. Brouwer: Collected Works*, vol. 1, ed. Arend Heyting (Amsterdam and Oxford: North-Holland, 1975), 15–101 (p. 97).
33. L. E. J. Brouwer, 'Synopsis of the Signific Movement in the Netherlands: Prospects of the Signific Movement', *Synthese*, 5.5 (1946), 201–8 (p. 201).
34. Brouwer, 'Synopsis of the Signific Movement', p. 201.
35. Walter P. Van Stigt, 'Brouwer's Intuitionist Programme', in *From Brouwer to Hilbert: The Debate on the Foundations of Mathematics in the 1920s*, ed. Paolo Mancosu (New York and Oxford: Oxford University Press, 1998), 1–22 (p. 3).

36. Brouwer, qtd in Dirk van Dalen, *L. E. J. Brouwer: Topologist, Intuitionist, Philosopher. How Mathematics is Rooted in Life* (London: Springer, 2013), p. 264.
37. Eric Herd, 'Hermann Brochs Romantrilogie *Die Schlafwandler* (1930–32)', in *Hermann Broch*, ed. Paul Michael Lützeler (Frankfurt am Main: Suhrkamp, 1986), 59–77 (p. 75). Jürgen Heizmann, 'A Farewell to Art: Poetic Reflection in Broch's *Der Tod des Vergil*', in *Hermann Broch, Visionary in Exile: The 2001 Yale Symposium*, ed. Paul Michael Lützeler (Rochester, NY and Woodbridge, Suffolk: Camden, 2003), 187–200 (p. 188).
38. Leo Kreutzer, *Erkenntnistheorie und Prophetie: Hermann Brochs Romantrilogie 'Die Schlafwandler'* (Tübingen: Niemeyer, 1966) and Hartmut Reinhardt, *Erweiterter Naturalismus: Untersuchungen zum Konstruktionsverfahren in Hermann Broch* (Cologne: Böhlau, 1972).
39. Hofmannsthal, *Selected Prose*, p. 131.
40. Adrian Stevens, 'Hermann Broch as a Reader of James Joyce: Plot in the Modernist Novel', in *Hermann Broch: Modernismus, Kulturkrise und Hitlerzeit*, ed. Adrian Stevens, Fred Wagner and Sigurd Paul Scheichl (Innsbruck: Institut für Germanistik, 1994), 77–101 (p. 101).
41. Hermann Broch, 'Joyce and the Present Age' [1932], in *A James Joyce Yearbook*, ed. Maria Jolas (Paris: Transition, 1949), 68–108 (p. 88).
42. Broch, 'Joyce and the Present Age', p. 88.
43. Broch, 'Joyce and the Present Age', p. 89.
44. Theodore Ziolkowski, 'Hermann Broch and Relativity in Fiction', *Wisconsin Studies in Contemporary Literature*, 8.3 (1967), 365–76 (p. 376).
45. Es 'wird deutlich, daß Bertrand Müller als das Erzähl-Ich der ganzen Trilogie vorzustellen ist' (Paul Michael Lützeler, *Hermann Broch – Ethik und Politik: Studien zum Frühwerk und zur Romantrilogie 'Die Schlafwandler'* (Munich: Winkler, 1973), p. 74).
46. Schlant, *Hermann Broch*, p. 51.
47. Ernestine Schlant, 'Hermann Broch and Modern Physics', *The Germanic Review*, 53.2 (1978), 69–75 (pp. 69–70).
48. Bendels, *Erzählen zwischen Hilbert und Einstein*, pp. 108–9.
49. Ziolkowski, 'Relativity in Fiction', p. 367.
50. 'daß die gegenwärtige revolutionäre Erschütterung der Gesamtwelt, einerseits die geradezu erdbebenhafte in allem äußeren Geschehen, andererseits die sozusagen präzise Revolution im Zentralgebiet der Erkenntnis, in der Physik und in der mathematischen Grundlagenforschung, schier unzweideutig auf eine gemeinsame Wurzel hindeutet' (Broch, *Das essayistische Werk und Briefe*, p. 471).
51. David Hilbert, 'Axiomatic Thought' [1918], in *From Kant to Hilbert: A Source Book in the Foundations of Mathematics*, vol. 2, ed. William Bragg Ewald (Oxford: Oxford University Press, 1996), 1105–15 (p. 1115).
52. Broch, *Das essayistische Werk und Briefe*, p. 97.
53. Broch, *Erkennen und Handeln: Essays, Band II*, ed. Hannah Arendt (Zürich: Rhein-Verlag, 1955), p. 194.
    'Natürlich handelt es sich da nicht um den empirischen Beobachter, sondern um einen abstrakten, um den "Beobachter an sich"' (Broch, *Briefe 3 1945–1951: Kommentierte Werkausgabe 9/1*, ed. Paul Michael Lützeler (Frankfurt am Main: Suhrkamp, 1975), pp. 3834).
54. Broch, *Erkennen und Handeln*, p. 202.
55. Ziolkowski, 'Relativity in Fiction', p. 376.
56. Raymond Williams, *Keywords: A Vocabulary of Culture and Society* (New York: Oxford University Press, 1983), p. 138.

57. Henry S. Turner, 'Lessons from Literature for the Historian of Science (and Vice Versa): Reflections on "Form"', *Isis*, 101.3 (2010), 578–89 (p. 582).
58. Janine Rogers, *Unified Fields: Science and Literary Form* (Montreal and Kingston: McGill-Queen's University Press, 2014), p. xvi.
59. 'unity of man': 'Einheit des Menschen' (DSW 624).
60. 'Dichten heißt, Erkenntnis durch die Form gewinnen wollen, und neue Erkenntnis kann nur durch neue Form geschöpft werden' (letter to Daisy Brody, 25 Nov. 1932) (Hermann Broch, *Briefe 1*, ed. Paul Michael Lützeler (Frankfurt am Main.: Suhrkamp, 1974–81), p. 223).
61. Mehrtens, *Moderne Sprache Mathematik*, p. 457.
62. Paul Bernays, 'Hilbert's Significance for the Philosophy of Mathematics' [1922], in *From Brouwer to Hilbert: The Debate on the Foundations of Mathematics in the 1920s*, ed. and trans. Paolo Mancosu (Oxford: Oxford University Press, 1998), 189–97 (p. 192).
63. David Hilbert, 'Mathematical Problems', trans. Mary Winston Newson, *Bulletin of the American Mathematical Society*, 8.10 (1902), 437–79 (p. 454).
64. Hermann Broch, 'The Spirit in an Unspiritual Age' [1934], in *Geist and Zeitgeist: The Spirit in an Unspiritual Age. Six Essays by Hermann Broch*, ed. and trans. John Hargraves (New York: Counterpoint, 2002), 41–64 (p. 45).
65. 'annäherbar' (DSW 715).
66. Turner, 'Lessons from Literature', p. 586.
67. Turner, 'Lessons from Literature', p. 584.
68. Alain Badiou, *Being and Event*, trans. Oliver Feltham (London and New York: Continuum, 2005), p. 6. Broch: 'Die Möglichkeit des mathematischen Seins ist die reinste ontologische Erkenntnis [...]: in ihr ist Seinsnotwendigkeit und logische Möglichkeit zur vollen identischen Evidenz gebracht' (Hermann Broch, 'Zum Begriff der Geisteswissenschaften', in *Die unbekannte Größe* (Zürich: Rhein-Verlag, 1961), 261–75 (p. 270)).
69. Moritz Epple, *Die Entstehung der Knotentheorie: Kontexte und Konstruktionen einer modernen mathematischen Theorie* (Braunschweig: Vieweg und Teubner, 1999), p. 209.
70. Susan J. Wolfson, 'Reading for Form', in *Reading for Form*, ed. Susan J. Wolfson and Marshall Brown (Seattle and London: University of Washington Press, 2006), 3–25 (p. 6).
71. Hermann Broch, *Geist and Zeitgeist: The Spirit in an Unspiritual Age. Six Essays by Hermann Broch*, ed. and trans. John Hargraves (New York: Counterpoint, 2002), p. 181.
72. Hermann Broch, 'Kommentare', in *Die Schlafwandler: Eine Romantrilogie* (Frankfurt am Main: Suhrkamp, 1996), 719–35 (p. 729).
73. Broch, 'Kommentare', p. 731.
74. Broch, 'Kommentare', p. 732.
75. Graham Bartram, '"Subjektive Antipoden"? Broch's *Die Schlafwandler* and Musil's *Der Mann ohne Eigenschaften*', in *Hermann Broch: Modernismus, Kulturkrise und Hitlerzeit*, ed. Adrian Stevens, Kurt Wagner and Sigurd Paul Scheichl (Innsbruck: Institut für Germanistik, 1994), 63–75 (p. 75).
76. Jacques Derrida, 'Structure, Sign and Play in the Discourse of the Human Sciences', in *Modern Criticism and Theory*, 2nd edn, ed. David Lodge and Nigel Wood (Essex: Pearson, 2000), 89–103 (p. 90).
77. Derrida, 'Structure, Sign and Play', p. 90.

3

MATHEMATICS, EPISTEMOLOGY, ETHICS: ROBERT MUSIL, *THE MAN WITHOUT QUALITIES*

'Musil?!! In a talk, I called his approach "rational writing", writing from reason. It is the opposite of my own abilities.'[1] Hermann Broch's forceful attempt to distinguish his own literary projects from *The Man without Qualities* by fellow Austrian author Robert Musil only draws the more attention to similarities between their works. Musil, having read an abstract of Broch's *The Sleepwalkers*, expressed concern that such overlaps could be extensive.[2] And indeed, like Broch's *The Sleepwalkers* trilogy – and Pynchon's much later *Against the Day* – Musil's work explores the development of European society towards the First World War, the disintegration of traditional values and Enlightenment beliefs, and, not least, the role of mathematics in these processes. Like Pynchon and Broch, Musil sets *The Man without Qualities* against the historical and mathematical developments of the 1880s to 1920s and beyond, but, unlike these works, its actual plot spans only one year. It approaches the First World War, yet, though overshadowed by the imminent catastrophe, never arrives at its outbreak in August 1914. The period is thus condensed into one year, and similarly the setting in the state Kakania, a name based on an abbreviation for the monarchy of the Austro-Hungarian Empire, illustrates a wider situation in modern Europe: 'On the pretext of describing the last year in the life of Austria, it raises questions about the meaning of modern man's existence and responds to these in a completely novel way, which is light and ironic but also philosophically deep', Musil sets out his project in an autobiographical sketch.[3] In a further step of condensation, *The Man without Qualities* introduces mathematics as 'the new method of thought itself, the mind itself, the very wellspring of the times and the primal source of an incredible transformation' (MwQ 35). As in Broch's trilogy then, *The Man without Qualities* accords maths a privileged position in understanding modern existence. The two Austrian works differ in more than their writing styles, however, and this chapter examines further relations of maths and modernist literature when arguing that, for Musil, maths becomes a model not only of exactitude but also of vagueness and that in this paradoxical double-function it serves to inspire the critical trust needed to adapt epistemology, ethics and aesthetics to a time of profound change.

The assertion in *The Man without Qualities* that mathematics should be considered as the source of modern times and the method of thought can appear rather surprising. Although the protagonist, Ulrich, works as a mathematician before he embarks on a year-long holiday from life, only modest space is dedicated to direct engagement with maths in Musil's enormous text that, designed as two books consisting of two parts each, remains a fragment. Both parts of book 1, 'A Sort of Introduction' and 'Pseudoreality Prevails', were published in 1930, and the first part of book 2 appeared in 1932 as 'Into the Millennium [The Criminals]'. A further twenty chapters were submitted to the printer but withdrawn in 1938; next to these so-called galley chapters, we have a fair copy of six chapters of a revised version as well as additional versions and chapters of this continuation of the first part of book 2. The envisioned last part, 'A Sort of Ending', exists as a copious collection of notes, a selection of which was published together with the galley chapters and revised versions in 1978.[4] Famously labelled a novel without a plot, *The Man without Qualities* can be described not only as unfinished but as unfinishable: there is no possible conclusion that would complete the scant storyline and turn the fragment into a closed whole. Musil explains the sparse plot with his focus on ethics: 'People want Ulrich to *do* something. But I'm concerned with the *meaning* of the action' (notes 1764). Like other modernist works, *The Man without Qualities* abandons plot and traditional narrative as these imply a direction and coherence that cannot be found in disintegrating reality, and it also shares with Broch's *The Sleepwalkers* and other modernist novels a concern with the absence of a moral framework that gives action meaning. Musil's philosophical novel consequently introduces various partial solutions to its central question of how to live a moral life in a time when scientific and technological progress radically transforms its conditions.

The role of mathematics in this moral endeavour is twofold. On the one hand, it is the shaping power of science and technology and, through it, modern society, and it also stands for one side in a characterisation of the time as dominated by diametrically opposed epistemological approaches: the period is split into 'mathematics and mysticism', Ulrich contends (MwQ 837). In his diaries, Musil similarly describes the early twentieth century as a time of epistemological polarities: 'rationality and mysticism are the poles of the time'.[5] Although maths here constitutes the symbolic extreme of rational engagement with the world, Ulrich ultimately pursues it in view of fundamental human and moral questions:

> If someone had asked him at any point while he was writing treatises on mathematical problems or mathematical logic [. . .] what it was he hoped to achieve, he would have answered that there was only one question worth thinking about, the question of the right way to live. (MwQ 275)

And Musil explains about his work: 'I have written about certain connections between moral and mathematical thinking on several occasions; not in a conventional manner, indeed, but I'm nevertheless happy to be able to point out that these exist.'[6] Unlike the traditional identification of maths and rationality, the moral dimension of maths in Musil's work is closely tied to its modern development and to the potential of its new methods to transform thinking and thereby arrive at the right way to live.

Across his diaries and novelistic writing, Musil uses 'mathematics' and 'rationality' interchangeably to name the opposition to mysticism, and scholars looking at maths in his work often do so to better understand the presentation of rational approaches to the world. Apart from a few exceptions, the specific role of mathematics in the contrast of rationality and mysticism is not considered, so Dale Adams rightly criticises.[7] To do exactly that, this chapter examines the specifically modern nature of maths in *The Man without Qualities*, including its historical development into a logicist-formalist and an intuitionist school. It explores how the novel fragment employs this modern notion to elaborate on the falsely perceived antagonism between rationality and its various Others and on abortive attempts at synthesising them. Rather than only presenting maths as exemplifying the side of rationality, the text uses it to transform the binary opposition into a relation described by a circle where the poles of rational maths and mysticism take diametrically opposed positions but are connected by transitional states on the circumference. *The Man without Qualities* introduces this dynamics between clear-cut distinctions and a more complicated relation between elements in relation to law. To make law practicable, it is based on the belief that 'between two contraries there is no third or middle state' (MwQ 261): a murderer will either be declared responsible for their actions or insane and therefore not guilty. Yet, such clear distinctions can be difficult to make in individual cases as these are more accurately examined taking into consideration nature's 'peculiar preference': '*Natura non fecit saltus*, she makes no jumps but prefers gradual transitions' (MwQ 261). In what follows, I look precisely at the gradual transitions of maths in view of demands for exactitude and pragmatic vagueness, and examine how it works as 'the primal source of an incredible transformation' in three interrelated domains: epistemology, ethics and aesthetics.

As we saw reflected in the novels by Pynchon and Broch, various thinkers perceived the beginning of the twentieth century as, in Ulrich's terms, splitting into 'mathematics and mysticism'. Europe experienced immense scientific progress and technological change that transformed city life, the workplace and, with new transport and communication systems, the sense of space and time. At the same time, it saw a wave of attraction to the irrational, the emotional and the supernatural: Sigmund Freud's psychoanalysis introduced the study of the unconscious and the drives of the id, scientific concepts such as the fourth dimension and the aether seemed to confirm the existence of realms beyond the immediately experienced, and séances fed into the wish to connect with the spirit world and the dead. The perceived gap between rational-technological and emotional-mystical approaches to the world animated philosophy and art in the early twentieth century, and Musil's metaliterary *The Man without Qualities* reflects on fictional efforts to locate literature between the spheres of 'mathematics and mysticism'. His own literary style, which Broch called 'rational writing', displays a split in language that reflects opposed exact-scientific and imprecise everyday approaches. Famously, the first eleven lines are taken up by a meteorological description:

> A barometric low hung over the Atlantic. It moved eastward toward a high-pressure area over Russia without as yet showing any inclination to bypass this high in a northerly direction. The isotherms and isotheres were functioning as they should. The air temperature was appropriate relative to the annual mean temperature. (MwQ 3)

The technical account is then rephrased in everyday language: 'In a word that characterizes the facts fairly accurately, even if it is a bit old-fashioned: It was a fine day in August 1913' (MwQ 3). As the more immediately graspable rephrasing suggests, technically exact language is not always preferable, and in his non-fictional work too, Musil does not advocate that literature merely turn to scientific diction. Rather, it is to employ science as a method, to say it with Ezra Pound's famous modernist dictum, to 'make it new'. According to Musil, 'all intellectual daring today lies in the natural sciences. We shall not learn from Goethe, Hebbel, or Hölderlin, but from Mach, Lorentz, Einstein, Minkowski, from Couturat, Russell, Peano ...'[8] Self-consciously exploring how to learn from modern mathematics in matters of conflicting epistemologies and literary aesthetics, *The Man without Qualities* contributes to establishing its place in modernist culture.

Mathematics and Morality

As a mathematician Ulrich is, so Thomas Sebastian claims, 'so well informed that the reader is forced to take several crash courses in scientific theory to appreciate the author's relentless appropriation of scientific ideas'.[9] Sebastian's example, namely 'Ulrich's familiarity with "the law of the large numbers" [which] demonstrates the author's declared intent to make him "a man equipped with the most advanced knowledge of his time"', is rather unhappily chosen, considering that the law of large numbers was described by Siméon Poisson in 1835, thus hardly constituting an instance of the most advanced knowledge in 1913.[10] Yet, we learn that Ulrich's knowledge is indeed up to date when he is concerned with contemporary questions regarding the foundations of maths: 'He was one of those mathematicians called logicians, for whom nothing was ever "correct" and who were working out a new foundational theory' (MwQ 939).[11] Ulrich's orientation suggests that it is not a specific mathematical law but rather the philosophy of maths that is at the core of his appropriation of scientific ideas, and this indirect employment makes a crash course in scientific theory even more necessary. Based on the earlier overview of formalist and intuitionist approaches to rebuilding mathematical foundations (see Introduction and Chapter 2), I examine the presentation of a specifically modern notion in relation to Ulrich's main reason for practising maths. To repeat his moral objective: 'he was writing treatises on mathematical problems or mathematical logic [. . . to think about] the question of the right way to live' (MwQ 275). Taking a closer look at the maths is not a sterile exercise, then, but immediately bound up with ethics.

Ulrich identifies as a logicist, and *The Man without Qualities* presents logicism as contributing to a modern loss of essence when it does not describe the inner qualities of nature but refers only to mathematics itself. Working in a self-contained field, mathematicians resemble 'racing cyclists pedaling away for dear life, blind to everything in the world except the back wheel of the rider ahead of them' (MwQ 37). The fact that Ulrich retires from the outside world to do his mathematical work further emphasises its disconnection: 'He had drawn the curtains and was working in the subdued light like an acrobat in a dimly lit circus arena rehearsing dangerous new somersaults for a panel of experts before the public has been let in' (MwQ 115). Removed from nature into an artistic sphere, Ulrich devises new moves that have to be approved by the mathematical community before being released for application to the world. And Ulrich reflects the self-referential turn of modern maths in his own life: realising that his 'connections to the world had become pale, shadowy, and negative' and that he has lost the capacity to apply his abilities, the eponymous man without qualities reverts to the realm of his own thoughts and decides to take a year-long holiday from life (MwQ 285–6). Ulrich is not prepared to embrace logicist self-referentiality and relinquish the possibility of impacting the world, however, as an encounter with fellow scientist Dr Strastil shows. Embarking on a more commonplace holiday to the mountains, Strastil implies that she has no more direct relation to physical reality than modern maths: she asks indignantly 'what she needed nature for. [. . .] She could lie on the mountain meadow for three whole days without stirring' (MwQ 940). Feeling no inclination to interact with or act upon nature, Strastil lives the self-containment of logicism, while Ulrich's reply that a farmer would be bored when lying on the grounds he usually ploughs illustrates his belief that nature has to be worked on in order to bear fruit and maths should help achieve these results.

The exchange between the two scientists further connects mathematical and moral concerns when Strastil advocates 'feeling on a sufficiently elementary level', just after pointing to foundational debates that negotiate notions of mathematical possibility, correctness and truth (MwQ 940). Strastil asks Ulrich whether he thinks a mathematical deduction possible, and she explains her own standpoint: 'I don't think Kneppler's deduction is mistaken, it's just that it's wrong' (MwQ 939). Claus Hoheisel maintains that Musil here criticises scientific discourse and makes fun of the restrictedness of the scientific approach.[12] While Strastil, described as a scientist with 'an exceptionally developed capacity for abstract thought and a notably retarded understanding of the soul', is obviously ridiculed, on a different level her distinction between 'mistaken' and 'wrong' points to the serious matter of the problematic transfer of precise mathematics to everyday language: 'She might have said with the same firmness that she did consider the deduction mistaken but nevertheless not essentially wrong. She knew what she meant, but in ordinary language, where the terms are undefined, one cannot express oneself unequivocally' (MwQ 941, 939–40). We will come back to issues of precision and vagueness below, but more important in this context is Strastil's suggestion that maths is not a field of indisputable statements, but that evaluations of correctness and truth can differ according to personal conviction. Indeed, when the mathematical community is divided into the schools of logicism, formalism and intuitionism, the decision whether a deduction is proclaimed right or wrong can depend on the adherence to a particular school, and it makes a difference whether there is a mistake in Kneppler's deduction or Strastil disagrees with his fundamental understanding of what mathematics is.

As a logician wanting to determine the foundations of maths, for Ulrich 'nothing was ever "correct"', and he advocates going back to the ancient Greek roots of logic before considering truth in maths (MwQ 939). Accordingly, his response to Stastil's question about Kneppler's deduction is a shrug. The fact that mathematicians can have disparate opinions or none at all questions the possibility of truth in general, and the foundational queries in maths mirror doubts that animate what we could call 'foundational research' in Kakania: only sure that it is not the country it used to be, Kakania sets up the Parallel Campaign, a group with the aim to determine the essential being of Austrian culture. The campaign is to define the country's innermost character and exhibit Kakania's unified nature in a celebration planned to make 1918 'a jubilee year for our Emperor of Peace' (MwQ 79). The jubilee year is then expected to free a unifying force and enable the modern world to find its true being, but the futility of the campaign is immediately obvious to readers: the year 1918 was hardly one of celebrating any 'Emperor of Peace', and equally evidently *The Man without Qualities* does not achieve unity – it remains a fragment.

Uncertainty in maths and the unsuitability of logical approaches to determine essential character in nature or Kakania have immediately moral consequences in the case of Moosbrugger. Having murdered several women, he waits for the authorities to agree whether to sentence him to death or declare him insane. His diminished responsibility constitutes a problem for legal categories, which allow either convicting culprits as guilty or declaring them mentally incapacitated, and his case induces a re-examination of the interrelated notions of reason and responsibility. Ulrich's father, a lawyer, explains the connection: 'as the intellect and reasoning power develops, the will comes to dominate desires or instincts [. . .]. Any willed act is accordingly always the result of prior thought and not purely instinctive' (MwQ 343). The legal term 'accountability' shares an etymological root with 'to count'; a relation that Gwyneth Cliver is at risk of overstating when she declares that 'the concept of sanity grows directly out of at least arithmetical, if not mathematical, capacity'.[13] Nevertheless, the text does exploit the suggestive connection between rationality, accountability and mathematics. It strengthens the shared relation of law and maths to reason when a calculation exercise constitutes part of the court's evaluation of Moosbrugger's accountability: while persons clearly irresponsible of their actions are thought to have no grasp of mathematics and 'when asked to multiply 7 times 7 stick out their tongue', Moosbrugger's abilities cannot be dismissed as easily. Asked to add fourteen to fourteen, he replies:

> 'Oh, about twenty-eight to forty.' This 'about' gave them trouble, which made Moosbrugger grin. It was really simple. He knew perfectly well that you get twenty-eight when you go on from fourteen to another fourteen; but who says you have to stop there? Moosbrugger's gaze would always range a little farther ahead, like that of a man who has reached the top of a ridge outlined against the sky and finds that behind it there are other, similar ridges. (MwQ 263, 259)

Moosbrugger's idiosyncratic calculation clearly deviates from the traditional rules, but it is not entirely wrong. Moreover, his inability to stop at a right answer points to the problems encountered in modern maths where attempts to determine its correct basis give rise to ever further questions. The association of Moosbrugger's calculation with an unending succession of obstacles thus implies that, since the grounds of maths itself are found to be elusive, it is no longer an entirely reliable means to determine reason. Indeed, if in law there is a belief that 'between two contraries there is no third or middle state', this assumption is no longer a given in modern maths: logicists and formalists do work from the premise that either a proposition is true or its negation is true, but the school of intuitionism does not accept the so-called 'law of excluded middle' as an axiom. Moosbrugger's case thus relates mathematics, accountability and reason on several levels: basic arithmetic is expected to determine the offender's accountability but reveals a more complex situation than expected, and the controversy on possible states in between a binary opposition compares to the foundational debate between different mathematical schools (MwQ 261). Since Moosbrugger's condition of diminished responsibility can be judged only once the grounds on which to determine reason are agreed upon, his case also depends on foundational research in mathematics, which thus becomes a vital moral task.

Epistemology: Between Mathematics and Mysticism

Set in a period when art and philosophy widely reflect diverging attraction to science and technology and, on the other hand, to irrational, emotional and supernatural perspectives, *The Man without Qualities* presents Ulrich as having been born at a time of 'growing rationality' that gives rise to the idea that 'life could be lived with precision' (MwQ 235, 265). While he continues to value this rational approach to knowledge and life, in 1913 the majority of Kakanians have turned to the pole of mysticism and explain all problems with the rule of cold calculation. Described in an exaggerated tone as 'screaming to have their sores rubbed with soul' and defining the soul as 'that which sneaks off at the mention of algebraic series', these adherents to the pole of mysticism and their simplified understanding of maths are clearly ridiculed (MwQ 269, 106). Sympathy lies with Ulrich's response: he asks for 'bringing together again what had fallen apart' in a synthesis of mathematics and mysticism (MwQ 648). Musil discusses possibilities of countering diverging mindsets in his non-fictional work too and coined the ungainly neologisms 'the ratioïd' and 'the non-ratioïd'. The ratioïd denotes any knowledge 'that science can systematize, everything that can be summarized in laws and rules; primarily, in other words, physical nature'.[14] The non-ratioïd, by contrast, is that which escapes systematisation and can be understood only in individual situations, and it encompasses values, ideas and aesthetics. Musil's unwieldy terminology reveals his intention not simply to oppose a rational and a non-rational domain or, indeed, mathematics and mysticism, but to contrast a sphere ruled by intellectual cognition and law and, on the other hand, a realm dominated by immediate intuitive knowledge and not by rules but by exceptions. As we shall see, maths in *The Man without Qualities* is precisely not an incarnation of the ratioïd, but it involves both domains and can therefore lend itself to exploring notions of synthesis.

In the early twentieth century Henri Bergson's philosophy presents the probably most popular criticism of the belief that science could measure and explain all phenomena, and Musil names him – along with Friedrich Nietzsche, Karl Marx and Otto von Bismarck – as exemplifying major trends in modern thinking.[15] While Musil stressed that he had not read Bergson's work and that similarities between their views could give only the appearance of influence, Bergson's popularity meant that Musil could not help being aware of his focus on the inner self that apprehends experience through intuition and whose spiritual essence escapes analytical examination. In a similar manner to Musil, Bergson distinguishes between rational analysis rooted in the intellect and focused on material reality, and the immediate and absolute knowledge of a thing in intuition. The widespread reception of Bergson's philosophy helps appreciate that *The Man without Qualities* articulates a general feeling with its opposition of maths and mysticism, but discussing Musil's text in view of Bergson also has another point: his writings allow us to see how the juxtaposition connects with attributions of national characteristics during the First World War. To repeat the quotation from the beginning of this chapter, *The Man without Qualities* explores 'the meaning of modern man's existence', but aspects of Bergson's writing alert us to the fact that Musil's text also addresses a specific situation and locates maths in between rival Prussian and Austrian mindsets. Although the novel fragment charts only the pre-war situation, it makes clear that the inability to synthesise opposed ratioïd and non-ratioïd orientations will lead to war. In historical reality, the opposed perspectives entered war propaganda through Bergson's philosophy, and his thinking was applied to military matters in sometimes peculiar ways: 'The French military took his ideas of an animating force in life – *l'élan vital* – to argue that spirit in soldiers was ultimately more important than weapons', Margaret MacMillan reports.[16] But with the little-known propagandist speech 'The Meaning of the War', Bergson also participated directly in connecting his concepts of matter and spirit to the warring parties.

Bergson delivered the speech as president of the *Académie des sciences morales et politiques* in December 1914, and it is clearly aimed at strengthening the belief in the moral righteousness of the First World War and France's ability to win. Like Musil, he presents Otto von Bismarck, the 'Iron Chancellor' who built up a powerful German Empire at the expense of Austria, as the personification of a mindset: 'There was a man on the spot in whom the methods of Prussia were incarnate [. . .]. He had just removed the only obstacle which could spoil his plan; he had got rid of Austria.'[17] For Bergson, the separation from Austria is not only of political significance, but it means severing ties to its mentality and cementing Prussian characteristics of mechanical discipline, rigid method, automatism and precise information. *The Man without Qualities* similarly presents Prussia as the epitome of intellectual discipline and as contrasted to Austria, which has managed to preserve its feeling. Even Arnheim, a German character modelled on the industrialist Walter Rathenau and seemingly connecting economics and the soul, ultimately turns out to reside in Vienna not to escape rationalism but to sell oil and guns. Where Ulrich demands to use mathematical knowledge to live morally, Arnheim's preparations to benefit from war stand for merely materialistic exploitation of science and technology. Bergson similarly singles out a Prusso-German inability to respond to scientific progress with corresponding advance in the domain of the soul:

> Each new machine being for man a new organ – an artificial organ which merely prolongs the natural organs – his body became suddenly and prodigiously increased in size, without his soul being able at the same time to dilate to the dimensions of his new body. From this disproportion there issued the problems, moral, social, international, which most of the nations endeavoured to solve by filling up the soulless void in the body politic by creating more liberty, more fraternity, more justice than the world had ever seen. Now, while mankind laboured at this task of spiritualization, inferior powers [... i.e. Prusso-Germany] plotted an inverse experience for mankind. What would happen if the mechanical forces, which science had brought to a state of readiness for the service of man, should themselves take possession of man in order to make his nature material as their own?[18]

In other words, where other European states work to spiritualise matter, Prussia is guilty of mechanising spirit: throughout its history there is 'the continuous clang of militarism and industrialism, of machinery and mechanism, of debased moral materialism'.[19] When Bergson ends by predicting the victory of French spiritual principles over Prussia's materialist doctrine, his speech reinforces the connection between the violent conflict of the First World War and the irreconcilability of what Ulrich associates with mathematics and mysticism.

Given that the conflict between epistemological orientations threatens to result in war, for *The Man without Qualities* the year 1913 is the last opportunity to mend the split. As Allen Thiher notices, it 'sometimes appears, indeed, that Ulrich actually wants to leave the modern world to go back to the scientific revolution of the seventeenth century and to reunite the irreconcilable epistemologies that emerged then'.[20] The quest for reintegration occupies Ulrich during his year-long holiday from life: roughly speaking, the first book presents his exploring possibilities of synthesis from a rational perspective, and book two focuses on his turn to mysticism. Both approaches fail. Ulrich does experience synthesis in what he calls the Other Condition when his sister Agathe, a female version of himself, makes him whole: he enjoys 'ecstatic moments in which a split has not yet occurred' and where morality exists 'without interruption' (MwQ 931, 898). This synthesis cannot serve as a model for moral living, however, since it entails withdrawing from reality into an Other Condition and losing the possibility of effecting change. Ulrich's attempts to instil precision in the domain of feeling and thereby adjust emotions to the progress made in science similarly fall short. In the first chapter, a statistical assessment of a traffic accident allows bystanders to see the incident as a necessary part of a general picture and relieves them from the need to feel unsettled or touched. Transforming calamity into an event that takes an 'entirely lawful and orderly' place in an organised system, the use of science is shown not to heighten the truth and freedom of feeling but to stifle it (MwQ 5). The subsequent chapter illustrates the similar failing of Ulrich's employing maths to determine the right way of living: observing passers-by from his window, he tries to calculate the effort of taking part in the flow of traffic and estimates that, summed up, such everyday actions create more energy than isolated extraordinary deeds. In the light of this everyday heroism, Ulrich concludes the futility of his inborn wish to become an important man; that is, his precise examination of life leads to a new evaluation of his ambitions. But a little later Ulrich abandons mathematical measuring of actions since it leads to favouring objective criteria over the imprecise values of real genius and greatness.

The brief sketch above shows that, when *The Man without Qualities* introduces maths as 'the new method of thought itself [. . .] and the primal source of an incredible transformation', this does not refer to a superficial transfer of mathematical precision to other domains (MwQ 35). Rather, one has to 'take flight' (MwQ 897) from the level that scientific knowledge has reached and transcend it, so Ulrich understands, and Musil uses similar imagery in an essay to make the point that there is a difference 'whether one [. . .] as a half-scientific person whose imagination is gripped by the pleasures of science writes a pseudoscientific novel [. . .], or whether one really goes all the way to the end of the trampoline of science and only then jumps'.[21] It is in this latter way that mathematics continues to play a decisive role in Ulrich's moral endeavour. More precisely, maths is part of a strategy to deal with the lack of a central organising idea that afflicts Austrian culture and, on an individual level, prevents Ulrich from settling on any personal quality. Peering through her wedding ring, Ulrich's friend Clarisse ponders: 'if we could be cut open our entire life might look like a ring, just something that goes around something. [. . .] There's nothing inside, and yet it looks as though that were precisely what matters most' (MwQ 401). The imagery of the empty circle helpfully illustrates that Ulrich's attempt to live with mathematical precision fails to fuse opposed parts of life at the centre of the 'circle of questions [...]: "How should I live?"' (MwQ 972). But the circle also describes an alternative understanding of the relation between antithetical positions: the binary opposites are not taken as endpoints of a one-dimensional opposition that have to be merged in the middle, but they take antipodal positions that are contrasted but also connected by the circumference. The extremes of rational maths and mysticism are joined through intermediate positions on the circle, enabling not a fusion at the centre but a transition between the poles. In what follows, I take a closer look at the presentation of maths in *The Man without Qualities* to argue that it appears not solely as the incarnation of Prussian rationality, but as a much more ambiguous domain that has ties to the domain of mysticism. In this different way of accounting for the ratioïd and the non-ratioïd, modern maths proposes a response to disintegration that, so Musil suggests with the novel fragment and elsewhere, constitutes a model for literary fiction.

TRANSITIONS: FROM MATHS TO MYSTICISM . . . AND BACK AGAIN

Moosbrugger's unusual but strangely accurate understanding of mathematics is removed from rational grasp and brings maths closer to the sphere of his madness or, more generally, the opposite of reason. This introduces a sense of diminished rationality in maths, and *The Man without Qualities* more immediately relates it to reason's Others at the transition from the first to the second book. The last chapter of book one, entitled 'The Turning Point', indicates a change in Ulrich's life, punctuated by his father's death. Ulrich is relieved of the ties with traditional morality that his father represents, and he also closes the chapter of rational research regarding the question of the right way to live when, shortly after the funeral at the beginning of book two, he finishes 'his interrupted mathematical investigation' which 'may well be the last piece of work that reaches back to that time' (MwQ 782, 783). In fact, it is implied that rational investigation destroys the old order embodied by Ulrich's father and to leave the remnants in a mess: when, according to his father's last wish, the body is put 'at the disposal of science; after which anatomical intervention it was only natural to assume that the old gentleman had been hurriedly sewn up again', the unity of the world of the father is literally destroyed by science, and the community of mourners at the funeral is not held together by an intact entity, but 'at the center of this great, beautiful, solemn pageantry, was an untidily recobbled object' (MwQ 772). The situation also illustrates the state of the modern world which has lost the moral order formerly guaranteed by God the Father and substitutes the empty place at the centre with a multitude of contradictory ideas that do not fit together properly. Moreover, the concurrence of the funeral and the completion of Ulrich's last mathematical problem invites a comparison with the situation of maths where research has destroyed the body of orthodox beliefs and left it in pieces fought over by different foundational schools. When intuition plays an important role in the solution of Ulrich's mathematical problem, it signals the move from his rational investigation of the right way to live to pursuing more mystical ways.

Working on his last mathematical question, Ulrich solves it helped by a flash of intuition. The solution is thus not entirely part of the semicircle of reason, but such intuitive answers are, Ulrich understands, 'prompted by some stimulus outside the scope of everyday scientific activity' and are 'never purely intellectual' (MwQ 748, 782). Nevertheless, the conclusions intuition arrives at are no less true than rational deductions, and intuition can, indeed, even be more accurate, the narrator suggests. Arnheim gives the example of playing billiards to illustrate that intuition can answer problems that are irresolvable by precise means: taking account of all the determining forces of a billiard shot results in incalculable complexity: 'we are abandoned by reason!', Arnheim exclaims (MwQ 622).[22] In contrast, dismissing reason from the outset and hardly thinking about playing the ball, the task almost solves itself. His similarly intuitive solution makes Ulrich experience that intuition may take precedence over reason even in maths.

The implications of relating mathematics to intuition on a basic level are profound, as the history of intuitionism and its role in the foundational debate reveal. While logicism and formalism refer only to rational means to secure the foundations of their field, intuitionism reacts against the implications of a purely logical or formal basis, and its founder L. E. J. Brouwer claims that 'mathematics is independent of the so-called *logical laws* (laws of reasoning or of human thought)'.[23] As Jeremy Gray explains, the foundational dispute thus also revolves around the question 'whether mathematics could be regarded as rational', and intuitionism implies its participation in the realm of reason's Others.[24] As examined in more detail in the introductory chapter and the discussion of Broch's *The Sleepwalkers*, the different evaluations of the place of reason in logicist-formalist and intuitionist mathematics have implications for the notions of knowledge, truth and value, and they thus affect Ulrich's investigations into the right way to live. While formalists 'stripped mathematics of any meaning at all' and it consequently has no intrinsic truth or value, intuitionism related it to reality via the human intuition, which then guarantees its value in the world.[25] The young Brouwer describes maths as a near-mystical realm characterised by unity: 'it develops from a single aprioristic basic intuition, which may be called *invariance in change* as well as *unity in multitude*'.[26] And he emphasises the relation to mysticism when explaining that 'mathematical understanding is something like "yes" or "no" just like sleeping is something like "yes" or "no"' and that '[m]athematics justifies itself, needs no deeper grounds than moral mysticism'.[27]

The well-known case of Brouwer shows that the connection of mathematics and mysticism in *The Man without Qualities* is not without precedent, but that it negotiates questions that were being discussed in the scientific and public sphere in the years prior to its publication. Moreover, when Ulrich's mathematical practice approaches the pole of mysticism and thus gets close to a state of morality 'without interruption', this echoes Brouwer's insistence on a moral dimension of maths. He intended to call his doctoral dissertation 'The Value of Mathematics' before settling on the title 'On the Foundations of Mathematics', and he demanded to pursue it not for its own sake but in view of moral value: 'Let the motivation behind mathematics be the craving for the good.'[28] In *The Man without Qualities*, Ulrich shares the intuitionist concern with value when his mathematical work is ultimately directed at finding the right way to live, and he consequently toys with the idea of transferring his intuitive insight from maths to life. Yet, seeing that purely intuitive ideas are only an excuse for 'all those who could not justify what they did by logic', he dismisses it as a comprehensive means of explanation and once again concludes that neither rational nor non-rational approaches are successful but that a synthesis of the two poles of life is needed (MwQ 595). Significantly, however, Ulrich's experience of non-rational solutions in maths reveals that the opposition between the poles is not absolute but that maths itself can pass over into the mystical domain. In its intuitionist notion, maths inhabits a transitional position between the extreme of reason and the pole of mysticism.

That maths takes an intermediate position between polar extremes informs Cliver's statement that 'the engagement with mathematics seems to adversely affect the sanity of Musil's characters and in fact displaces the very distinction between the rational and the irrational'.[29] Yet, the relation between maths and the characters goes deeper than allowed for by Cliver. Clarisse and Moosbrugger are not overexposed to maths, but it is their engagement with underlying rational-logicist and intuitionist perspectives that encourages their escapes into the unambiguousness of their own minds and appearances of madness. As developed in relation to Broch's *The Sleepwalkers* in Chapter 2, logicist-formalist and intuitionist perspectives are divided on the question whether mathematics is to be seen as a language. Moosbrugger and Clarisse address related positions in their respective language scepticism. Clarisse's words disintegrate into meaningless components: 'My dar*ling* – my duck*ling* – my *ling*! Do you know what a *ling* is? I can't work it out' (MwQ 773). Moosbrugger similarly despairs of the unreliability of words, even if not reaching Clarisse's eloquence: all the 'words he did have were: hm-hm, uh-uh' (MwQ 428). Nor does he engage in the rational dissection of language that reveals its meaninglessness, but, in contrast, is overwhelmed by the significance and power of words:

> It had happened that he said to a girl, 'Your sweet rose lips,' but suddenly the words gave way at their seams and something upsetting happened: [...] there was a rose sticking out of it [her mouth] on a long stem, and the temptation to take a knife and cut it off, or punch it back into the face, was overwhelming. (MwQ 259)

The quotation illustrates how ambiguous figural language aggravates the incomprehensibility of the world and runs counter to Moosbrugger's need for clarity and unity that he achieves by killing the disconcerting Other, namely women. We can note common structures between Clarisse's breakdown of language into its basic units, revealing its arbitrariness and inherent meaninglessness, and developments in formalist-logicist maths. And Moosbrugger's seeking refuge from the ambiguous nature of language in perfect mysticism mirrors the intuitionist belief in the prelinguistic nature of meaning. There is a risk of overstretching the connection between positions in the foundational debate and the characters' versions of modernist language scepticism. Yet, in early drafts to the book, Musil more clearly presented Ulrich as a logician – a plan he dropped because he found it too difficult to communicate – and in the first chapter, entitled 'Dream of a Logician', connected maths and speechlessness when a man bites off a woman's tongue. The draft thus more clearly implicates maths in problems of communication and in the epistemological crisis that derives from being unable to trust language, a major means of representation. The wider implications of mathematical positions thus suggest that it is not 'an overzealous exploration of rational mathematics [that] ironically leads to [characters'] flirtation with irrational thought', but with a view to intuitive, moral and prelinguistic aspects, *The Man without Qualities* presents maths itself as moving away from the pole of pure reason and crossing over into the realm of mysticism.[30]

Next to the crossover from the pole of mathematics as the extreme of reason to the pole of mysticism, Musil's novel fragment presents a corresponding transition from the individuality of mysticism to the generality of maths. A childhood memory shared by Agathe and Ulrich points to the opposition of general maths and a concrete individual: when a house is being built in the garden, the young siblings plan to smuggle slips of paper with beautiful verses into the walls, but as they do not come up with a poem Agathe copies an arithmetic sentence from her schoolbook and Ulrich writes 'I am' and adds his name (MwQ 768). Apart from highlighting the opposed qualities of impersonal maths and an individual name, the contributions also exemplify a division inside modern maths: forced to act when the walls 'were already rising out of the foundations', Agathe throws her arithmetic sentence into the building pit and thus helps construct a building on 'mathematical grounds'; in contrast, when Ulrich slips his name into the wall, the individual is involved in the building – corresponding to the place of the human being in intuitionist maths (MwQ 767). Shortly after remembering his childhood decision to become part of the construction, Ulrich translates the intuitionist impulse to solving his mathematical problem.

The memory might inspire Ulrich's solution by intuition, but, pitting against each other the generality of mathematics and a concrete individual, it also leads him to reconsider the convergence of maths and mysticism. That is, immediately after finding an intuitive solution to his last mathematical problem, Ulrich reminds himself that progress does not rely on the inner qualities of an individual: 'what it finally amounts to is something remarkably impersonal [. . .] everything serves an evolution that is both unfathomable and inescapable' (MwQ 784). Having accepted that maths remains impersonal despite the intuitive part in his final exercise and does therefore not lend itself to making a personal impact on the world, he plunges himself into the city crowd where he comes to feel that individual achievement is not only insignificant in science but that in general 'it is not oneself that matters but only this mass' (MwQ 785). Individual characteristics dissolve in the face of the multitude which can display completely different qualities. The narrator muses: 'Water, for instance, is less of a pleasure in excessive than in small doses, by exactly the difference between drowning and drinking' (MwQ 321–2). In a world where personal destiny is, as Ulrich feels, displaced by collective processes, a general meaning might emerge from statistical description. Agathe even suggests statistical order as a means of transcendence: 'wouldn't it be lovely to be dissolved by statistics? [. . .] It's been such a long time since love could do it!' (MwQ 785). Walking among the city crowd, Ulrich indeed feels that being part of an impersonal mass could include one into a greater significance. Instead of the individual, the average or most probable would carry meaning. Probability becomes a key concept in the chapters not published in Musil's lifetime, where Ulrich proposes that the advance of the average person means that 'gradually "probable man" and "probable life" would emerge in place of "true" man and life'.[31] Considering the traffic accident in the very first chapter, however, where the bystanders come to think of the victim not in terms of his true life or death but in relation to accident probabilities, it remains doubtful whether the significance of statistics is a satisfactory alternative to dissolving in love. It is not a mathematical way to achieve the Other Condition, then, but – connecting random single cases and a general order, the meaningful and the meaningless – statistics constitutes a transformative step between the realms of mysticism and rational maths.

The presentation of transitional states breaks down the binary opposition between mathematics and mysticism, and a potential synthesis has to take account not only of the poles but also of the crossovers between them. As we have seen, considering *The Man without Qualities* in the historical mathematical context shows that it is not primarily characters' exposure to maths that relates it to the irrational, but that mathematics itself encompasses non-rational elements. It is not solely part of the pole of rationality but also participates in at least two states of transition: mathematical exactitude draws on intuitive and mystical elements, while linking individual cases to the regularity of a general law marks the corresponding transition from mysticism to rational maths, or, in Musil's less memorable terms, from the non-ratioïd to the ratioïd. Given that maths features both as the extreme of reason and in transitional states, it does not lend itself to a synthesis of the poles. Rather, its modern development suggests that it could be used as a method of answering the circle of questions 'How should I live?' from various positions – that is, it responds to the circle of questions with a circle of answers. As the next sections develop, it is in this less unequivocal way that modern maths works as a model for moral living and writing, and introduces in the domains of ethics and aesthetics an appreciation of the vague.

Transitions in Literature: Between Mathematics and Mysticism

When *The Man without Qualities* presents mathematics as taking different positions between analytical exactitude and mystical states outside of language, it speaks to Megan Quigley's reassessment of the influences on literary modernism: she aims to rectify the impression that literary modernism was shaped more by the mathematised language of analytic philosophy than by pragmatism's 're-instatement of the vague'.[32] As discussed in Chapter 2, the introduction of mathematical symbols in analytic philosophy, for example by Gottlob Frege and Bertrand Russell, answers the wish for concrete, precise language in philosophical reasoning. Russell defines the 'process of sound philosophizing' as 'passing from those obvious, vague, ambiguous things, that we feel quite sure of, to something precise, clear, definite'.[33] In his talk 'Vagueness', he contrasts common speech with the more precise language of logic and his own attempt to invent 'a special language with a view to avoiding vagueness'.[34] Many modernist writers celebrated precise expression, among them T. S. Eliot who, as mentioned in the last chapter, lauded Russell and Whitehead's *Principia Mathematica* as 'perhaps a greater contribution to our language than [. . .] to mathematics'.[35] Against this tradition in literary criticism, Quigley explains modernist experimentation focusing on authors who embrace 'the elusive and the unfixable' and revel 'in "psychological commentaries," indecisiveness in plot and action, and "absolute" vagueness in style'.[36] Where she explores vagueness relating to subjective perception in works by Virginia Woolf, James Joyce's verbal punning, and Henry James's engagement with his brother William James's pragmatist philosophy, the opening of *The Man without Qualities* presents itself as a direct challenge to Russell's 'process of sound philosophizing': the first paragraph moves from the technical language of a meteorological description to the unspecific phrase 'It was a fine day'. To most readers, the latter expression is more useful, and the novel fragment thus immediately introduces the productiveness of vagueness and qualifies Dr Strastil's later complaint that one cannot express oneself unequivocally in ordinary language. From its beginning, then, Musil's text presents vagueness as a potentially practical choice and vindicates trust in its usefulness.

Pragmatism, with its focus on the practical effects of science, language or beliefs, is intimately connected to vagueness. Indeed, pragmatism can be seen as the opposite pole of foundational research and its aim for certainty: it is '*the attitude of looking away from first things, principles, "categories," supposed necessities; and of looking towards last things, fruits, consequences, facts. So much for the pragmatic method!*'[37] The author of this description, William James, is one of the founding fathers of pragmatism and uses vagueness as a tool in his philosophy. He argues that vagueness in language adequately represents a vague reality and accordingly aims for a 're-instatement of the vague to its proper place in our mental life'.[38] As even precise means of representation could only record the vagueness of reality, James shifts his focus from the conditions of language to its effects:

> You must bring out of each word its practical cash-value, set it at work within the stream of your experience. It appears less a solution, then, than as a program for more work, and more particularly as an indication of the ways in which existing realities may be *changed*.[39]

As *The Man without Qualities* suggests in its opening paragraph, the 'cash-value' or effects of words might be greater if using non-specific language. We will come back to the metaphor of the cash-value below and relate it to the notion that fictional assets open up scope for changing existing realities. But, before turning to pragmatist trust in fictional credit, a brief look at the presentation of literature in *The Man without Qualities* reveals how its various positions between the epistemological opposites mirror modern maths's circling around the poles and questioned impact on the world.

Just as Ulrich employs mathematics to determine the right way of living, he considers the possibility of living 'like a character in a book' and thus achieving an ethical existence (MwQ 646). This aesthetic strategy emerges as far from clear-cut when, like maths, literature takes various positions between the epistemological extremes. Maybe least surprisingly, the novel fragment presents literature as a means to express individuality and apprehend unity that is associated with the pole of mysticism: the poet is presented as 'the voice of the inner life', who feels himself to participate in a 'great irrational power' and to be the medium of 'the mysterious whole' (MwQ 323). Ulrich voices criticism of this notion of literature when complaining about the 'emotional excess' of writing and its inadequate response to a time dominated by scientific and technological progress (MwQ 1042). Like maths that comes to be associated with Moosbrugger's madness, literature threatens to tip over into dangerous irrationality; for example when literature relates to Moosbrugger through the figure of the philosopher Dr Meingast. Where Moosbrugger attains a quasi-mystical feeling of unity through sexual offence and murder, Meingast, whose writings are hoped to make the world into a mystical whole, is compared to an exhibitionist: Clarisse calls an exhibitionist a 'swine' and Meingast connects this to his own behaviour and Clarisse's identical exclamations in their youths (MwQ 857). Associated with Moosbrugger via the sexual offender, Meingast's writing towards a mystical whole is suggested to result in killing the Other that threatens to destabilise his unambiguous worldview. The capacity of literature to get closer to unity and inner order thus also makes it vulnerable to insanity and disconnect from the world. At the same time, the proposed introduction to rationalise handwriting with the shorthand system Oehl and the '"Thirty-five Mile" poem' that celebrates the flight over the English Channel at thirty-five miles per hour constitute merely rational responses to the reality of the period's scientific progress and disregard the moral request to change the world for the better (MwQ 436).

While literature at the poles of mathematics and mysticism appears flawed, writing also marks the transition between general order and the individual views related to mysticism. Narrative as the 'thread of the story' of life can be a primary means to bring the chaos of reality into a 'unidimensional order, as a mathematician would say' (MwQ 709, 708–9). But maths no longer proves reliable and the ordering function of narrative similarly fails: the contradictory pre-war society is no longer narrative, and the thread of the story manages to order only the individual domain. Correspondingly, writing can turn the individual into the general when it establishes a distance from life. Ulrich holds that, if people lived life in an aesthetic manner, 'more or less as they read', this would give them the critical distance necessary to change it (MwQ 399). Yet, completely living life as art entails an inability to interact with reality: the exhibitionist is unable to talk to the girl he observes, since '[h]is imagination, ready to conjure up any possibility that could even be suggested by a woman, became fearful and awkward when confronted with the natural possibility of admiring this defenseless little creature' (MwQ 860).[40] And, more drastically, Ulrich understands the suggestion that 'our existence should consist wholly of literature' to imply that 'reality ought to be done away with' (MwQ 397, 396). Modelling life on literature thus does achieve a distance from individual life, but the aesthetic detachment detrimentally affects the ability to change reality.

In the metaliterary discussions in *The Man without Qualities*, writing takes on various positions on the circle that connects the poles of mathematics and mysticism. Taking positions between the rational and the irrational, the individual and the general, the exact and the vague, literature does not emerge as a synthesis of fundamental elements of life but, like maths, as a way to explore aspects from different perspectives. Presented as part of the poles as well as of transitional states, and subject to pragmatic considerations of its effects on the world, the epistemological and moral potential of literature mirrors that of maths, and solutions developed in relation to mathematics reflect back on fiction. Accordingly, the next section takes a closer look at how pragmatist dealing with vagueness in maths informs Musil's vision of modernist literature, before the last section turns to examining, in the light of the mathematical discussion, essayism as a literary answer to the modern circling around opposed tendencies.

Mathematics and Pragmatist Use of Possibilities

With a focus on the practical cash-value of words by which reality may be changed, William James considers the possibilities language opens up rather than how it represents reality. *The Man without Qualities* similarly lauds what it calls a sense of possibility over a sense of reality and uses monetary imagery to stress that the same amount of possibility opens up vastly different options: 'To try to readily distinguish the realists from the possibilists, just think of a specific sum of money. Whatever possibilities inhere in, say, a thousand dollars are surely there independently of their belonging or not belonging to someone' (MwQ 11). Possibilities remain the same whatever the balance in the bank account, and they have, to use James's term, 'practical cash-value':

> the sense of possibility could be defined outright as the ability to conceive of everything there might be just as well, and to attach no more importance to what is than to what is not. The consequences of so creative a disposition can be remarkable. (MwQ 11)

The sense of possibility dominates the novel when Ulrich contemplates various approaches to life during his year-long holiday, and it permeates the text down to the level of grammatical structure when the subjunctive of possibility is the dominant mood. Modern maths is part of this presentation as it encourages the sense of possibility: not directly referring to the physical world, it opens up a vast domain of alternative structures. In his study on mathematics and modernism, Herbert Mehrtens explicitly refers to the sense of possibility in *The Man without Qualities* and characterises modern maths in young Ulrich's terms as quasi set in the subjunctive.[41] As maths exemplifies foundational research as well as the opposite focus on possibility and its creative consequences, further examining its role in Musil's writing can shed light on modernism's oscillation between the certainty of precise methods and trust in productive vagueness.

When talking about the creative potential of possibilities, it is not a big step to consider it in relation to fiction. Musil encountered the idea that mathematical structures constitute fictions when writing his doctoral thesis on Ernst

Mach, a physicist and philosopher whose work was also known to the founders of pragmatism. Mach is a precursor to constructivist approaches to science and for example holds that the mathematical concept of the continuum is a useful fiction and should be employed as such: 'There can be no objection to such a system, considered as a fiction merely.'[42] When Mach suggests to use a convenient fiction as long as it does not contradict experience, his position and Musil's evaluation of it can appear surprising if we expect a stereotypical division between a scientist's view on truth and a literary perspective. As Thiher summarises: 'the writer defends the truth of reality against the scientific epistemologist for whom the knowledge of laws or recurring functions is essentially a fiction created by autonomous scientists'.[43] The potential fictionality of maths is not a focus of Musil's dissertation, even though he was deeply involved with mathematics at the time. In later essays and his creative work, however, Musil engages with the possible relation of maths to fiction and the epistemological and ethical consequences. He thus participates in a discussion that animates both the sciences and the humanities in the decades around 1900. To bring up again some positions that are more closely examined in the introductory chapter: on the mathematical side, Georg Cantor puts freedom at the heart of maths, Henri Poincaré states that 'mathematical reasoning has of itself a kind of creative virtue', and in the non-mathematical sphere Friedrich Nietzsche, Ernst Cassirer, Oswald Spengler and Hans Vaihinger engage with ideas of employing maths as a means to turn incomprehensible reality into understandable fictions.[44]

Musil's essay 'The Mathematical Man' from 1913 explores relations between maths, fiction and literature in a humorous and exaggerated tone. Here, too, maths exhibits what in *The Man without Qualities* is called the sense of possibility: it is described as an 'ideal intellectual apparatus whose task and accomplishment are to anticipate in principle every possible case' (MM 40).[45] The hyperbolic speaker, not to be confused with Musil himself, explains that although maths conceives cases other than reality, one of its 'remarkable' consequences is that it creates life: 'All the life that whirls about us, runs, and stops is not only dependent on mathematics for its comprehensibility, but has effectively come into being through it and depends on it for its existence' (MM 41). Like *The Man without Qualities*, the essay presents maths not only as the pinnacle of reason but depicts it as more ambiguous, as also relying on non-rational elements and suffering from questionable foundations. And since maths is used extremely widely, from calculations in building houses and machinery to predicting the rise in populations, problems in its foundations threaten the very basis of existence:

> [T]he pioneers of mathematics formulated usable notions of certain principles that yielded conclusions, methods of calculation, and results,

and these were applied by the physicists to obtain new results; and finally came the technicians, who often took only the results and added new calculations to them, and thus the machines arose. And suddenly, after everything had been brought into the most beautiful kind of existence, the mathematicians [. . .] came upon something wrong in the fundamentals of the whole thing that absolutely could not be put right. They actually looked all the way to the bottom and found that the whole building was standing in midair. But the machines worked! We must assume from this that our existence is a pale ghost; we live it, but actually only on the basis of an error without which it would not have arisen. (MM 41–2)

Despite its crisis, maths does not lose its affinity with precision or reason, but, as Justice Kraus points out, in 'The Mathematical Man' it appears as 'the epitome of rationality and simultaneously a structure without a base. It is systematic and anti-systematic at the same time.'[46] Moreover, notwithstanding the sense of crisis and the 'ghostly existence' that originates from foundational questions, Musil's humorous essay arrives at a pragmatic celebration of the still useful mathematical methods. These might have been developed on an erroneous basis but nevertheless enable productive developments: maths 'makes it possible under favourable circumstances to perform in a few moments an operation that one could in principle never complete, like the enumeration of an infinite series', and it gives rise to machines and other aspects of life that 'in principle' could not arise out of thin air (MM 40). The ambiguity of maths does not injure its results, then, and mathematicians' continued belief in their field is praised as an exemplary response to modern uncertainty.

'The Mathematical Man' presents mathematicians as responding to foundational problems with a pragmatist focus on its productive consequences – that is, they face the crisis in their field by holding on to its achievements and continuing to use a challenged but still operational system. The conclusion of the essay establishes this as a model for literature. By shifting attention to the questioned but useful tool of reason, the period's dull literature, which the essay describes as exclusively focused on feeling, could find invigoration: 'in their field they [mathematicians] do what we ought to be doing in ours. Therein lies the significant lesson and model of their existence; they are an analogy for the intellectual of the future' (MM 42). The mathematical model that Musil's essay devises is not primarily one of precision, then, but it is led by pragmatic considerations: its uncertain foundations are epistemologically and ethically acceptable since the system continues to work and sustain life. Here, maths, the ideally precise language of analytic philosophy, features as a model for pragmatically embracing uncertainty.

Mathematics and Trust in Fiction

That 'The Mathematical Man' advocates following mathematicians' continued trust in their field despite questioning its foundations illustrates, quite literally, the *'fundamental* importance of trust to an understanding of modern societies' (my emphasis).[47] John Attridge argues that 'the moment of cultural modernism more generally, [was] characterized by a concern with the question of trust, and especially with how trust, like "human character", might be said to have changed, and even to have entered a period of crisis'.[48] Where Musil's essay depicts confidence in maths as necessary to creating life, Attridge cites Georg Simmel as an early twentieth-century view on the importance of trust in society. Like James, Simmel notes the openness of possibilities that money encapsulates – superficially a number on a piece of paper, money has 'as its content the most objective practices, the most logical, purely mathematical norms, the absolute freedom from everything personal'.[49] The closeness to objectivity, logic and maths does not guarantee its truth and value, however; money works on trust: the trust that it can be spent later at the same value. Early copper coins from Malta that could be exchanged for real silver pieces acknowledge that the value of the coins depends on their acceptance: they bear the inscription *non aes sed fides* – 'not money but trust'. Simmel uses this example to illustrate a more general need for trust in society:

> Without the general trust that people have in each other, society itself would disintegrate, for very few relationships are based entirely upon what is known with certainty about another person, and very few relationships would endure if trust were not as strong as, or stronger than, rational proof or personal observation.[50]

Simmel does not argue here that maths relies on faith, as Musil's essay does, but equating the strengths of confidence and rational proof he contends the insufficiency of any purely intellectual evidence. In both Musil's and Simmel's views, the possibilities that ultimately enable life depend on trust and a crisis of trust threatens existence.

In modern societies that see the questioning of traditional certainties, trust is no longer a given but in need of justification itself – it enters a period of crisis. Pragmatist philosophy provides such justification by arguing that the productive effects of placing trust in systems warrants doing so in the first place. So, the advice in 'The Mathematical Man' to continue making use of maths introduces a view that finds clear expression in one of the key texts of early pragmatist philosophy, William James's *Pragmatism* (1907):

> Truth lives, in fact, for the most part on a credit system. Our thoughts and beliefs 'pass', so long as nothing challenges them, just as bank-notes

> pass so long as nobody refuses them. But this all points to direct face-to-face verifications somewhere, without which the fabric of truth collapses like a financial system with no cash-basis whatever.[51]

James here explains that truth relies on a credit system and only, we could add taking up his imagery from an earlier quotation, has 'cash-value' if it is trusted. Truth depends on confidence as it rests on inaccessible foundations, but trust in it is warranted in James's view, since, theoretically, it could be verified, even if this is not possible in practice. This notion of secure credit ultimately relies on a gold standard – that is, it resembles a monetary system in which the value of a banknote is directly linked to a gold reserve for which it could, theoretically, be exchanged. In contrast to James's trust in at least theoretical verifiability, in Musil's essay there is no far-off point at which face-to-face correspondence still holds, and the modern mathematical man has to hold on to beliefs even though they no longer pass unchallenged. As Rob Hawkes points out, it is precisely the absence of such stable grounds that 'makes trust so crucial. Under the conditions of modernity, we cannot *know*, so we have to rely instead on *trust*'.[52]

Musil, Simmel and James all identify trust as a way to deal with the epistemological crisis at the beginning of the twentieth century. However, Musil does not agree with the implication of James's view that trust could take the place of knowledge, and neither do 'The Mathematical Man' and *The Man without Qualities* point to ultimately secure grounds of truths. In Musil's texts, confidence does not entail abandoning foundational research, but trust is combined with persistent questioning of the grounds and limits of knowledge. It is such critical trust that modern mathematicians exemplify in Musil's essay: they examine their field as well as maintain confidence in reason, acknowledge that they stand in mid-air but continue their work. As Cornelia Blasber emphasises, keeping the problematical foundations in view is a moral quality for Musil:

> Musil considered mathematicians the pathbreakers of a new epistemology because they seemed to pair a sharp intellect with an extraordinary moral quality, namely, the courage of wanting to penetrate the foundations of their own science and the rational worldview even at the risk of undermining their own foundations.[53]

Only in combination with a reflection on the conditions and limits of knowledge-making does trust in reason make mathematics and its practitioners exemplars of the right way to live. The modern crisis of trust thus partly turns into trust in crisis – both in the sense of maintaining confidence in times of crisis but also of trusting in the value of disturbing foundational questioning. By paradoxically joining critical examination and trust in the usefulness of its outcomes, modern maths connects tendencies respectively associated with analytic philosophy and pragmatism.

To some degree, *The Man without Qualities* is a literary implementation of the mathematical model developed in 'The Mathematical Man' and its negotiation of foundational and pragmatist orientations. Where, in the essay, confidence in the usefulness of reason does not entail abandoning foundational research, the novel fragment similarly advocates rational examination, emphasising its role again and again in various responses to the absence of central ideas in Kakania and Ulrich's personal life. Similar to his aim of connecting 'mathematics and mysticism', Ulrich attempts to join knowledge with faith since he understands that 'people's goodness and beauty come from what they believe, not from what they know' (MwQ 897). The relation between rational knowledge and faith, which Ulrich also calls 'knowledgeable intuition', has to be re-established in the early twentieth century (MwQ 898). He learns, however, that as in the case of maths and mysticism, a synthesis is not practicable, and that his theoretical analysis is stifling and a simple man far more likely to succeed.

When opposing knowledge and faith, stifling theory and enabling practice, *The Man without Qualities* portrays trust without simultaneous critical examination in decidedly negative terms. In the Moosbrugger case, while the scientific enquiry of psychiatrists describes Moosbrugger's mental state in detail but reaches no practicable conclusion, juridical precision works with 'the imaginary concept of cumulative law' and, disregarding Moosbrugger's actual mental state, renders possible a verdict based on the fiction of absolute responsibility (MwQ 267). Law here exemplifies the ratioïd domain where all cases fit rules, while for psychologists every case is an exception. The opposed responses also denote the extremes of absolute trust in an imaginary concept, namely law, and, on the other hand, utmost focus on critical examination. Ulrich is convinced that practicality will ultimately decide Moosbrugger's fate and result in his execution, suggesting that people dispense with critical evaluation of the reality of facts in favour of the feasibility granted by trusting fiction even in matters of life and death. Next to leading to ethical quandaries, trust and practicality can also, and maybe surprisingly, perpetuate stagnation, as it does in the case of the Parallel Campaign. On the one hand, the Parallel Campaign develops quickly even without an actual aim, that is, without having determined a fundamental idea that expresses the essence of the epoch. Documents are collected and increase in number, so that Count Leinsdorf considers the Campaign to be progressing well. But while propositions are amassed, their value cannot be judged until the essential aim of the Campaign is settled. Suggestions are therefore marked 'Fi' for being filed for later decision. Leinsdorf praises the technique of filing when it averts an impasse in the Campaign's meetings: a member 'has come up with a really saving idea; we've decided to continue this evening's meeting another time' (MwQ 1130). As 'one of the basic formulas of the structure of life', 'Fi' does not enable action but leaves worrying pragmatic gaps (MwQ 243). Since the Count's comment closes the second book, it also emerges as a formula of the novel fragment itself and thus as a literary manifestation of mathematicians' holding fast to their field despite foundational concerns. Whereas Leinsdorf's naive belief is ridiculed, with its self-ironic meta-comment the novel fragment takes on modern maths's strategy of critical trust: building on faith while simultaneously examining its own conditions.

While *The Man without Qualities* is critical of unlimited trust, its waning emerges as a main problem of the period in crisis. Like Simmel and James, Musil connects the notion of trust with the concept of credit and explores the modern period as a time that does not only struggle with confidence in any concrete belief but suffers a loss of trust itself. A production credit allows real transactions to be performed with fictive capital, despite missing funds, and pre-war Kakania adapts the religious phrase '*Credo ut intelligam*' – 'I believe so that I may understand' – to the time with the translation: 'O Lord, please grant my spirit a production credit!' (MwQ 575). While its citizens acknowledge that belief is necessary for spiritual growth and for any action to be performed successfully, Kakania is unable to believe in itself and has lost confidence in an enabling fiction. It is 'the first country in our present historical phase from which God withdrew His credit': 'So what has been lost? Something imponderable. An omen. An illusion' (MwQ 575, 56). In other words, in a credit crunch of belief in pre-war Kakania, the country does not lack anything concrete but the loss of fictive capital renders it unable to act. A comparison with Bergson's similar application of economic terms to a rationalised country clarifies that the loss of trust entails both material and spiritual dimensions. In a short article that Bergson wrote a month before his propagandist speech discussed above and on a similar topic, he sets out the economic and spiritual loss of credit as a cause of Germany's inevitable downfall: Germany 'has money, but her credit is falling, and one does not see where she is to borrow'.[54] While Bergson begins with the notion of financial and material credit, he extends his concept to the moral sphere. The two connect when Germany's moral force 'is only the confidence which her material force inspires in her', and it is therefore limited to that material force and cannot replenish itself.[55] Opposed to Germany and its self-imposed moral blockade that hinders the emergence of new life, France can rely on the sympathy of other countries and renews its moral force by finding value outside the material. That the country keeps 'her credit intact' will be the source of France's ultimate victory, so the article concludes.[56] In Musil's and Bergson's writings, then, credit and the illusion on which it is based are central to the reality of a nation's disintegration or survival. The loss of credit, that is, the loss of trust in a fictive element, leads to stasis and defeat.

As we have seen in 'The Mathematical Man', Musil uses maths as an area in which critical trust averts stagnation. Echoing the essay, the narrator in

The Man without Qualities presents maths as a field that 'sometimes resorts to the absurd in order to arrive at the truth' and whose non-realistic elements nevertheless have cash-value in the world: scientists come up with hypotheses and mathematical symbols and 'the technicians use all these fictions to build up a world of new things' (MwQ 826, 553). Ultimately based on mathematical fictions, the physical world cannot work without trust in the validity of the imaginary. More broadly, when rationalisation can be grasped in terms of failing spiritual credit, the fictive nature of this loss – a loss of imaginary rather than real funds – suggests that the truth of fiction in general might be at stake. Attridge sets out: 'questions of trust intersect with the main lines of modernist culture, focusing in particular on language, complexity, sincerity and fictional truth'.[57] Regarding fictional truth, the literary critic I. A. Richards reconsiders the value of literary fiction in his 1926 *Principles of Literary Criticism* and manifesto *Poetry and Science*, where he contrasts 'the *scientific* use of language' in empirical writing with fiction's '*emotive* use of language' that is not verifiable.[58] But many modernist writers claim their fictions to be true precisely because they do not try to get close to empirical reality and illustrate flawed individual perspectives and inner worlds. The notion that a fictive or absurd element could allow approaching and impacting on the world animates modernist writers to abandon conventions of literary realism, and a number of authors, including Musil, consciously aim to redefine fiction as a moral force for change. As we have seen, for Musil this redefinition of fiction is intimately bound up with modern mathematics, not least because it answers to two major, and seemingly opposed, instances of modern crisis: the failing of reason and the loss of trust. Paradoxically combining critical questioning of its foundations and confidence in its usefulness, modern maths connects the approaches of analytic philosophy and outcome-focused pragmatism. The next section analyses how in its form *The Man without Qualities* reflects simultaneous examination of its conditions and trust in the credit of fiction, thus translating the model of modern mathematics into literary aesthetic.

Aesthetic Transitions; or Essayism: Running in Circles

The above referred to Ulrich and Agathe's shared childhood experience of planning to write poems and, unable to do so, putting an arithmetic sentence and Ulrich's name on two slips of paper, and it related the episode to formalist and intuitionist tendencies in maths. On a broader level, the idea of composing a literary piece splits into a general mathematical part and an individual component, and the possibility of combining both aspects in literature is implied. Explicitly in its discussion and also through its style, *The Man without Qualities* suggests essayism as a literary form in which such a combination can be achieved. Essayism has received intense scholarly attention, but it is nevertheless worth reiterating key characteristics of the essay upon which Musil's concept draws. An essay is a literary form that does not attempt to provide a full picture of an issue but examines it under specific aspects: 'A composition of moderate length on any particular subject, [...] a composition more or less elaborate in style, though limited in range.'[59] Ulrich's idea of essayism as a strategy of life proposes to examine the right way of living in the manner of a literary essay, considering an issue from several perspectives without encompassing it entirely. Although partly following the literary model, the novel fragment emphasises that the 'translation of "essay" as "attempt"' or 'trial, testing, proof; experiment' invokes scientific methods and the mathematical examination of possibilities (MwQ 273).[60] Drawing on roots of essayism in science and in literature, the essayist is neither a scientist 'who wants the truth' nor a writer 'who wants to give free play to his subjectivity' but a man 'who wants something in between' (MwQ 274). *The Man without Qualities* displays characteristics of essayism when Ulrich examines aspects of life and morality from rational and mystical perspectives and his views are further explored through reflections in other characters. The novel fragment is an amalgamation of perspectives and alternatives to the point that, as Thiher notes, '[a]t times the novel ceases to be a narrative to become something like an encyclopedia that includes a series of essays'.[61] In a metafictional comment, the narrator acknowledges: 'The story of this novel amounts to this, that the story that ought to be told in it is not told' (notes 1760).

In his non-fictional work, Musil describes essayism as a never complete method of reaching 'the strictest form attainable in an area where one can*not* work precisely'.[62] He here exhibits an attitude that, in the quotation at the beginning of this chapter, Broch calls 'rational writing': the aim for precision. At the same time, Musil acknowledges that vagueness is a necessary characteristic both of the problem and the form in which it is discussed. And, as the opening paragraph of *The Man without Qualities* shows, vague everyday language can have a clearer meaning and thus a greater cash-value than precise scientific expression. Indeed, Musil's focus is not primarily on rational writing as Broch claims, but on literature's potential for change that derives from 'a combination of exact and inexact, of precision and passion' (MwQ 272). The relation to reality and impact on it is crucial, as Musil emphasises in his non-fictional work on essayism:

> It takes its form and method from science, its matter from art. [...] [I]t proceeds from facts, like the natural sciences [...]. Except that these facts are not generally observable, and also their connections are in many cases only a singularity. [...] But the essay does present evidence, and investigates.[63]

That the essay 'proceeds from facts' meets Ulrich's concern for reality and a critical evaluation of it; even in the first book, he contemplates 'with revulsion' that purely logical thinking resembles 'piling one ladder upon another, so that the topmost rungs teetered far above the level of natural life' (MwQ 649, 648–9). As Musil formulates elsewhere: 'If I want to have a worldview, then I must view the world. That is, I must establish the facts.'[64] Crucially, then, trust in a system is not to replace facts but it is part of critically determining them. Critical trust, based on a methodology of constant questioning, is never to lose sight of its relevance to reality.

The concept of essayism is part of the level of plot when Ulrich discusses it, of the level of form when *The Man without Qualities* can be characterised as an unfinished succession of essays on the overarching topic of how to live in modern reality, and of the metaliterary level of aesthetic reflection on modernist responses to the challenges of the time. To some degree, essayism emerges as a literary answer to the exemplary behaviour of modern mathematicians that 'The Mathematical Man' humorously advertises, and it also constitutes an ethical approach: 'For me, ethics and aesthetics are associated with the word *essay*', Musil explains.[65] As in literature, essayism in the ethical domain does not advocate any particular action but continuous exploration. Using maths as an example of a method of exploration rather than in terms of content, *The Man without Qualities* employs it in a pragmatist manner. As William James sets out, pragmatism works with theories to increase possibilities and openness rather than to narrow down an answer:

> *Theories thus become instruments, not answers to enigmas, in which we can rest.* We don't lie back upon them, we move forward, and, on occasion, make nature over again by their aid. Pragmatism unstiffens all our theories, limbers them up and sets each one at work.[66]

'Unstiffened' by pragmatic acceptance of uncertainty, maths becomes a model not only of exactitude but also of vagueness, and in this paradoxical double-function it serves to inspire the critical trust needed to adapt epistemology, ethics and aesthetics to a time of rapid change. Maths thus takes on a mediating or bridging function between seeming opposites, not least between the domains of science and literary fiction. As the symbolic extreme of rationality, maths is a shorthand for one of the two cultures, but it also emerges as a way of transitioning between these and thus connecting them. Thus, the seemingly straightforward advice to literary writers to see in mathematicians' continued trust in reason a 'significant lesson and model of their existence' yields to a much more ambiguous mathematical model in *The Man without Qualities*: taking on diverse positions at the opposed poles as well as at transitions on the circumference, maths appears not as a precise but as a vague model and showcases the simultaneous need for pragmatist trust and analytic foundational examination (MM 42). Modern maths is precise and vague: bent on foundational analysis and on pragmatist ways to keep it working, it is both absurd and eminently useful in reality. It is precisely this encompassing of ambiguities that suggests maths as 'the new method of thought itself' and as a model to literary writers (MwQ 35).

The focus on method and movement rather than on giving final 'answers to enigmas' coheres with the incompleteness of the novel fragment and Ulrich's belief in the value of continued preoccupation with the 'whole circle of questions [...]: "How should I live?"' (MwQ 972). As the narrator sets out, the open-endedness of the examination is preferable, since 'a thing wholly encompassed suddenly loses its scope and melts down to a concept' (MwQ 270). The German word for 'scope' – *Umfang* – also signifies a circle's circumference and thus relates the strategy of complete explanation to diminishing the circle to a centre (MoE 250). In contrast, essayism, giving only partial answers, maintains the scope of the object of investigation. Concerning the relation between part and whole, this means that parts do not form into a closed whole, yet all perspectives, even those from diametrically opposed poles, are connected in the whole circle of life and its ever-open questions. When regarding Musil's request to read the text 'twice, in parts and as a whole' in view of the fact that the novel has remained a fragment, it similarly becomes clear that the whole is not to be understood as determinate but as the total of ever-changing reality (notes 1766).

The presentation of a specifically modern mathematics in *The Man without Qualities* works to support both rationality and fiction in the early twentieth century, and it suggests that, if maths relies on reason as well as on trust in fictional concepts, then an analogous state in literature might promise similarly consequential outcomes. As an aesthetic as well as epistemological and ethical model, modern maths is deeply implicated in Musil's modernism, and encompassing modernism's opposed tendencies of precision and vagueness, of foundational research and pragmatist trust, of Prusso-German mathematical rationality and mysticism, we can usefully talk of modernist maths in Musil's work. Following the chapters on Broch's *The Sleepwalkers* and Musil's *The Man without Qualities* as texts produced at the height of modernism and in close relation with a specifically (Prusso-)German mindset, in Chapter 4 we turn to a view from a greater cultural and temporal distance that sets the modernist developments into a broader context, from the beginnings of modernity in the scientific revolution to the postmodern period.

Notes

1. 'Musil?!! Ich habe seine Art in einem Vortrag "rationales Dichten" genannt, Dichten aus der Ratio. Es ist der Gegensatz zu meinen eigenen Möglichkeiten' (Hermann Broch, *Briefe: Dokumente und Kommentare zu Leben und Werk*, ed. Paul Michael Lützeler (Frankfurt am Main: Suhrkamp, 1981), p. 345).
2. Musil qtd in Karl Sigmund, *Sie nannten sich der Wiener Kreis: Exaktes Denken am Rand des Untergangs* (Wiesbaden: Springer, 2015), p. 177.

3. 'Unter dem Vorwand, das letzte Lebensjahr Österreichs zu beschreiben, werden die Sinnfragen der Existenz des modernen Menschen darin aufgeworfen und in einer ganz neuartigen, aber sowohl leicht-ironischen wie philosophisch tiefen Weise beantwortet' (Robert Musil, *Gesammelte Werke II. Prosa und Stücke. Kleine Prosa, Aphorismen, Autobiographisches, Essays und Reden, Kritik*, ed. Adolf Frisé (Reinbek bei Hamburg: Rowohlt, 1978), pp. 950–1).
4. In the following, quotations from the parts not published in Musil's lifetime are marked 'galley', 'drafts' or 'notes'. Citations from the fair copy, which is not included in the translation by Wilkins and Pike, are my translations and the original is given in a footnote.
5. Robert Musil, *Diaries 1899–1941*, ed. Mark Mirsky, trans. Philip Payne (New York: Basic Books, 1998), p. 216.
6. 'Ja, ich habe sogar einige Male über gewisse Zusammenhänge zwischen moralischem und mathematischen Denken geschrieben; zwar nicht in herkömmlicher Weise, aber es freut mich doch, darauf hinweisen zu können, dass es auch eine solche gibt' (Musil qtd in Sigmund, *Sie nannten sich der Wiener Kreis*, p. 181).
7. Dale Adams, *Die Konfrontation von Denken und Wirklichkeit: Die Rolle und Bedeutung der Mathematik bei Robert Musil, Hermann Broch und Friedrich Dürrenmatt* (St. Ingbert: Röhrig Universitätsverlag, 2011), p. 45.
8. Robert Musil, *Precision and Soul: Essays and Addresses*, ed. and trans. Burton Pike and David S. Luft (Chicago and London: University of Chicago Press, 1990), p. 13.
9. Thomas Sebastian, *The Intersection of Science and Literature in Musil's* The Man without Qualities (Rochester, NY: Camden House, 2005), p. 64.
10. Sebastian, *The Intersection of Science and Literature*, p. 64.
11. 'Fundamentallehre' (MoE 865).
12. Claus Hoheisel, *Physik und verwandte Wissenschaften in Robert Musils Roman Der Mann ohne Eigenschaften. (dmoe) Ein Kommentar*, Diss. (Berlin et al.: European University Press, 2004), p. 385.
13. Gwyneth Cliver, 'Maddening Mathematics: The Kinship of the Rational and the Irrational in the Writing of Robert Musil', *Journal of Romance Studies*, 7.3 (2007), 75–85 (p. 84).
14. Robert Musil, 'Sketch of What the Writers Knows', in *Precision and Soul: Essays and Addresses*, ed. and trans. Burton Pike and David S. Luft (Chicago and London: University of Chicago Press, 1990), 61–7 (p. 62).
15. Robert Musil, Eithne Wilkins and Ernst Kaiser, 'A Conversation with Robert Musil', *The Transatlantic Review*, 8 (1961), 9–24 (p. 19).
16. Margaret MacMillan, *The War That Ended Peace: The Road to 1914* (New York: Random House, 2013), p. 258.
17. Henri Bergson, *The Meaning of the War: Life & Matter in Conflict* (London: Fisher Unwin, 1915), p. 20.
18. Bergson, *The Meaning of the War*, pp. 34–5.
19. Bergson, *The Meaning of the War*, p. 33.
20. Allen Thiher, *Understanding Robert Musil* (Columbia: University of South Carolina Press, 2009), p. 232.
21. Musil, *Precision and Soul*, p. 67.
22. 'der Verstand läßt uns einfach im Stich!' (MoE 570).
23. Luitzen Egbertus Jan Brouwer, 'On the Foundations of Mathematics' [1907], in *L. E. J. Brouwer: Collected Works*, vol. 1, ed. Arend Heyting (Amsterdam and Oxford: North-Holland, 1975), 15–101 (p. 72).
24. Jeremy J. Gray, *Plato's Ghost: The Modernist Transformation of Mathematics* (Princeton and Oxford: Princeton University Press, 2008), p. 407.
25. Herbert Breger, 'A Restoration That Failed: Paul Finsler's Theory of Sets', in

Revolutions in Mathematics, ed. Donald Gillies (Oxford: Oxford University Press, 1992), 249–64 (p. 253).
26. Brouwer, 'On the Foundations', p. 97.
27. Brouwer qtd in Dirk van Dalen, *Mystic, Geometer, and Intuitionist: The Life of L. E. J. Brouwer; vol. 1: The Dawning Revolution* (Oxford: Clarendon, 1999), pp. 83 and 84.
28. Brouwer qtd in Dalen, *Mystic, Geometer, and Intuitionist I*, p. 82.
29. Cliver, 'Maddening Mathematics', pp. 75–6.
30. Cliver, 'Maddening Mathematics', p. 75.
31. 'Durchschnittsmenschen'; 'das Durchschnittliche ist immer auch etwas Wahrscheinliches'; 'nach und nach der "wahrscheinliche Mensch" und das "wahrscheinliche Leben" anstelle des "wahren" Menschen und Lebens emporzukommen begännen' (MoE fair copy 1209).
32. William James, *The Principles of Psychology* (New York: Holt, 1910), p. 254.
33. Bertrand Russell, 'The Philosophy of Logical Atomism', in *Logic and Knowledge: Essays, 1901–1950*, ed. Robert Charles Marsh (London and New York: Routledge, 2004), 175–281 (p. 179).
34. Bertrand Russell, 'Vagueness', in *Russell on Metaphysics: Selections from the Writings of Bertrand Russell*, ed. Stephen Mumford (London and New York: Routledge, 2003), 211–20 (p. 213).
35. T. S. Eliot, 'A Commentary', *The Monthly Criterion*, 6.4 (1927), 289–91 (p. 291).
36. Megan Quigley, *Modernist Fiction and Vagueness: Philosophy, Form, and Language* (New York: Cambridge University Press, 2015), p. 6; Megan Quigley, 'Modern Novels and Vagueness', *Modernism/Modernity*, 15.1 (2008), 101–29 (p. 104).
37. William James, *Pragmatism: A New Name for Some Old Ways of Thinking; Together with Four Related Essays Selected from* The Meaning of Truth (New York, London and Toronto: Longmans, Green, 1949), pp. 54–5.
38. James, *The Principles of Psychology*, p. 254.
39. James, *Pragmatism*, p. 53.
40. 'jede Möglichkeit' (MoE 791).
41. Herbert Mehrtens, *Moderne Sprache Mathematik: Eine Geschichte des Streits um die Grundlagen der Disziplin und des Subjekts formaler Systeme* (Frankfurt am Main: Suhrkamp, 1990), pp. 403 and 57.
42. Ernst Mach, *Principles of the Theory of Heat*, ed. Brian McGuinness, trans. P. E. B. Jourdain and A. E. Heath (Dordrecht et al.: Reidel, 1986), p. 73.
43. Thiher, *Understanding Robert Musil*, p. 46.
44. Henri Poincaré, *Science and Hypothesis*, trans. W. J. G. (London and Newcastle on Tyne: Walter Scott, 1905), p. 3.
45. Robert Musil, 'The Mathematical Man' [1913], in *Precision and Soul: Essays and Addresses*, ed. and trans. Burton Pike and David S. Luft (Chicago and London: University of Chicago Press, 1990), 39–43. From here on abbreviated in the text as 'MM'.
46. Justice Kraus, 'Musil's *Die Verwirrungen des Zöglings Törleß*, Cantor's Structures of Infinity, and Brouwer's Mathematical Language', *Scientia Poetica. Yearbook for the History of Literature, Humanities and Sciences*, 14, ed. Andrea Albrecht et al. (Berlin and New York: De Gruyter, 2010), 72–103 (p. 89).
47. John Attridge, 'Introduction: Modernism, Trust and Deception', in *Incredible Modernism: Literature, Trust and Deception*, ed. John Attridge and Rod Rosenquist (Farnham: Ashgate, 2013), 1–20 (p. 1).
48. Attridge, 'Modernism, Trust and Deception', p. 2.

49. Georg Simmel, *The Philosophy of Money*, trans. Tom Bottomore and David Frisby (London and New York: Routledge, 1978), p. 128.
50. Simmel, *The Philosophy of Money*, p. 179.
51. James, *Pragmatism*, pp. 207–8.
52. Rob Hawkes, 'Bogus Modernism: Impersonation, Deception and Trust in Ford Madox Ford and Evelyn Waugh', in *Reconnecting Aestheticism and Modernism: Continuities, Revisions, Speculations*, ed. Bénédicte Coste, Catherine Delyfer and Christine Reynier (New York and London: Routledge, 2017), 175–86 (p. 177).
53. Cornelia Blasber, 'A City "Under Glass": Vienna in Robert Musil's *The Man without Qualities*', in *Vienna: The World of Yesterday, 1889–1914*, ed. Stephen Eric Bronner and F. Peter Wagner (New York: Humanity Books, 1999), 150–67 (p. 153).
54. Bergson, *The Meaning of the War*, p. 43.
55. Bergson, *The Meaning of the War*, p. 46.
56. Bergson, *The Meaning of the War*, p. 44.
57. Attridge, 'Modernism, Trust and Deception', p. 4.
58. I. A. Richards, *The Principles of Literary Criticism* (London and New York: Routledge, 2003), p. 250. I. A. Richards, *Science and Poetry* (New York: Norton, 1926).
59. 'essay, *n.*', *The Oxford English Dictionary*. OED Online (Oxford: Oxford University Press, March 2017), Web, 5 Apr. 2017.
60. 'essay, *n.*', *The Oxford English Dictionary*.
61. Thiher, *Understanding Robert Musil*, p. 265.
62. Musil, *Precision and Soul*, p. 48.
63. Musil, *Precision and Soul*, p. 49.
64. Musil, *Precision and Soul*, p. 155.
65. Musil, *Precision and Soul*, p. 48.
66. James, *Pragmatism*, p. 53.

4

MATHEMATICS AND FICTION: THOMAS PYNCHON, *GRAVITY'S RAINBOW*

'Yes, sort of *German*, these episodes here' (GR 285, emphasis in the original), the narrator states at one point in *Gravity's Rainbow*. Set predominantly in Great Britain and Germany in the year between September 1944 and 1945, Thomas Pynchon's 1973 novel acknowledges its German focus even before Tyrone Slothrop, the closest we get to a main character, enters the country after the war. Its culture is pervasive in the text, as Thomas Moore observes,

> It is a quite remarkable fact about a novel so wholly American in its general personality that nearly all of its most important sources, father figures, oracular voices, and invited guests are German-speaking: from the mythological Nibelungen, Gottfried von Strassburg's Tristan and other ancients resurrected by Wagner, to Leibniz, Goethe, and Wagner himself, through Rilke, Freud, Jung, Max Weber, and the great twentieth-century physicists (Planck, Einstein, Heisenberg), to Rathenau, Stinnes, and the men of I. G. Farben, to the Weimar moviemakers, all the way through National Socialism and to Rocketman Wernher von Braun.[1]

The narrator's comment on the German flavour of the novel follows one of three equations in mathematical notion that are printed in *Gravity's Rainbow*. Next to a well-known probability distribution and a formula that amounts to a mathematical joke, the second equation presents maths in all its fascinating and intimidating complexity:

$$\Theta \; \frac{d^2 \varphi}{d t^2} + \delta^* \frac{d \varphi}{d t} + \frac{\partial L}{\partial \alpha}(s_1 - s_2)\,\alpha = -\frac{\partial R}{\partial \beta} s_3 \beta \qquad \text{(GR 284)}$$

Slothrop encounters the equation as part of his education on the mathematics and technology of the V-2 rocket, a German weapon developed by Wernher von Braun during the Second World War and used in attacks on London, among other targets. Slothrop, who has a special connection to the rocket, is fed information on the V-2 and then sent to post-war Germany to locate the mysterious Rocket 00000. Getting to know the mathematical language of rocket flight and learning German are linked for Slothrop: 'Well, these days Slothrop is even dreaming in the [German] language. Folks have been teaching him dialects [. . .]. Along with the language teachers come experts in ordnance, electronics, and aerodynamics' (GR 285). Associating German with the language of technology and the remarkable instance of mathematical notation in the text, *Gravity's Rainbow* calls up an image of German technocracy that takes particularly inhuman forms during the Second World War. Pynchon's novel thus picks up where the German-speaking texts by Hermann Broch and Robert Musil leave off: at the dangers of a German mindset tied to mathematics and the question of whether aspects of modern maths lend themselves to resisting rationalisation and promoting ethical action.

Although *Gravity's Rainbow* establishes a relation between mathematical and Nazi thinking in Germany, it also presents the Second World War as only the culmination of concepts and thought structures having emerged three centuries earlier, during the Age of Enlightenment. Pynchon's novel, for example, traces the prerequisites for building the V-2 rocket back to the seventeenth century when mathematicians developed the scientific concepts needed to describe and control its flight path. Following a well-established narrative, *Gravity's Rainbow* relates the beginning of the Enlightenment to the publication of Isaac Newton's *Principia Mathematica*. Published in 1687, it spread, according to Alexis Clairaut's assessment in 1745, 'the light of mathematics on a science which up to then had remained in the darkness of conjectures and hypotheses'.[2] Alexander Pope's famous epitaph consolidates the link between Newton and the Enlightenment: 'Nature and Nature's laws lay hid in night: / God said, Let Newton be! and all was light.'[3] While Enlightenment thinkers celebrated mathematics as illuminating the laws of nature, it acquired a more ambiguous image in the course of modernity. The development culminates in Theodor Adorno and Max Horkheimer's criticism of excessive focus on Newton's legacy: 'the fully enlightened earth radiates disaster triumphant', they write in *Dialectic of Enlightenment* (1944).[4] *Gravity's Rainbow* immediately acknowledges modern anxieties about excessive rationality when its first sentence – 'A screaming comes across the sky' – announces the destructive consequences of scientification and, in particular, German technological developments such as the rocket (GR 3). When this chapter takes account of *Gravity's Rainbow*'s use of science from the seventeenth to the twentieth centuries, it sets the literary illustrations of interrelations between mathematics and modernist culture in the broader context of modernity, from its foundations in the Enlightenment to its postmodern legacies.

The negotiation of mathematics is crucial to *Gravity's Rainbow*'s move beyond modernism and its pioneering features that have come to exemplify postmodernist literature. Martin Paul Eve calls Pynchon the 'godfather of American postmodernity', and, according to Ali Chetwynd, the 2012 *Cambridge Companion to Thomas Pynchon* 'constitutes an extended claim that Pynchon's career can stand for the precedence of postmodernism'.[5] In that *Companion*, Brian McHale contends: 'we might go so far as to say, not that postmodern theory depends on Pynchon's fiction for exemplification, but that, without Pynchon's fiction, there might never have been such a pressing need to develop a theory of literary postmodernism in the first place'.[6] *Gravity's Rainbow* is as much a key text in the emergence of literature and science studies as it is of literary postmodernism. Analyses of science in Pynchon's work 'promoted the interdisciplinary study of literature and science, and thus played a role in the founding of the Society for Literature and Science in 1985', so Lance Schachterle remembers.[7] *Gravity's Rainbow* in particular, so Alan Friedman claims, has invigorated the field: '*Gravity's Rainbow* demonstrates more clearly than any other work of modern fiction how science can be incorporated as a tool for metaphor and style.'[8] The two aspects that Pynchon's 1973 novel has come to epitomise – postmodernism and literary engagement with science – cannot be viewed in isolation. Rather, this chapter shows how its employment of modern maths illuminates the need to investigate the status of reality and explore new literary ways to engage with it. Putting relations between maths and fiction at its centre – a topic that has run through the previous chapters – the discussion of *Gravity's Rainbow* shows that a renegotiation of mathematics is a decisive factor in the novel's introduction of postmodernist features.

Physico-Theology and Mathematico-Ethical Concepts in *Gravity's Rainbow*

Like Musil in *The Man without Qualities*, Pynchon connects ethical and mathematical thinking in *Gravity's Rainbow*. The title relates the scientific concept of gravity to the biblical image of the rainbow, which signifies God's promise not to destroy the world in another Flood. The novel thus places itself in the tradition of physico-theological discourse. Eighteenth-century physico-theology links the study of nature to that of religion, for example using scientific knowledge to argue for the existence and wisdom of God. Newton's work, and particularly the *Principia Mathematica* in which he formulated the law of universal gravitation, quickly achieved a leading position in this context: 'soon after its publication his work became closely associated with the cause of Christian apologists'.[9] Theological implications of Newton's work on gravity also inform the criticism by the German mathematician and philosopher Gottfried Wilhelm Leibniz. In *Gravity's Rainbow*, the clash between Newton's and Leibniz's views, which animated English–German conflict in the early eighteenth century, signals the beginning of a scientific and moral competition that finds its heights in the Second World War. Pynchon's novel does not only trace its roots in physico-theological debates, however, but brings these up to date with twentieth-century knowledge and develops new, postmodern mathematico-ethical positions.

Newton's and Leibniz's thinking signal the increasing importance of mathematics across all branches of seventeenth-century natural philosophy. As Paolo Mancosu points out: 'the mathematical method [...] represented for many authors a guarantee of clarity and order in the development of a discipline'.[10] Newton's *Principia Mathematica* acknowledges the importance in its title and pioneers a mathematical engagement with gravity that had effects far beyond immediately scientific applications. The universal character of gravitation that Newton posits means that it applies to the heavens as well as to earth, leading to the far-reaching conclusion that the order presumed to rule the heavens should similarly govern the below and that all natural phenomena should be calculable. As further laws and regularities were formulated, the universe increasingly appeared to be mechanistic and science a means to reveal its predetermined development. By the beginning of the nineteenth century Pierre-Simon Laplace maintained the drastic view that the 'discoveries in mechanics and geometry, added to that of universal gravity, have enabled it to comprehend in the same analytical expressions the past and future states of the system of the world'.[11] Laplace's mention of gravity confirms the decisive role of Newton's discovery in the advent of deterministic views and the belief in a world ruled by causality and predictable by science.

Given the significance that *Gravity's Rainbow* accords to Enlightenment science and mathematics, I disagree with John Stark's opinion that 'Pynchon refers most often to scientific information that was discovered or became important during World War II.'[12] Indeed, Pynchon goes back to Enlightenment science to retrieve alternative views that were suppressed by later developments, and recovers their potential. Considering this, Friedman's identification of three coexisting scientific images is more helpful: 'the eighteenth-century clockwork universe, the nineteenth-century statistical rules [...], and the essential uncertainties of twentieth-century quantum theory'.[13] These concepts line up on a scale between two extreme positions in *Gravity's Rainbow*: connectedness, control and paranoia are linked to the determinateness of mechanical explanations in science, while, on the other side, randomness, freedom and anti-paranoia do not allow making meaningful connections between phenomena. The novel uses the concepts of gravity, the infinitesimal calculus and probability theory to highlight positions between the extremes of these worldviews and explore possibilities to undermine perspectives that have become dominant.

Gravity's Rainbow uses the concept of gravity and its relation to mechanism and determinism as a metaphor for the inescapable force that a privileged group, the Elect, exercises over the disadvantaged majority of the Preterite. Gravity is a main metaphorical force when underpinning causality and accordingly belief in the Elect's ability to control the Preterite, but characters also try to overcome it physically. 'Does no one recognize what enslavement gravity is[?]', Achtfaden wonders and hopes to defeat it with the help of a rocket (GR 540). Like von Braun, the German engineer mainly responsible for developing the V-2, various characters in the novel dream that the rocket might 'free man from his remaining chains, the chains of gravity which still tie him to this planet. It will open to him the gates of heaven'.[14] Although von Braun was brought to the United States after the Second World War to engineer the first vehicle to the moon, rockets in *Gravity's Rainbow* do not leave the planet behind or lead to heaven but bring death and destruction. The metaphorical flight from gravity, that is, escaping the control of the Elect to lead a free, self-determined life, is similarly futile. Slothrop realises the extent of Their control when learning that, as a toddler, he was conditioned to respond to the rocket with an erection. Conditioning deliberately creates a causal relationship between phenomena and thus constitutes a tool to increase control. In the novel, Edward Pointsman, among the strongest advocates of causality, follows in the footsteps of Ivan Pavlov and forcefully turns mere correspondences into cause-and-effect relations. In Pavlov's famous experiment of classical conditioning, a dog is presented with food while a bell rings. The sight of the food causes the dog to salivate, while the bell has no effect on the animal. The salivation and the bell have no causal connection then but only occur simultaneously. With a certain amount of repetition however, the dog starts to salivate when hearing the bell, even when there is no food. Thus, the correspondence of the ringing and the dog's salivation has become a causal relation: the ringing of the bell *causes* the dog to salivate. As Friedman points out, *Gravity's Rainbow* presents conditioning as an extension of Newtonian mechanism: 'the behavior of the dogs can be described entirely in terms of forces (now physiological and psychological) and universal laws (such as conditioned reflex)', just as in the wake of the *Principia Mathematica* the universe came to be seen as completely comprehensible in terms of physical forces and laws.[15]

True to his Pavlovian training, Pointsman pursues the theory that Slothrop was conditioned to respond to rockets with an erection and that, therefore, Slothrop's sexual encounters cause the rockets to fall where they do. The consequences of Pointsman's explanation are far-reaching: if there is a causal stimulus, 'then the rockets follow from it, 100% of the time. No exceptions. When we find it, we'll have shown again the stone determinacy of everything, of every soul' (GR 101). In such a mechanical explanation, effects can be controlled by manipulating the stimuli that cause them, and Pointsman accordingly concludes the necessity of controlling the stimulus Slothrop: 'he is [. . .] a monster. *We must never lose control*' (GR 171). In contrast to the Elect whose conditioning forcefully turns correspondences into causal relations and thus enables control, the narrator admits: 'The rest of us, not chosen for enlightenment [. . .], at the mercy of a Gravity we have only begun to learn how to detect and measure, must go on blundering inside our front-brain faith in Kute Korrespondences' (GR 699). Correspondences can be accidental and do not provide a meaningful causal explanation between the phenomena they relate, so the Preterite are not in a position to execute control and institute change.

The contrast between the Elect's unchecked control and the Preterite's ineffective reliance on Kute Korrespondences underlies the novel's central ethical notion, namely the necessary coexistence of opposites. With a nod to the role of Newton's work for physico-theology, *Gravity's Rainbow* introduces the ethical idea in reference to his third law of motion. Newton's law states that an action always occurs together with a simultaneous reaction of opposite direction; it thus constitutes a scientific formulation of William Slothrop's theological insight that '[e]verything in the Creation has its equal and opposite counterpart' (GR 658). Tyrone Slothrop's forefather criticises the Puritan doctrine that a small group receives God's grace and rules over the others, and he argues holiness for those not chosen for divine salvation, seeing them as a necessary counterpart to the Elect, who rely on the passed-over mass to distinguish themselves. The narrator presents William's insight as connected to Newton's scientific discovery that forces always arise in pairs: 'It was a little early for Isaac Newton, but feelings about action and reaction were in the air' (GR 657). While Newton's discovery became widely influential, William's corresponding realisation is suppressed: the theological potential of the discovery in physics is not realised. The interrelation of science and ethical positions remains central to understanding the Slothrop family, however, and, as we shall see in the next section, with a secular and mathematical focus it offers explanations for Tyrone Slothrop's eventual disappearance from the text and for further postmodernist features of the novel.

Mathematics and Fiction: Gravity

In accordance with William Slothrop's call to taking account of opposites, *Gravity's Rainbow* recovers physico-theological positions apart from the dominant Newtonian interpretations. Pynchon particularly draws on Leibniz's objections to Newton's work on the force of gravity and uses discoveries in twentieth-century physics to transform notions of eighteenth-century physico-theology into a modern mathematico-ethical position. With the recovery of lesser-known alternative views and taking into account modern science, *Gravity's Rainbow* puts into question the notion of gravity as a force and suggests that the metaphorically connected force of the Elect might similarly be less certain than it appears. Thus, Pynchon uses competing scientific and mathematical views to develop a modern mathematico-ethical position that offers tentative possibilities for resistance.

Leibniz opposed Newton's conception of a universal gravitational force, largely because of its philosophical and theological implications, and formulated his objections in a lengthy letter exchange with Samuel Clarke, a defender of the Newtonian view. Leibniz criticised the very idea of a *force* of gravity, since to attract matter gravity would have to have a determined origin and Newton was precisely unable to clarify its source. Newton claimed: 'to us it is enough that gravity does really exist, and act according to the laws which we have explained, and abundantly serves to account for all the motions of the celestial bodies, and of our sea'.[16] But, as he admitted in a letter to Richard Bentley, 'the cause of gravity is what I do not pretend to know'.[17] Leibniz was not satisfied with Newton's taking observable phenomena – apples falling down from trees, for example, and not upwards – as evidence that 'gravity does really exist', and he criticised that, as explanation is lacking, adherents to this idea have to believe that gravitational attractions are 'effected by *miracle*; or else have recourse to absurdities, that is, to the *occult qualities* of the schools; which some men begin to revive under the specious name of *forces*; but they bring us back again into the kingdom of darkness'.[18] Since the cause of gravity remained obscure and belief in it unwarranted in Leibniz's view, he dismissed Newton's premise: 'it is a strange fiction to regard all matter as having gravity', Leibniz held and proposed an alternative explanation of gravitation that carries different theological implications.[19]

For Leibniz, gravity appears to have an attractive effect only while the relation between apparent cause and apparent effect could be different. In other words, Leibniz argues that there is no force of gravity but that God harmonises events into a *'constant and regulated relation'*.[20] The philosopher of science Ian Hacking summarises this idea: 'actively rejecting any law of gravity, Leibniz had the idea of "constant conjunction". Minds and bodies "express" each other, and one body, in being, as we say, "affected" by another, is better described as "expressing" the other.'[21] In Leibniz's words: 'One thing expresses another, in my manner of speaking, when there is a *constant and regulated relation* between what is true of the one and what is true of the other' (my translation).[22] Such a relation does not necessarily describe a cause-and-effect connection, then, but the correlation only 'give[s] the appearance of causal interaction' while really being harmonised by God.[23] This understanding also gives rise to different ethical implications: while in Newton's view of a force of gravity causal relations strengthen a mechanistic worldview and threaten human freedom and self-determination, Leibniz's concept of a constant and regulated relation does not imply causality and therefore leaves room for free will. With his own notion of gravitation, Leibniz could accordingly argue that human beings are free and morally responsible for their actions.

In the terminology of *Gravity's Rainbow*, Leibniz's 'constant and regulated relation' is a 'Kute Korrespondence'. The term is introduced precisely as a contrast to what Leibniz calls the occult force of Newtonian gravity: unlike the Elect Lyle Bland who learns to control 'eerie' gravity when leaving his body and 'flying', the disadvantaged majority of people are 'at the mercy of a Gravity' they do not really understand and 'must go on blundering inside our front-brain faith in Kute Korrespondences' (GR 698, 699). The opposition of eerie Newtonian force and Leibnizian correspondence mirrors the contrast between control and powerlessness, but the competition between different understandings of gravitation also challenges the belief in causality on which the control of the Elect is based. If universal 'gravity does really exist', then it legitimately gives rise to the belief in causality and mechanism that the Elect exploit.[24] If, however, as Leibniz proposed, 'it is a strange fiction to regard all matter as having gravity', the power of the Elect is based on a correspondence that has become constant but that might potentially change and thus allow for liberation from Their system.[25]

The character Gottfried eludes the grip of gravity when, as the first passenger in a rocket, he experiences that 'Gravity dips away briefly' (GR 901). This reminds us of his namesake Gottfried Wilhelm Leibniz's rejection of gravity as a causal force, and, further mirroring Leibniz's theory, the flight in *Gravity's Rainbow* reaffirms the constant relation: 'This ascent will be betrayed to Gravity' (GR 900). Gottfried might enjoy a moment of free flight, but it is clear that the rocket will not elude the 'enslavement' of Gravity, the capitalised, personified force that stands for the Elect (GR 540). Regardless of whether it is understood as a Newtonian causal force or as a Leibnizian Kute Korrespondence, then, gravity has very real consequences that Pynchon's novel does not deny. What Gottfried's ascent does achieve, however, is to uphold the possibility of free flight: he 'rises on a promise, a prophecy, of Escape . . .' and keeps alive its theoretical possibility (GR 900). Correspondingly, the realisation that the Elect's control might be based not on a causal force but only exploit a correspondence upholds the possibility of freedom and self-determination. Viewing gravity and its theological and ethical implications in historical context thus helps specify that, even though it might be physically undefeatable – Lyle Bland has to leave his body behind to float and Gottfried's technologically induced flight is temporary only – gravity is not a force unproblematically in control, and by metaphorical extension neither are the

Elect. Indeed, in accordance with twentieth-century scientific developments, *Gravity's Rainbow* proposes that gravity is not a force at all but rather, to use Leibniz's words, 'a strange fiction'.[26]

The narrator in *Gravity's Rainbow* points to the fact that the cause of gravity remained obscure until the twentieth century, claiming that we are 'at the mercy of a Gravity we have only begun to learn how to detect and measure' (GR 699). In the nineteenth century the correspondence between scientists James Clerk Maxwell and Michael Faraday reiterates the points made by Newton and Leibniz over two hundred years earlier: discussing 'the great mystery [. . .] how like bodies attract (by gravi[ta]tion)', Maxwell argues for 'get[ting] over that difficulty [. . .] by simply admitting it [i.e. gravity]', while Faraday takes a position closer to Leibniz's when warning against using the term 'force' and criticising people 'who receive that description of gravity as a physical truth'.[27] The exchange illustrates that, as David Darling summarises, for scientists before the twentieth century '*gravity* was no more than an empty name for a phenomenon they didn't really understand'.[28] Albert Einstein's work finally significantly advanced the knowledge about gravity. With his theory of relativity, he could explain Newton's inability to give the cause of gravitation and partly affirmed Leibniz's understanding of gravity as a 'strange fiction'. Pointing to the changed notions of time and space to which Einstein's theory gave rise, Lyle Bland rises 'out of his body, about a foot, face-up' and feels that his gravity-defying journeys are travels in time as well as space: 'The Bland who came back to rejoin the inert white container he'd seen belly-up on the sofa, thousands of years beneath him, had changed forever' (GR 697). Travels in time – 'thousands of years' – and space – 'beneath him' – take up Einstein's idea of four-dimensional space-time and gesture towards the related, and profoundly changed, understanding of gravitation that the theory of relativity introduces. While numerous critics have noted the importance of relativity theory for Pynchon's writing, there is an overwhelming focus on new notions of space and time, and its impact on the understanding of gravity, the scientific concept in the title of the novel, has remained surprisingly under-examined. A closer look at the implications of Einstein's work reveals how *Gravity's Rainbow* brings gravity-based physico-theological interpretations up to date with modern developments and shows that mathematics plays an important role in this process.

Crucially for physics and for *Gravity's Rainbow*'s Elect who base their power on it, Einstein dispensed with the understanding of gravity as a *force*. According to the theory of relativity, there is no physical force that attracts objects, but Einstein explains the effects as due to distortions in four-dimensional space-time. As Arthur Eddington, the foremost populariser of the theory of relativity in the 1920s, explained: 'Einstein's law of gravitation controls a geometrical quantity *curvature* in contrast to Newton's law which controls a mechanical quantity *force*.'[29] In the well-known story of Newton sitting under a tree and formulating his law of universal gravitation after seeing a falling apple, he concludes that the apple falls to the ground because the force of gravity attracts it. Since the cause of attraction remained obscure, Eddington explains, 'Newton had to invent a mysterious force dragging the apple down.'[30] In contrast, according to the theory of relativity, the apple falls down not because of a force that attracts it, but it moves because of a curvature in space-time. The mass of the earth creates a 'dent' in space-time, and the apple has no choice but to follow the curve and come to rest in that dent. Einstein thus replaces the understanding of gravity as a force with a geometrical explanation. Gravity, treated as a physical phenomenon by Newton, turns into a mathematical issue.

Gravity's Rainbow refers to another modern scientific concept when introducing physico-theological thinking in relation to Newton's law on the correspondence of action and reaction: the equivalence principle in the theory of relativity. The equivalence principle states that in accelerating surroundings the effects of inertia equal those of gravity. And with the character Tyrone Slothrop – who carries 'sloth' or inertia in his very name – the novel illustrates that inactivity can be as harmful as oppression by the Elect. The Slothrop family has a history of failing to act: although at first 'assimilated in life to the dynamic that surrounded them', they 'did not prosper ... about all they did was persist' while the world around them moves on, and instead of following the progress west, 'out of some reasoned *inertia* the *Sloth*rops stayed east' (GR 33, my emphasis). But Tyrone Slothrop falls prey not only to physical but also to moral inertia. As one of the seven capital sins, sloth has religious meanings, and most importantly for Pynchon is the Puritan interpretation of sloth as the absence of conviction and inactivity in the face of suffering. He refers to this Puritan view in a newspaper article from 1993: 'Sloth – defiant sorrow in the face of God's good intentions – was a deadly sin.'[31] Tyrone Slothrop becomes slothful according to this religious meaning of the word: he ceases to care about others and grows less and less able to act as the novel progresses. When he is being handed a bomb with a lit fuse, for example, he does nothing except think: 'Gee, sometimes I wish I wasn't so indecisive' (GR 817). Saved from his predicament, Slothrop does not help his rescuer who is abused and tortured in his stead, but he 'slips away, [. . .] dragging reluctantly, off of his grease-chevroned head, the shining wig of innocence . . .' (GR 818). Allowing others to suffer by failing to act, Slothrop becomes guilty, and his example constitutes a translation of Einstein's equivalence principle to ethics: in physics the effects of inertia can equal those of gravity, and in the moral domain the effects of sloth can equal those of the Elect's control.

Physico-theology, which in the wake of relativity theory and loss of religious belief can be better understood as a connection of mathematical and ethical ideas, sheds light on Slothrop's trajectory through *Gravity's Rainbow*: while the post-war world quickly changes around him, he becomes more and more divided between different possibilities until he ceases to act, only appearing in scattered references in the text and ultimately completely disappearing from the novel. In an attempt to save Slothrop from his growing inertia, Seaman Bodine tries to persuade him to care and take action, that is, to defy inertia that equals gravity and fly. In contrast to his friend's sloth, Bodine praises the questionable actions of the bank-robber John Dillinger that at least are a protest against the unsatisfactory state of things: 'he still did what he did. He went out socked Them right in the toilet privacy of Their banks. Who cares what he was *thinking* about, long as it didn't get in the way?' (GR 879). According to Bodine, Slothrop's inertia remains a bloodless enterprise as it bars him from acting on the world. He therefore wants Slothrop to have a cloth stained with Dillinger's blood and to understand that 'what we need isn't right reasons, but just that *grace*. The physical grace to keep it working' (GR 879–80). Bodine fails to reinfuse Slothrop with blood, however, and he remains emotionally inert: short of the human feeling and active frame of mind to fight the system of the Elect and keep up with the quickly changing post-war world, he is weighed down by gravity-like sloth and lacks the 'physical grace to keep it working' (GR 880).

Slothrop could also be said to lack the 'mathematical grace' to keep it working, since in relativity theory gravity is understood to be a geometrical concept. By failing to view gravitation as a geometrical issue, he misses the opportunity to revive Leibniz's notion of it as 'a strange fiction' and the ethical freedom this entails. The historical reception of Einstein's theory does recover Leibniz's idea and language, as we can, for example, see in a mathematics textbook from 1938: 'Today it is believed by many scientists that gravitational force is merely a fiction and that we live in a type of space in which the behavior of bodies can be explained without recourse to that fiction.'[32] If anything, the contemporary understanding is even more radical; for instance, the physicist Michio Kaku states: 'In some sense, gravity does not exist; what moves the planets and the stars is the distortion of space and time.'[33] Since, however, gravity *appears* to act as a force, it is now scientifically termed a *fictitious force*: inside a certain system it is experienced as a force, but when observing the system from the outside, the effect of gravitation can be revealed not to be due to a force but, for example, due to inertia in accelerating surroundings. In analogy, Slothrop could notice the fictitiousness of the force bearing him down if stepping outside his frame of reference, and he could then, like Bodine, conclude that it is possible to act against the Elect. Only considering his own view, however, he becomes convinced of the universality of gravity and his non-action furthers its effects. Lacking the mathematical and ethical ability to consider the relativity of viewpoints and expose claims to universal laws as fictitious, Slothrop becomes part of the problem himself.

The notion of fictitious force might seem to imply that gravity is merely a fiction that a change in perspective could dispel or whose effects could be evaded. Einstein warned against such inferences:

> [W]e might easily suppose that the existence of a gravitational field is always only an *apparent* one. We might also think that, regardless of the kind of gravitational field which may be present, we could always choose another reference-body such that *no* gravitational field exists with reference to it. This is by no means true for all gravitational fields, but only for those of quite special form. It is, for instance, impossible to choose a body of reference such that, as judged from it, the gravitational field of the earth (in its entirety) vanishes.[34]

Gravity's Rainbow is equally cautious not to deny the very real consequences of gravity. Bland does not achieve bodily flight, and Gottfried's ascent can only promise escape but not achieve it: the rocket will descend, regardless of whether it finds its path due to a force, a 'constant and regulated relation', or a 'strange fiction'. Pynchon's novel does not propose the possibility of opting out of gravity, then, but highlights the value of staying critical of the inevitability of forces, suggesting that by taking an outside position, apparently inevitable and real aspects can be discovered to be subject to specific conditions.

With over four hundred characters and a multitude of voices and perspectives, *Gravity's Rainbow* does not offer a stable frame of reference itself but forces readers to compare points of view, and metafictional passages remind them of the world outside the novel, encouraging an outside perspective from which the Elect's force can be identified as fictitious and inertia as adding to its effects. This does not dispute the inescapability of the force that characters experience inside the novelistic system, but it at least questions its seemingly irrefutable reality and reveals the Preterite to have some impact on the situation: they are free and morally responsible to avoid inertia. *Gravity's Rainbow*'s use of a twentieth-century understanding of gravity thus recovers possibilities of free will and moral responsibility that Leibniz championed with his idea of correspondence against Newton's belief in causality and force. But the freedom not to add to the effects of gravity can give rise to very limited hope only: it does not curtail Their control but merely keeps in view the possibility of an alternative. In correspondence with the impossibility to physically overcome gravity, characters do not escape the control of the Elect: although Seaman Bodine and several others launch a Counterforce, their actions achieve very little, doing nothing more than annoy the Elect with jokes and pranks. However, these helpless actions prevent the force of the Elect from becoming universal and, keeping in view its fictitiousness, maintain the possibility of freedom if not freedom itself. Thus, reshaping the tradition of physico-theology in view of modern mathematical and ethical ideas, *Gravity's Rainbow* uses the notion of scientific fictitiousness to revaluate the reality of domination and uphold the possibility of freedom without questioning the reality of practical constraints. Gravity has to be grasped as a mathematical rather than physical concept in order to identify its fictitiousness, and *Gravity's Rainbow* draws on further concepts to establish a relation between maths and fiction and explore implications for literary writing.

MATHEMATICS AND FICTION: INFINITESIMAL CALCULUS

The different understandings of gravity as Newtonian force, Leibnizian 'constant and regulated relation', and Einsteinian fictitious force illustrate a move from apparent causality to fiction, as well as a shift in focus from physics to mathematics. *Gravity's Rainbow* emphasises that, in contrast to the physical sciences, maths does not aim at causal explanations and uses mathematical concepts to further develop how identifying fiction in seemingly fully determined systems might open up possibilities for resistance and change. In this way, the novel's presentation of mathematical functions and, in particular, the infinitesimal calculus works to propose possibilities inherent in Enlightenment maths, pointing to a path that does not lead to the disaster of a fully enlightened earth but, including uncertainty and fiction at its core, towards possibilities of freedom.

Establishing relations between phenomena is a key concern of both physics and mathematics. But, unlike physics, maths does not offer reasons for the relations it describes. Characters in *Gravity's Rainbow*, trying to make sense of their surroundings and find ways to influence their future, nevertheless seek explanations for a functional relation between rocket hits in London and marks on a map in Slothrop's office with which he seems to record his sexual encounters in the city. The distribution of rocket hits matches the marks on Slothrop's map: 'The two patterns also happen to be identical. They match up square for square' (GR 100–101). The relation between the patterns is therefore organised by a function, that is, a rule that relates to each element x exactly one element y: each mark on Slothrop's map is assigned a corresponding site of impact on the map of London. The textbook *Introduction to Mathematics* explains that functions correlate quantities but do not make any statement as to the nature of the relation by using the example of two columns, one giving the value of Siamese imports from the United States in each year of a period of time, and the other showing the number of marriages in New York City in the same years: 'Thus to each amount of imports in the table there is made to correspond a definite number of marriages, and vice versa. The correspondence is therefore a functional relation.'[35] The obvious arbitrariness of the relation between the two columns is of no concern to mathematicians: 'the definition of a functional relation does not require that one variable should be the *cause* of the other. It only requires that to each value of one variable there shall correspond a value of the other variable.'[36] The textbook points out that the correspondence between Siamese imports and New Yorker marriages is 'a functional relation of no practical value. No one would think of basing any predictions on it.'[37] This is certainly not true in the paranoid universe of *Gravity's Rainbow*: in order to explain the matching maps, several characters speculate that Slothrop was conditioned to respond to the rocket with an erection or that he directs the rockets at will.[38] But *Gravity's Rainbow* exposes the dangers of giving in to the desire for causal explanation: in analogy to the notion of gravity, the connection between the maps turns out not to be a cause-and-effect relation and ultimately not a correspondence either, but to be based on a fiction.

In an essay Bernard Duyfhuizen collects clues that indicate the problematic nature of Slothrop's map. For example, Pointsman's post-war investigations reveal 'a number of cases where the names on Slothrop's map do not appear to have counterparts in the body of fact' (GR 323). Several of the names do not correspond to actual women in London, and the remark that the names on the map 'are mostly all first names, you see, the, the Xs without the Ys so to speak' points to the similarly functional relation between the maps and the assumed but missing counterparts in reality (GR 324). As an abstract science maths is not concerned with questions of reality, and, so it turns out, neither is Slothrop when telling stories about his amorous adventures: he remembers 'the gentlemanly reflex that made him edit, switch names, insert fantasies into the yarns he spun' (GR 360). Such reminiscences reveal that his map refers to stories, and, as Duyfhuizen argues, readers have to dismiss explanations of – causal or kute – relations between rocket hits and Slothrop's amorous adventures and 'realize the map's fictional quality'.[39] As in the case of gravity, then, what some characters interpret as a causal connection is better described as a mathematical function and, ultimately, suggested to have a basis in fiction.

References to functions in *Gravity's Rainbow* highlight the fact that maths does not lend itself to the control exercised by the Elect. Bland's use of an eerie physical force of gravity is contrasted with the Preterite's inability to control their surroundings and their living with 'Kute Korrespondences, [. . .] trying to string them all together like terms of a power series hoping to zero in on the tremendous and secret Function' (GR 699). Even if the powerless majority could connect all correspondences into a mathematical function, they would not arrive at the deeper meaning they crave since functions offer no explanations of the relations they describe and consequently no way to influence these. On the other hand, however, mathematics as a realm of non-necessity proposes openness to alternatives, and *Gravity's Rainbow* further explores the, not least ethical, possibilities inherent in mathematical views. The novel closely connects these possibilities with the realm of fiction, and with the presentation of the infinitesimal calculus it illustrates that fiction is at the heart of one of the major mathematical achievements of the Enlightenment period. The implications of this are profound: Enlightenment maths appeared to be a perfectly rational and entirely transparent area of knowledge that Newton could use as a base for his physics and that consequently underlies the physico-theological views of the period. Uncertainty or fiction in maths could consequently undermine the mechanical view of the world on which the Elect base their power and put into question their moral prerogatives.

Gravity's Rainbow refers to the infinitesimal calculus as an instrument to calculate a rocket's path and to determine the moment when fuel is cut off, after which the rocket begins its descent. The description of the point of fuel cutoff, the so-called *Brennschlusspunkt*, as 'a point in space, a point hung precise as the point where burning must end, never launched, never to fall', alerts to the artificiality of determining a single moment in a continuous movement: of course, the Rocket does not hang motionless, and the apex of its path cannot be dissociated from its launch or fall (GR 360). This both mathematical and philosophical issue features in another controversy between Newton and Leibniz, in which they quarrelled over who was first to invent the calculus and also over the basic interpretation of what the calculus is and does. Newton understood motion as a continuous process and the parabolic curve of a rocket's trajectory as described by a moving point, namely the rocket. In contrast, Leibniz regarded the curve as made up of discrete points: the parabola is pieced together from an infinite number of separate points that have no spatial extension but are infinitesimally small. Unlike Newton's notion of continuous motion, Leibniz's description of a rocket's path divides it into discrete positions – an idea that *Gravity's Rainbow* takes up in the *Brennschlusspunkt* as a point in space independent of the rocket's launch or fall. Leibniz's opponents argued that it is impossible to break up a continuous movement into components and vehemently opposed his use of infinitesimals. This mathematical concept remained highly disputed up to the twentieth century, and in *Gravity's Rainbow* it features as an example of the value of fiction in maths and ethical systems related to it.

A formal definition of an infinitesimal reads: 'An infinitely small quantity or amount, a quantity less than any assignable quantity' (*OED* 'infinitesimal'). In other words: an infinitesimal number is not quite zero but smaller than any determinable number. As the definition does not point to a stable existence but only to a shifting and ungraspable 'smaller than', the nature and reality of infinitesimals was highly contested when the term was coined in the seventeenth century, and uneasiness regarding their elusiveness persisted over the next centuries. As philosopher of mathematics John Bell sets out, infinitesimals were '[d]erided by Berkeley in the eighteenth century as "ghosts of departed quantities", in the nineteenth century execrated by Cantor as "cholera-bacilli" infecting mathematics, and in the twentieth roundly condemned by Bertrand

Russell as "unnecessary, erroneous, and self-contradictory"'.[40] In view of Newton's rejection of their use, Leibniz admitted that infinitesimals do not really exist but contended that they, like any part of an infinite, constitute useful fictions: 'I maintain, strictly speaking, that an infinite composed of parts is neither one nor a whole, and it is not conceived as a quantity except through a fiction of the mind.'[41] Leibniz argued for the practical usefulness of such 'fictions of the mind', and *Gravity's Rainbow* accords the concept of infinitesimals a similar value, not least in view of its ethical vision.

The infinitesimal calculus can be used to determine a rocket's path, despite being based on the indeterminate 'ghosts of departed quantities' and 'erroneous, and self-contradictory' 'cholera-bacilli' of mathematics. Indeed, to use Leibniz's terms, a rocket explodes at its target because of calculations with a 'fiction of the mind'. Obviously, then, even though fiction enters mathematics with infinitesimals, they cannot be discarded as ineffectual. In the novel, the engineer Pökler accordingly understands that the reality or fictivity of infinitesimals is not significant when determining the moment of fuel cutoff by use of the fiction that the time span Δt (delta t) becomes zero: 'The important thing is taking a function to its limit. Δt is just a convenience, so that it can happen' (GR 188). Despite the fact that the term Δt never actually becomes zero, the calculus treats it as effectively doing so and arrives at results with practical consequences. In this respect, as the literary scholar James Earl puts it, '[t]he delta-t is not just another mathematical tool, it is a compromise with reality' – that is, it realises what is by definition indeterminable.[42] However, despite its intricate relation to reality, Δt is precisely 'just another mathematical tool' and an example of how *Gravity's Rainbow* uses the discipline at the forefront of Enlightenment scientification to introduce ideas of the 'real' value of fiction.

Amir Alexander conducts research on the historical reception of infinitesimals and argues that infinitesimals implied maths not to be entirely rationally ordered and thus encouraged questioning other seemingly fixed systems, not least giving rise to movements advocating social and political change. In contrast, '[t]o groups invested in the existing hierarchy and social stability, infinitesimals seemed to open the way to sedition, strife, and revolution'.[43] *Gravity's Rainbow* similarly locates in infinitesimals a notion of other possibilities and a space for change. These ideas take on a mathematico-ethical dimension for readers when, at the end of the novel, a falling rocket threatens to destroy a cinema, and 'we' – a term referring to the cinema audience but also including the reader – wait for a disrupted film to start again (GR 902). Mirroring the break in the film's continuity, the rocket 'reaches its last unmeasurable gap above the roof of this old theatre, the last delta-t', and this disruption of motion might open up a possibility for change (GR 902). In the infinitesimally small moment when impact is just about to arrive, there remains time, so the narrator points out, to overcome sloth and act and show compassion. The closing words of the novel – 'Now everybody' – invite participation and, referring to an earlier song that advocates treating people as partners rather than passing them over, work towards infusing the uncaring Neuters of the world with human feeling: 'just turn to the Glozing Neuter nearest you, even your own reflection in the mirror, and . . . just . . . sing,

> [. . .]
> Maybe we should stick together part o' the way, and
> Skies'll be bright-er some day!
> Now *ev'*rybody –' (GR 902, 802)

At the close of the novel, with the reader only a moment away from putting the book down and returning to their reality, the text suggests that 'fictions of the mind' such as infinitesimals and literary works such as *Gravity's Rainbow* are indispensable for keeping open possibilities that might never lead to the reality of escape but at least maintain hope for a brighter future. This is not a hopeful ending, not a vision of grace as in *Against the Day*, but a call to recognise one's freedom to take moral responsibility for (non-)action and not become part of the problems associated with gravity. Like gravity, which cannot be overcome regardless of whether it is understood as force or fictitious force, the mental fictions of infinitesimals and literature offer no viable escape but demonstrate the value of an outside view that can question reality and reveal hidden possibilities.

Mathematics and Fiction: Probability Theory

When *Gravity's Rainbow* focuses on the possibility of freedom rather than freedom itself, questions arise regarding the relation of this possibility to reality and its chances of becoming real. Pynchon's novel draws on probability theory as a mathematical way to gauge the likelihood of an outcome in order to explore the possibilities inherent in the less-than-certain states it describes. It roundly condemns naively literal 'calculations' of future possibilities, doing so with reference to Leibniz's attempt to use mathematics for real-life decision-making. Leibniz, an early proponent of probability theory, argues for turning to a theory of games in cases that lack causal explanations and transfers the mathematical concept of combinatorial analysis to questions such as politics. For example, he uses calculation to determine the future king of Poland: he sets out four possible candidates, establishes the political reasons for electing each of them, and weighs their respective chances. As Jérémie Griard clarifies, Leibniz does not calculate probabilities but weighs political reasons; a process that Leibniz nevertheless describes as 'a type of mathematics'.[44] Indeed, Leibniz aimed to submit all decision-making to mathematics, as he writes in 'Art of Discovery' (1675):

> The only way to rectify our reasonings is to make them as tangible as those of the Mathematicians, so that we can find our error at a glance, and when there are disputes among persons, we can simply say: Let us calculate, without further ado, in order to see who is right.[45]

To many modernist thinkers such a mathematisation of all areas of life and the implied, overly literal connection of maths and ethics felt threatening, and apprehensions of a rule of rationality not least inform Adorno and Horkheimer's warning of a 'fully enlightened earth [that] radiates disaster triumphant'.[46] *Gravity's Rainbow* highlights the futility of straightforwardly applying mathematical means to non-scientific domains of life. In the novel, Brigadier Pudding employs Leibniz's combinatorial analysis to determine possible developments in European politics, and he despairs as ever-changing reality makes it impossible to keep up with the task: '"Ramsay MacDonald can die." By the time he went through resulting party alignments and possible permutations of cabinet posts, Ramsey MacDonald had died' (GR 90–1). Moreover, Pudding's predictions do not fit the actual development: 'the permutations 'n' combinations of Pudding's *Things That Can Happen in European Politics* [...] don't give Hitler an outside chance' (GR 328). Too slow and disregarding unlikely scenarios, Pudding's combinatorial analysis fails for similar reasons as Leibniz's attempt to calculate the royal election: not only did Leibniz's essay appear too late to have any influence on the election, but none of the four candidates he considered was chosen. Instead, a fifth man – the outside chance – became king. Recalling Leibniz's practice, Pudding's use of combinatorial analysis attests to the attractiveness of seeking security in calculating future developments, while his failing points to the impracticality of Leibniz's method.

In *Gravity's Rainbow*, Roger Mexico and Edward Pointsman personify the contrast between probabilities and the certainties of cause-and-effect relationships. Pointsman accepts only unambiguous, reliable relations between causes and the effects these determine and is therefore said to 'only possess the zero and the one', numbers which in probability theory denote events that certainly will not take place (0) or that will certainly occur (1) (GR 64). In contrast to Pointsman's deterministic answers, Mexico, the 'Antipointsman', provides statistical explanations that cover the realm in between the certainties of absolute presence and absolute absence: all uncertain probabilities are expressed by fractions; for example, the probability to obtain 'heads' when flinging a coin is ½; the probability to roll a six with a die is ⅙ (GR 64). While zero and one denote certain events and therefore constitute reliable prognoses for the future, all other probabilities indicate the chance of an event only and are not predictions: despite knowing the probability of an event, it is impossible to tell whether a coin will show heads or what number is rolled; and obviously the coin will not show half heads, half tails. Yet, as Mexico explains in *Gravity's Rainbow*, regarding a large number of cases, statistics seems to forecast an outcome: when throwing a die many times, approximately a sixth of the rolls will show the number six. This does not mean that predicting an individual event is possible, however; the statistical rule applies only if considering a large number of cases. As during the Second World War rockets fall on London in large numbers, Mexico can plot their distribution, noting down how many hits a quadrant of the city has received. As the distribution follows a statistical law, some characters think that he is able to predict where the next rocket will hit, but Mexico insists that he cannot forecast individual events: 'It's not precognition [. . .] all I'm doing is plugging numbers into a well-known equation, you can look it up in the book and do it yourself . . .' (GR 64). A hundred pages later, the so-called Poisson equation is given in the text, and a mathematically inclined reader could indeed plug in the numbers and dispel all doubts as to the difference between the unpredictability of an individual event and the calculability of a large number of cases (GR 166).

Even statistically unlikely possibilities can occur in individual cases, and in *Gravity's Rainbow* improbable events happen very often indeed: ignored by Brigadier Pudding's calculations, Hitler comes into power, Ludwig is reunited with his lemming Ursula against all odds, and Slothrop recovers his lost harmonica in a journey down a toilet. The statistical unpredictability of individual events and the possibility that even highly unlikely events become real harbour potential for resistance. Mexico, having joined the Counterforce that opposes the Elect, uses his mathematical background to threaten his ex-girlfriend's new partner, Jeremy. He confronts him with: 'Little sigma, times P of s-over-little-sigma, equals one over the square root of two pi, times e to the minus s squared over two little-sigma squared' (GR 841). And Jeremy is right to feel unsettled as the formula describes the so-called normal distribution, the most common probability distribution: it has a peak at the mean value, and the probability of events outside the mean decreases symmetrically on both sides. Significantly, although probabilities further distanced from the mean value can quickly become very small, they never actually become zero: in an event described by the normal distribution, no outcome is completely unfeasible. Accordingly, as Lance Schachterle and P. K. Aravind convincingly argue, by citing the equation Mexico draws attention to the fact that, however small the probability of succeeding against the Elect, he might pay Jeremy back.[47] Indeed, after the encounter, Mexico and Bodine demonstrate the power of the outside chance when subverting a dinner of the Elect by talking about invented dishes that are both alliterative and highly disgusting. Their protest might not be very effective in destroying Their system, but it creates, at least, a moment when the Elect are not in control.

The frequent occurrence of improbable events stresses the fact that probabilities are not predictions of the future: already Aristotle argues in his *Poetics* that 'it is probable that improbable things occur'.[48] Or, as sociologist Elena Esposito maintains, '[r]eality is improbable, and that is the problem', since even the most likely future development is by no means guaranteed.[49] As a probability does not refer to the future reality and does not eradicate uncertainty, the question arises as to how it relates to reality. Esposito elaborates that probabilities indicate possible futures, some with higher, others with lower probability of actually taking place. Since probability theory takes into account all possibilities rather than predicting the future course, it opens up a domain apart from the actual or real, and in this sense, probability theory encompasses fictive realities – imaginable but not actualised versions of reality.[50] Since the alternative, fictive realities of probability theory do not compete with real reality, Esposito compares the workings of probability theory to literary fiction and its creation of worlds that are coherent according to fictive premises.[51] In other words, describing consistent worlds apart from the given, literary fiction and probability theory have comparable relations to reality. It is in this sense that we can say that mathematical probabilities are not predictions but fictions.

The seventeenth and early eighteenth centuries saw the conception of probability theory as well as the rise of the novel, making this Age of Reason a decisive period for the valuation of fictive systems. Following the premise that fiction had to seem like fact, the early novel introduced realistic characters and settings, to the extent that readers of Daniel Defoe's *Robinson Crusoe* took the text to be a record of real events, written by the protagonist. Like the contemporaneously emerging probability theory, then, the early novel sets a possible and realistic reality next to real reality. In a book on early modern conceptions of the nature of truth, Barbara Shapiro argues for the related emergence of realistic novelistic reality and the notion of truth created by probability theory, and Esposito similarly contends that at the time when, with the early novel, fiction approaches reality, the conceptualisation of probability theory and the consequent concern with fictive future realities means that mathematics takes a turn towards fiction.[52] Both Shapiro and Esposito assert that a new relation to reality emerges when the domains of fiction and fact converge, and that with the emergences of the novel and probability theory formerly uniform reality comes to be seen in terms of a coexistence of different possible and realistic realities. The result is a 'pluralism of realities', as Esposito calls it, a variety of realities that might be fictive but that each claims the status of reality rather than of fantasy, hallucination or arbitrary creation.[53] In other words, literary fiction and probability theory can be understood to disturb the notion of a determinate reality and point towards plural actualisations that all take the status of possible reality. So, if, as historian of science Lorraine Daston claims, 'it has been one of the glories of mathematical statistics that it can deal with events in which conditions weaker than causation obtain', probability theory and literary fiction also deal with events in which conditions weaker than reality obtain.[54]

Gravity's Rainbow revisits early modern questions about the relation of probabilities to reality in terms of twentieth-century experiences and draws from it conclusions for literary fiction. The novel explores ways in which conditions weaker than causation can extend to questions of reality, and it is populated by entities in conditions weaker than existence: the dead communicate from the afterlife, the minds of hallucinating characters shift in and out of realities, Slothrop scatters into small parts, and gravity turns out to be a fictitious force. The universe of *Gravity's Rainbow* is thus not determined only by what is, but conditions weaker than existence have to be taken into account. Drawing on the similar relationships of probability theory and fiction to reality, the novel presents probability theory as a way of dealing with being that is neither fully present nor fully absent and uses it to perform the move from the epistemological questions that emerge when attending to conditions weaker than causation, to ontological concerns about conditions weaker than existence. Thus, mathematics is a vital part in a development that, as Brian McHale has argued, makes *Gravity's Rainbow* a quintessential postmodernist text.

Mathematics, Fiction, Ontology: Towards Postmodernism

Gravity's Rainbow is decisively plural and attentive to different realities, sporting hundreds of characters and a great variety of voices and perspectives including those of animals, objects and existences beyond death. In an influential study of the novel's diverse worlds, Brian McHale shows that readers can never fully trust the text, as passages read as real turn out to be characters' fantasies or hallucinations: 'the minds of *Gravity's Rainbow* give us access only to provisional "realities" which are always liable to be contradicted and cancelled out'.[55] For example, the narrator first describes how: 'A fly lands belly-up on the front fender of Roger's motorcycle, thrashes ten seconds, folds its veined and sensitive wings, and dies' (GR 748). A few sentences later, this course of events is cancelled by a different fictional reality: 'The fly, who was not dead, unfolds its wings and zooms off to fool somebody else' (GR 748). McHale argues that with the destabilisation of novelistic ontology, *Gravity's Rainbow* performs the decisive move from modernism to postmodernism: 'The breakthrough [. . . comes in] *Gravity's Rainbow*, where, no longer constrained by the limits of modernism, he [Pynchon] will freely exploit the artistic possibilities of the plurality of worlds, the transgression of boundaries between worlds.'[56] He defines the difference between modernist and postmodernist texts as precisely a shift towards concern with being and away from questions of knowledge about reality. Where modernist texts ask what can be known in the world, the ontological questions of postmodernist texts go along the lines of: 'Which world is this? What is to be done in it? Which of my selves is to do it?'[57] While texts usually contain both epistemological and ontological concerns, a dominant of one over the other can serve to distinguish modernist from postmodernist works.

In *Gravity's Rainbow*, Thanatz's puzzled query aptly summarises the questions arising from the novel's different worlds that coexist and turn into each other: 'Isn't this an "interface" here? a meeting surface for two worlds ... sure, but *which two?*' (GR 791). Thanatz's experience of a meeting of unknown worlds is symptomatic of the precarious and plural nature of reality in *Gravity's Rainbow* and also applies to the relation between states with differing degrees of reality and fiction. The domains are not clearly distinguishable but, so the novel illustrates not least with the example of mathematics, interfaces connect and put into question the distinction between reality and fiction: probability theory regards states weaker than existence and proposes fictive realities, calculus employs the mental fiction of infinitesimals to initiate a compromise with reality, drawing on the impossible to arrive at real outcomes, and gravity turns out to be a fictitious force but to nevertheless be inescapable. When *Gravity's Rainbow* closes in the fiction of an infinitesimal Δt, it gives readers a chance to realise the potential for change inherent in maths. The direct addresses to readers in the final paragraphs draw attention to the coexisting levels of novelistic fiction and reality, and *Gravity's Rainbow* encourages readers to take advantage of this crossover and use the singular point of the ending, where continuity is broken, not just to jump back into their 'real reality' but to realise the 300-year-old attempt to acknowledge the importance of both realities and fictions.

Moreover, *Gravity's Rainbow* employs probability theory as an interface between an epistemological and an ontological dominant, from regarding relations weaker than causation to questioning being in view of conditions weaker than existence. Mexico suggests:

> [T]here's a feeling about that cause-and-effect may have been taken as far as it will go. That for science to carry on at all, it must look for a less narrow, a less ... sterile set of assumptions. The next great breakthrough may come when we have the courage to junk cause-and-effect entirely. (GR 104–5)

Here, Mexico does not speak as a scientist in the Second World War who would probably be familiar with decisive developments in twentieth-century physics, but he assumes a state of mind much closer to the opposition of the concepts of causality and probability in the seventeenth century. Where Pointsman's determinism and Mexico's statistical view play out a conflict from the beginnings of modern science, Enzian, a Herero who witnessed the quasi-extinction of his people, fully embraces – and exaggerates – the twentieth-century discovery that, on the subatomic level, existence is only probable: 'Well, I think we're here, but only in a statistical way. [. . .] [O]ur own chances of being right here right now are only a little better than even – the slightest shift in the probabilities and we're gone – schnapp! like that' (GR 430). Twentieth-century scientific developments reveal that, on the subatomic level, prediction is possible only in probabilities, not due to human beings' limited knowledge but because unknowability is intrinsic in the basic building blocks of the universe. While in classical physics an object exists in a specific place and time, an object in quantum physics exists in probabilities only: it has a certain probability of being at a certain place at a certain time. It is not only our knowledge that is uncertain here, but being itself. Hacking emphasises: 'Quantum physics takes for granted that nature is at bottom irreducibly stochastic.'[58] As probability replaces determination and causal relations on the subatomic level, Mexico is right in saying that science has to adapt a less 'sterile set of assumptions' than cause-and-effect and accept the randomness of existence that Enzian, having survived the genocide ordered by the German General Lothar von Trotha on the Herero, is particularly apt to understand: 'Forty years ago, in Südwest, we were nearly exterminated: There was no reason. Can you understand that? *No reason*' (GR 430). Replacing cause-and-effect with statistics means jettisoning possibilities for meaningful explanation, and, more drastically, Enzian suffers the uncertainty of living in probabilities as an ontological situation. Readers of *Gravity's Rainbow* are similarly subject to a feeling of perpetual ontological danger when experiencing multiple possibilities and continuously shifting degrees of reality and fantasy, hallucination and fiction: what has been taken as novelistic reality might be eradicated with the next sentence 'schnapp! like that'.

McHale claims the genre of science fiction to be 'the ontological genre *par excellence*'.[59] Science fiction is usually concerned with meetings of different planets and civilisations and thus precisely foregrounds the concern with worlds that characterises postmodernist fiction according to McHale. *Gravity's Rainbow* is not science fiction in the classical sense, and the juxtaposition of worlds is much more pronounced in Pynchon's later novels. Rather, *Gravity's Rainbow* is 'science fiction' when it begins to address notions of fiction in science and to explore mathematics as a realm independent of physical reality – a process Pynchon continues in *Mason & Dixon* and *Against the Day* (see Chapter 1). In this respect, Pynchon is careful to distinguish maths from the natural sciences: where physics stands for cause-and-effect relationships that can be exploited by the Elect, maths encompasses greater uncertainty but also greater freedom. Not representing physical reality or causal connections but Kute Korrespondences and using fictive elements in concepts such as infinitesimals, there resides potential in mathematics for alternative states and realities. Comparing the positions of Newton and Leibniz again illustrates the difference. Where Newton ropes in mathematics for explaining the real part of existence, exploring what we could call, with Leibniz, the fictive aspects of maths opens up realms apart from the existing: probabilities, infinitesimals and fictitious forces, and even a complete mathematical world. And, fittingly, Leibniz is closely associated with the idea of possible worlds that permeates the novel. The first to introduce this term, he held that there are several possible worlds out of which God chose to create the actual world. Thus, Leibniz does not only stand for the identification of fictions in mathematics and for suspecting the fictivity of a gravitational force but also for the idea of a plurality of worlds.

In the seventeenth century mathematics itself takes on the status of reality as its descriptions are trusted to be more real than physical ones: most importantly, even without being able to determine a physical cause of the force of gravity, the mathematical explanation is taken to prove its existence. Isaac Barrow, a contemporary of Newton, consequently held: 'mathematics, as it is vulgarly taken and called, is co-extended and made equal with physics itself'.[60] A little later, Camille Falconet identified a competition between the reality of maths and the physical world:

> There is, so to say, two very different worlds; one mathematical, the other physical. The mathematical [...] only exists in the ideas of the geometer: he supposes the infinitely small, dots without dimensions, lines without width [...]; as well as vacuum and gravitation. [...] But nothing of this can be found exactly in nature [...] and this is a strange illusion to abuse of the abstractions in transposing them in the physical world as if they were real beings.[61]

Falconet aimed to counter what he saw as his contemporaries' tendency to bypass the real world in favour of maths: 'instead of accommodating their ideas to Nature, they want to submit Nature to their ideas', he complained.[62] His was far from the only voice in the seventeenth century to deplore the fact that, while specific mathematical concepts such as probability theory contributed to considerations of a pluralism of realities, more generally the growing importance of maths introduced a competition between physical reality and an independent mathematical world.

Calling mathematics and physical reality 'two very different worlds', Falconet offers a neat formulation to explore the idea that the relation between maths and reality gives rise to a main concern of postmodernism and science fiction, namely the juxtaposition of worlds. The Enlightenment engagement with maths thus already foreshadows ways in which Pynchon's works draw out the ontological implications of 'science fiction'. More precisely, for Pynchon, in the tradition of Falconet and other seventeenth-century thinkers, not science fiction but what we could call 'maths fiction' is the ontological genre *par excellence*, since mathematics opens up a different world and confronts physical reality with an alternative. So, *Gravity's Rainbow* does not only identify fictional concepts in maths but it also reactivates the idea that maths constitutes a different world – an idea that remained suppressed by the grand narratives of Enlightenment rationality and physical reality. When *Gravity's Rainbow* shows how with its mathematical discoveries the Enlightenment witnesses conflicting concepts of truth and reality, it suggests that the age misses an opportunity to widely acknowledge the interrelations of reality and fiction and the plurality of worlds. With this ontological focus on the world of mathematics, the maths fiction of *Gravity's Rainbow* accords this specific science a crucial place in its development of a postmodernist response to the grand narratives of modernity.

Closing the Circle: The Ethical Limits of Mathematics and Fiction

Gravity's Rainbow constitutes a world in which historical reality and exuberantly imaginative writing, mathematics and fiction, and various discourses, possibilities, probabilities and realities coexist, connect and turn into each other. Not least, it brings together its own opposed halves of mathematical description and narrative exploration. Before reading the novel, its title might seem to forcibly combine a scientific term with a poetic image, bringing to mind John Keats's famous accusation that, through its scientific investigation, Newton 'had destroyed all the poetry of the rainbow'.[63] Conversely, Newton might have claimed gravity to belong only to the scientific sphere. In the course of *Gravity's Rainbow*, however, the respective attributions to the domains of science and literature are reversed: the rainbow, similar in form to the parabola-shaped path of a rocket, is related to the mathematical concept of the calculus, while gravity is revealed to be a fictitious force.

The link between the rainbow and the rocket's trajectory goes further when, like the rainbow which appears to be a semicircle but would form into a full circle if it did not meet the horizon, the Rocket 00000 does not end with its explosion: it passes underneath the earth, completing the other half of its path to arrive at its starting point as the reborn Rocket 00001. The calculus, which can be used to calculate the rocket's flight trajectory, cannot represent this complete circular passage: a function demands that each value x corresponds to only one value y, so it can describe a semicircle and a parabola, but not a circle where a point on the horizontal middle axis corresponds to two values y – one on the upper semicircle, one on the lower semicircle. A circle can be described by mathematical means, of course, but not in the language of the calculus as employed in *Gravity's Rainbow*. The novel's maths is thus insufficient to take account of the Rocket's complete route, and its metaphorical burial and dark passage through the earth is instead rendered in a Herero myth: the

Herero believe that the sun lives until in the evening it is speared to death and colours the sky red. Then, 'under the earth, in the night, the sun is born again, to come back each dawn, new and the same' (GR 383). Relating the sun's death and rebirth, the Hereros' story addresses a part of existence that the enlightened calculus cannot cover.

The image of the complementarity of science and story in *Gravity's Rainbow* illustrates an idea that similarly informs Jean-François Lyotard's argument in *The Postmodern Condition*: 'scientific knowledge does not represent the totality of knowledge; it has always existed in addition to, and in competition and conflict with, another kind of knowledge, which I will call narrative'.[64] Lyotard's limiting the relevance of science and his valuation of small, contradictory narratives fuelled the association of the postmodern with relativism and led to accusations of his abandoning objective truth. The misleading attractiveness of systems that do not accord with reality is not limited to stories, however, but in *Gravity's Rainbow* appears most clearly in Pointsman's belief in the causal connection between Slothrop's sexual encounters and the rocket hits, which eventually turns out to be unfounded in 'the body of fact' (GR 323). Moreover, while Pynchon's novel questions and expands any notion of objective truth, it is also cautious not to abandon the reality of facts. Indeed, it is worth pointing out again that, when *Gravity's Rainbow* moves from a modernist to a postmodernist stance in close connection with a nuanced view of the mathematical and ethical value of fiction, its explorations of ontological uncertainty and plurality do not lead to unbounded relativism. As set out in Chapter 1, Pynchon's *Against the Day* is extremely careful not to suggest the possibility of abandoning the real: even its flights to the greatest imaginative heights are stabilised by what Yashmeen calls the 'spine of reality'. And *Gravity's Rainbow*, too, emphasises the precedence of 'real reality' and the ways in which, as Esposito notes in relation to probability theory, '[t]he relation to the world serves as the corrective to fiction'.[65] The novel illustrates that the facts of the world limit mathematical fiction when an engineer reports a problem with the Rocket, complaining that the measured data indicates a much smaller value than the calculated pressure of 40 atü. Enzian, although most attuned to living in probabilities and conditions weaker than existence, argues for dismissing the calculation in favour of the reality of the facts: 'What are these data, if not direct revelation? [. . .] How do you presume to compare a number you have only derived on paper with a number that is the Rocket's own?' (GR 374–5). When declaring the precedence of reality, Enzian acts as a voice of caution, pointing out that the facts of reality inhibit both the construction of purely fictional and of entirely mathematical systems.

The use of gravity in Pynchon's novel further clarifies the limits of fictional and mathematical systems. Although gravity is exposed as a fictitious force, the novel does not present the possibility of physically escaping it: Gottfried's flight is temporary, Lyle Bland travels in his mind only, and the Counterforce is nowhere near overcoming the system of the Elect. Attentive to the inevitability of gravitational effects to which the inertia of inaction and carelessness further add, *Gravity's Rainbow* does not embrace complete ontological uncertainty or relativity. What is possible, so the novel suggests, is to realise that what was considered to be a force and therefore inescapable might not be as all-encompassing as previously thought. Although this does not show a clear path to escaping the very real effects of gravity, it can at least keep alive hope for alternatives and the work of counter-movements. So, when bringing Enlightenment physico-theology up to date, *Gravity's Rainbow*'s modern mathematico-ethical perspective promotes a postmodernist proliferation of worlds and establishes that seemingly universal forces can be found not to be so, but it also shows that there are physical facts that no change in reference frames can deny. Even more important than physical facts, however, is the gravity of ethical concerns. The metaphorical use of gravity suggests that a proliferation of perspectives is not to lead to inertia, but that the exact nature of reality, its perspectives, causes and meanings, have to take a backseat: what ultimately matters is commitment to some kind of action that maintains compassion and the 'physical grace to keep it working' (GR 880). In this respect, the ethical dimension of gravity even takes precedence over the ontological: in view of ethical demands, questions of reality are secondary. Thus, long before the 1990s criticism of scientific relativism and, in the 2000s, the call by Bruno Latour and others to move beyond the dichotomy of fact and fiction and establish a 'fair' position, Pynchon's novel highlights the ethical dimensions of science, fiction and of doing nothing.[66]

Gravity's Rainbow with its use of various concepts from modern maths – from the Enlightenment period to the Second World War – sets into broader context the specifically modernist features explored in earlier chapters. Focusing on the relation of maths and fiction that has also run through the discussions of *Against the Day*, *The Sleepwalkers* and *The Man without Qualities*, the novel addresses the roots and legacies of modernist maths: considering gravity in terms of geometry reveals it to be a fictitious force; calculus makes use of the 'fiction of the mind' of infinitesimals to arrive at 'real' solutions; and probability theory sets several fictive realities next to each other. With these examples across its modern history, *Gravity's Rainbow* suggests that mathematics does not only lend itself to rationalisation and technological invention but similarly supports the 'reality' of fiction. It thus contributes to the novel's postmodernist dedication to a plurality of possibilities and, indeed, worlds. Gesturing to the seventeenth century when maths becomes an instrument of physics as a decisive fork in the path, and to the twentieth century when a new focus on mathematics recovers its potential to deal with uncertainty and fictive concepts and points the way forward to a postmodernist pluralisation of reality,

Gravity's Rainbow takes account of the inextricable relation between modernism, its roots in early modernity, and its postmodernist legacies. The novel keeps closely in view the aberrations to which mathematical mindsets and their applications in science and technology have given rise over four centuries, and it ends with only an infinitesimal moment of hope – a mathematically described moment that is almost but never really inexistent and whose minute probability does not alleviate demand for compassion and action. Where Gravity's Rainbow uses the combined force of physical forces and imaginative grace to argue for the reality of ethical demands but gives little reason for hope, Pynchon invests maths with more positive potential in Against the Day: here, it might help us to, in some way at least, 'fly toward grace' (AD 1220). Until then, however, Gravity's Rainbow suggests that maths and literature, allowing us to identify outside perspectives and moments of chance and change, can at least help us maintain the physical grace to keep it working.

NOTES

1. Thomas Moore, *The Style Connectedness:* Gravity's Rainbow *and Thomas Pynchon* (Columbia: University of Missouri Press, 1987), p. 196.
2. Newton 'a répandu la lumière des Mathématiques sur une science qui jusqu'alors avait été dans les ténèbres des conjectures & des hypothèses' (Alexis Clairaut, 'Du système du monde, dans les principes de la gravitation universelle', in *Histoire de l'Académie royale des sciences, année M. DCCXLV, avec les mémoires de mathématique & de physique* (Paris: L'Imprimerie royale, 1745), 329–64, p. 329).
3. Alexander Pope, 'Intended for Sir Isaac Newton', in *Collected Poems*, ed. Bonamy Dobrée (London, Melbourne and Toronto: Dent, 1983), p. 122.
4. Theodor W. Adorno and Max Horkheimer, *Dialectic of Enlightenment*, trans. John Cumming (London and New York: Verso, 1997), p. 3.
5. Martin Paul Eve, 'Thomas Pynchon, David Foster Wallace and the Problems of "Metamodernism": Post-Millennial Post-Postmodernism?', *C21 Literature: Journal of 21st-century Writings*, 1 (2012), 7–25 (p. 8). Ali Chetwynd, Review of *The Cambridge Companion to Thomas Pynchon*, ed. Inger H. Dalsgaard, Luc Herman and Brian McHale, *College Literature*, 39.4 (2012), 142–5 (pp. 142–3).
6. Brian McHale, 'Pynchon's Postmodernism', in *The Cambridge Companion to Thomas Pynchon*, ed. Inger H. Dalsgaard, Luc Herman and Brian McHale (Cambridge: Cambridge University Press, 2012), 97–111 (p. 97).
7. Lance Schachterle, 'Introduction', in Joseph W. Slade, *Thomas Pynchon* (New York: Peter Lang, 1990), vii–x (p. ix).
8. Alan J. Friedman, 'Science and Technology', in *Approaches to* Gravity's Rainbow, ed. Charles Clerc (Columbus: Ohio State University Press, 1983), 69–102 (p. 100).
9. John Gascoigne, 'From Bentley to the Victorians: The Rise and Fall of British Newtonian Natural Theology', *Science in Context*, 2.2 (1988), 219–56 (p. 221).
10. Paolo Mancosu, *Philosophy of Mathematics and Mathematical Practice in the Seventeenth Century* (New York and Oxford: Oxford University Press, 1996), p. 3.
11. Pierre-Simon, marquis de Laplace, *A Philosophical Essay on Probabilities* [1814], ed. E. T. Bell (New York: Dover, 1951), p. 4.
12. John O. Stark, *Pynchon's Fictions: Thomas Pynchon and the Literature of Information* (Athens, OH: Ohio University Press, 1980), p. 46.
13. Friedman, 'Science and Technology', pp. 94–5.

14. Walther von Braun qtd in Walter Sanders, 'The Seer of Space: Lifetime of Rocket Work gives Army's Von Braun Special Insight into the Future', *Life* (18 November 1957), 133–9 (p. 133).
15. Friedman, 'Science and Technology', p. 77.
16. Isaac Newton, *The Mathematical Principles of Natural Philosophy*, vol. II, trans. Andrew Motte (London: H. D. Symonds, 1803), p. 314.
17. Richard Bentley, *The Works of Richard Bentley*, vol. 3, ed. Alexander Dyce (London: Macpherson, 1838), p. 210.
18. Gottfried Wilhelm Leibniz, *Philosophical Writings*, ed. G. H. R. Parkinson, trans. Mary Morris and G. H. R. Parkinson (London and Vermont: Everyman, 1995), p. 377.
19. Leibniz, *Philosophical Writings*, p. 228.
20. Gottfried Wilhelm Leibniz, *Briefwechsel zwischen Leibniz, Arnauld und dem Landgrafen Ernst von Hessen-Rheinfels*, ed. C. L. Grotefend (Hanover: Hahnsche Hof-Buchhandlung, 1846), p. 109.
21. Ian Hacking, *The Emergence of Probability: A Philosophical Study of Early Ideas about Probability, Induction and Statistical Inference*, 2nd edn (Cambridge: Cambridge University Press, 2006), p. 184.
22. 'Une chose exprime une autre (dans mon langage) lorsqu'il y a un rapport constant et reglé entre ce qui se peut dire de l'une et de l'autre' (Leibniz, *Briefwechsel*, p. 109).
23. Nicholas Jolley, *Leibniz* (New York: Routledge, 2005), p. 49.
24. Newton, *Mathematical Principles*, vol. II, p. 314.
25. Leibniz, *Philosophical Writings*, p. 228.
26. Leibniz, *Philosophical Writings*, p. 228.
27. Lewis Campbell and William Garnett, *The Life of James Clerk Maxwell; With Selections from His Correspondence and Occasional Writings*, 2nd edn (London: Macmillan, 1882), pp. 203 and 289.
28. David Darling, *Gravity's Arc: The Story of Gravity, from Aristotle to Einstein and Beyond* (Hoboken: Wiley, 2006), p. 141.
29. Arthur Eddington, *The Nature of the Physical World* (New York: Macmillan, 1929), p. 133.
30. Arthur Eddington, *The Theory of Relativity and Its Influence on Scientific Thought* (Oxford: Clarendon, 1922), p. 25.
31. Thomas Pynchon, 'Nearer, My Couch, to Thee', *The New York Times Book Review* (6 June 1993), p. 57.
32. Hollis R. Cooley et al., *Introduction to Mathematics: A Survey Emphasizing Mathematical Ideas and Their Relations to Other Fields of Knowledge* (London, Bombay and Syndey: Harrap, 1938), p. 597.
33. Michio Kaku, 'Theory of Everything', *Nova Science Now*. Available at <http://www.pbs.org/wgbh/nova/blogs/secretlife/physical-science/michio-kaku/> Transcript at <http://p-i-a.com/Magazine/Issue6/MichioKaku.htm> (last accessed 21 June 2017).
34. Albert Einstein, *Relativity: The Special and the General Theory*, trans. Robert W. Lawson (New York: Henry Holt, 1920), p. 82.
35. Cooley et al., *Introduction to Mathematics*, p. 263.
36. Cooley et al., *Introduction to Mathematics*, p. 263.
37. Cooley et al., *Introduction to Mathematics*, p. 263.
38. Even concerning reality, the mathematics textbook rather overestimates the hold of rationality: during the 2010 Football World Cup, Paul the Psychic Octopus was said to predict the outcome of Germany's matches by taking food from the container with the flag of the winning team. Paul was right on each occasion, and the correspondence between his preferred food container and the victorious team

can be described as a functional relation. Not only was this obviously arbitrary relation taken to predict the result of the matches, but threats to cook Paul for dinner if he did not pick the right team attest to the even less rational idea that the octopus could actually influence the outcome. Although obviously part of an entertaining hype and not to be taken too seriously, the incident shows the attraction of promises to predict and influence the future.

39. Bernard Duyfhuizen, 'Starry-Eyed Semiotics: Learning to Read Slothrop's Map and *Gravity's Rainbow*', *Pynchon Notes*, 6 (1981), 5–33 (p. 20).
40. John L. Bell, *The Continuous and the Infinitesimal in Mathematics and Philosophy* (Milan: Polimetrica, 2006), p. 17.
41. Gottfried Wilhelm Leibniz, *The Leibniz–Des Bosses Correspondence*, ed. and trans. Brandon C. Look and Donald Rutherford (New Haven and London: Yale University Press, 2007), p. 53.
42. James W. Earl, 'Freedom and Knowledge in the Zone', in *Approaches to* Gravity's Rainbow, ed. Charles Clerc (Columbus: Ohio State University Press, 1983), 229–50 (p. 241).
43. Amir Alexander, *Infinitesimal: How a Dangerous Mathematical Theory Shaped the Modern World* (New York: Scientific American/Farrar, Straus and Giroux, 2014), p. 24.
44. 'qu'il y a une espece de mathematique' (Gottfried Wilhelm Leibniz, *Sämtliche Schriften und Briefe* 1/13, ed. Akademie der Wissenschaften Göttingen (Berlin: Akademie Verlag, 2010), p. 551). Jérémie Griard, 'The *Specimen Demonstrationum Politicarum Pro Eligendo Rege Polonorum*: From the Concatenation of Demonstrations to a Decision Appraisal Procedure', in *Leibniz: What Kind of Rationalist?*, ed. Marcelo Dascal (New York et al.: Springer, 2008), 371–82 (pp. 378–9).
45. Gottfried Wilhelm Leibniz, 'The Art of Discovery' [1675], in *Leibniz: Selections*, ed. Philip P. Wiener (New York: Scribner's, 1951), 50–8 (p. 51).
46. Adorno and Horkheimer, *Dialectic of Enlightenment*, p. 3.
47. Lance Schachterle and P. K. Aravind, 'The Three Equations in *Gravity's Rainbow*', *Pynchon Notes*, 46–9 (2000), 157–69 (p. 168).
48. Aristotle, *Poetics*, ed. and trans. Stephen Halliwell (Cambridge, MA: Harvard University Press, 1995), p. 135.
49. 'Die Realität ist unwahrscheinlich, und das ist das Problem' (Elena Esposito, *Die Fiktion der wahrscheinlichen Realität* (Frankfurt am Main: Suhrkamp, 2007), p. 50).
50. See Esposito, *Die Fiktion der wahrscheinlichen Realität*, p. 21.
51. See Esposito, *Die Fiktion der wahrscheinlichen Realität*, pp. 55–6.
52. Barbara J. Shapiro, *Probability and Certainty in Seventeenth-Century England: A Study of the Relationships between Natural Science, Religion, History, Law, and Literature* (Princeton: Princeton University Press, 1983).
53. See Esposito, *Die Fiktion der wahrscheinlichen Realität*, p. 68.
54. Lorraine Daston, 'The Doctrine of Chances without Chance: Determinism, Mathematical Probability and Quantification in the Seventeenth Century', in *The Invention of Physical Science: Intersections of Mathematics, Theology and Natural Philosophy since the Seventeenth Century*, ed. Mary Jo Nye, Joan L. Richards and Roger H. Stuewer (Dordrecht, Boston, MA and London: Kluwer Academic Publishers, 1992), 27–50 (p. 47).
55. Brian McHale, 'Modernist Reading, Post-Modern Text: The Case of *Gravity's Rainbow*', *Poetics Today*, 1.1–2 (1979), 85–110 (p. 91).
56. Brian McHale, *Postmodernist Fiction* (London and New York: Routledge, 1996), pp. 24–5.

57. Dick Higgins qtd in McHale, *Postmodernist* Fiction, p. 10.
58. Ian Hacking, *The Taming of Chance* (Cambridge: Cambridge University Press, 1990), p. 2.
59. Brian McHale, 'Change of Dominant from Modernist to Postmodernist Writing', *Approaching Postmodernism*, 21 (1986), 53–79 (p. 67).
60. Isaac Barrow qtd in Antoni Malet, 'Isaac Barrow on the Mathematisation of Nature: Theological Voluntarism and the Rise of Geometrical Optics', *Journal of the History of Ideas*, 58.2 (1997), 265–87 (pp. 280–1).
61. Camille Falconet qtd in Yves Gingras, 'What Did Mathematics Do to Physics?', *History of Science*, 39 (2001), 383–416 (p. 402).
62. 'au lieu d'accommoder leurs idées à la Nature, ils voidroient soumettre la Nature à leurs idées' (Camille Falconet, 'Preface', in Bernard Le Bovier de Fontenelle, *Théorie des tourbillons cartésiens* (Paris: Guerin, 1752), iii–xxxi (p. xxxi)).
63. John Keats qtd in Benjamin Robert Haydon, *The Autobiography and Journals of Benjamin Robert Haydon*, ed. Malcolm Elwin (London: Macdonald, 1950), p. 317.
64. Jean-François Lyotard, *The Postmodern Condition: A Report on Knowledge*, trans. Geoff Bennington and Brian Massumi (Manchester: Manchester University Press, 1984), p. 7.
65. 'Der Bezug zur Welt dient der Korrektur der Fiktion' (Esposito, *Die Fiktion der wahrscheinlichen Realität*, p. 114).
66. Bruno Latour, 'Why Has Critique Run out of Steam? From Matters of Fact to Matters of Concern', *Critical Inquiry*, 30.2 (2004), 225–48 (p. 243).

CONCLUSION: MODERNISM, FICTION AND MATHEMATICS

In his 2015 overview of the study of literature and science from the early modern period to the present, Martin Willis identifies the topic of mathematics as a gap in scholarship:

> One distinct scientific discipline that has played only a small role in literature and science criticism is mathematics. Despite being central to many other sciences [. . .] that literature and science scholars have investigated, pure (rather than applied) mathematics has not received the same attention which its status in the sciences afford it.[1]

Differences between pure and applied mathematics become particularly evident in modern maths when a close relationship with philosophy and the discovery of concepts without direct counterparts in nature encourage the discipline to turn away from application and towards self-referential concerns with mathematical existence, truth and meaning. As the specific characteristics of maths and its exceptional relation to physical reality gain attention with its modern transformation, the need to account for the unique status of mathematics in the spectrum of the disciplines becomes urgent in studies of twentieth-century literature and science. At the same time, maths becomes a necessary and fruitful concern of modernist studies.

With its focus on Pynchon's, Broch's and Musil's imaginative negotiations of the place of maths, this book reflects the notion of mathematical modernism through the lens of interrelations with literary fiction, and it thus helps us understand the modernist condition from the interdisciplinary perspective of literature and mathematics studies. The novels accord maths and its modernist development a central place in their visions and employ it as interrelated with and exemplary of transformations in the modern West, the wider loss of absolute truth, and the increasing scepticism towards Enlightenment values. More surprisingly, however, they also explore the freedoms and opportunities that the mathematical crisis implies and relate the growing acceptance of imaginary and fictional concepts to the possibilities of literature and their own literary practices. Engaging with questions of representation and the value of fiction for a highly rational field, the novels use maths and its history to provide new perspectives on reason and on modernist experimentation with literary form. The texts reflect challenges to traditional perceptions of maths, negotiate the place of a new modernist mathematics, and explore the fruitfulness of considering shared characteristics of maths and literature.

Broch's *The Sleepwalkers* trilogy most explicitly considers maths as a structural science that lends itself to exploring changes in the very notion of structure, including opposed ideas of complete dissolution and finding cohesion in intuition. With reference to these modern and counter-modern positions, the trilogy connects the foundational debate in mathematics to ideas of literary form and uses it as a model for its own narrative structure. Similarly concerned with opposed ways to approach the world, Musil's *The Man without Qualities* does not suggest that it is possible to decide for either a ratioïd, logicist-formalist or a non-ratioïd, intuitionist outlook but presents maths as a model for productively dealing with the unsolvable contradiction by incorporating the aims and methods of both exactitude and pragmatic vagueness. Standing for ideal precision and, at the same time, pragmatically embracing uncertainty, mathematics answers to two main aspects of modern crisis: the failing of reason and the loss of trust. Combining the two equally challenged concepts into critical trust, Musil's novel fragment does not propose a solution but a way to avert stagnation in crisis, that is, a way to keep it working by drawing on the method of essayism that includes aspects of both science and literature. Pynchon's novels demonstrate the continued relevance of modernist maths for postmodernist considerations. *Gravity's Rainbow* explores ways in which mathematics incorporates fiction as part of its challenging the dominant status of one-dimensional rational reality, and *Against the Day* uses maths to locate in the modern crisis of representation a promise of possibilities inherent in imaginary domains. Both novels are careful to keep in sight the, to use Pynchon's expression that reminds us of the German dimension of all the texts, '*Rückgrad von Wirklichkeit*' that ensures continued relation to the real and its responsibilities (AD 679). Pynchon's, Broch's and Musil's literary visions thus point to unrealised potential that lies in aspects of uncertainty and fictionality in maths that Enlightenment rationality has suppressed. Suggesting that Enlightenment beliefs have to be re-examined and adjusted to the situation in the twentieth or twenty-first century, each of the works examined here contrasts negative associations of rationalisation with notions of modernist mathematics as a domain of an-archistic liberation from foundations.

On a more general level, the notion of a mathematical modernism reinforces the 'growing awareness of the need to understand modernism as a more diverse field; characterized by an aesthetic and ideological challenge that goes beyond a narrow canon of writers and works' and, we could add, disciplines.[2] Attention to mathematical modernism and literature engaging with it also leads to questioning interpretations of modernism as mainly focused on negative aspects of modernisation and instrumental rationality. Fiction written in and about the period, as well as mathematical prose texts of the time, reconsider the foundations of reason and rediscover neglected aspects of rational domains, including, counter-intuitively, non-rational and imaginary dimensions. Modernist literature does not only combat a spiritually impoverished rationality, then, but locates in it ways to avoid becoming complicit with problematic developments of rationalisation. Examining the place of maths thus leads to a more nuanced understanding of modernism's complex engagement with its Enlightenment roots and processes of modernisation.

Attention to maths also provides new insights into responses to the first of eight fundamental problems that Michael Whitworth identifies as motivating modernist writers: 'How can we justify art in a world dominated by commerce, quantification, and instrumental rationality?' As Whitworth explains, '[n]o modernist would have put the question in exactly this way, because "instrumental reason" is a phrase indebted to Adorno and Horkheimer's *Dialectic of Enlightenment*'.[3] Indeed, reason retains more ambiguous connotations in some areas of early twentieth-century thinking, not least in those aware of challenges to the foundations of mathematics. Mathematical discussions at the time and modernist engagements with maths also suggest that the opposition between art and what came to be called instrumental reason was less entrenched than in later assessments: mathematics could be seen as a main tool of rationality but also as an art independent from reality and its demands. The question of the role of art in a rationalied world is, so Whitworth points out, related to what Andrew Brighton calls the 'inaugurating problem' of modernism, namely 'the status and possibility of imaginative and ethical consciousness in a culture dominated by modern rationality'.[4] Where his phrasing implies an opposition, texts engaging with modernist maths explore the imaginative and ethical dimensions of precisely this most rational discipline. They thus resist a rationalisation of reason, that is, the tendency to see maths and reason as means of rationalisation only. Viewing maths on its own terms, the texts identify in it imaginative and ethical potential and explore new relations to reality and fiction.

Texts engaging with a specifically modernist mathematics can suggest alternatives to the dominant reaction to a changed relation between reason and reality. Up to the twentieth century, reason was understood to exist in the real world in various manifestations: 'This view asserted the existence of reason as a force [...] in the objective world – in relations among human beings and between social classes, in social institutions, and in nature and its manifestations.'[5] Max Horkheimer argues that this theory of objective reason posits a 'universal rationality from which criteria for all things and beings were derived. The emphasis was on ends rather than on means.'[6] The theory that reason is inherent in reality is not least put into question by the realisation that mathematics is not a direct expression of the physical world. Reason being unmoored from a foundation in reality, it becomes, so Horkheimer holds, a subjective faculty of the mind and shifts to instrumental rationality. While various modernist texts derive from the dissociation of reason and reality an argument for questioning the rule of instrumental rationality, works focusing on maths also draw attention to the rationality of fiction: as rationality does not imply reality, it supports a much broader realm of possibilities or, indeed, fictional realities.

The novels by Pynchon, Broch and Musil engage with a specifically modernist maths that exhibits characteristics such as self-referentiality and a sense of crisis, but also view maths in its connections to the larger period of modernity, considering its roots in the Enlightenment and relation to postmodern ideas of structure and writing. As developed in detail in Chapter 4, in the wake of the rising importance of maths in the scientific revolution, not least initiated by Newton's *Principia Mathematica*, seventeenth- and eighteenth-century thinkers contemplated the implications of valuing abstract mathematical reasoning over empirical observation of reality. To quote Camille Falconet again: 'There is, so to say, two very different worlds; one mathematical, the other physical.'[7] Falconet and other Enlightenment thinkers pondered the possibility of transposing mathematical abstractions to the physical world 'as if they were real beings', and while questions regarding the legitimacy and value of this other world never completely vanished, they revived when around 1900 mathematicians aimed to prove the foundations of their field with purely mathematical means and without recourse to physical referents.[8] Reactions to the failure of this attempt and the resulting foundational crisis demonstrate that the uncertainties regarding the world of maths unsettle the real world too. No longer understood as a Platonic realm of ideas and absolute truth, mathematics now appears as flawed but still constitutes a domain apart from the real that suggests alternatives to the given. For the novels by Pynchon, Broch and Musil, the value of maths lies precisely in its deficiencies, meaning that occupying oneself with it does not equal escape into a perfect world but engagement with possibilities that are imperfect but full of potential to illuminate and change the real.

In a historical account of the relationship of maths and empirical investigations of the world, evocatively entitled 'What Did Mathematics Do to Physics?', Yves Gingras traces it from Aristotle's argument that mathematical exactness cannot be found in physical matter and maths consequently not be a method in the natural sciences, to a revival of physicist David Bohm's declaration in the mid-1980s that 'the current emphasis on mathematics has gone too far'.[9] Indeed, the conflict between mathematical and empirical approaches, referring to what Falconet calls two 'very different worlds', continues to take place at present. Current examples include the demand in climate research to do more work 'with the help of a pick and shovel (as opposed to a computer)'.[10] While it would go too far here to examine ways in which mathematical computer models can be considered as fictions, the conflict between empirical and theoretical research shows that debates regarding the relation of maths and reality have a long and continuing history and share with literary scholarship concerns with representation.

The examination and historicising of modernist interrelations between maths and fiction point to implications for the field of modernist studies. Attention to informed engagements with mathematics can encourage nuanced views of modernism's reaction to the growing rule of instrumental rationality: while, generally speaking, modernist fiction questions the uninhibited rule of reason, texts focusing on modernist maths also reveal its limits and its making use of imaginary aspects. The examination of the mathematical novels and their contexts also contribute to distinguishing the specific conditions of studying maths in the wider field of literature and science. Not least, the comparative analysis of the works by Pynchon, Broch and Musil reminds us that, if the relationship between literature and reality and the usefulness of fiction continues to be debated, so are the relationship between mathematics and the physical world and its role in the natural sciences. The novels use these questions around maths to explore similar concerns in relation to literature and its potential value at times when political turmoil and threatening scientific progress demand attention to the real. Since modernist maths and literary fiction, both lacking a direct representational connection to nature, have a comparable relation to reality, the 'unreasonable effectiveness of mathematics' might point to a similarly 'unreasonable' but undeniable relevance of literature for real concerns.[11] In this respect, the notion of fictional elements in mathematics is of central interest as it strengthens hope that responses to the crisis of modernity could be achieved with the help of fiction but without abandoning the benefits of rational investigation. *Against the Day*, *The Sleepwalkers*, *The Man without Qualities* and *Gravity's Rainbow* suggest that awareness of the history of maths can help avoid repeating the Enlightenment's mistake of failing to acknowledge the potentials of fiction and the plurality of worlds.

It is notable that all four literary works discussed here show concern with the relevance of fiction for the real world and establish strong connections between mathematics and ethics. They thus stand in the physico-theological tradition that, since early modernity, views religious issues as related to scientific ones, but the works by Pynchon, Broch and Musil relocate religious to secular ethical questions and the examination of the physical world to the exploration of possibilities: the translation of physico-theology to a mathematico-ethical focus entails shifting emphasis from existence to possibility, from what is to what could be. Pynchon's, Broch's and Musil's works examine both maths and literature as realms of possibility that can have real effects: in the modernist understandings of maths as well as in literary fiction, working with language extends possibilities and makes worlds. Given that maths, the peak of rationality, can be seen as a different world but also as crucially related to understanding and creating reality, it lends itself to modernist and postmodernist renegotiations of rationality, reality and fiction.

Let me conclude the circle of this book with a story. When Michael Faraday received a scientific paper by James Clerk Maxwell in 1857, he admitted that the younger scientist's much more mathematical approach intimidated him: 'I was at first almost frightened when I saw such mathematical force made to bear upon the subject.'[12] If even the celebrated scientist Faraday respectfully feared the power of maths, it might seem unsurprising that laypersons and scholars in the humanities have shied away from it, even in the field of literature and science, in what Steven Connor has diagnosed as a 'contemporary allergy to number in the humanities'.[13] Yet, the second part of Faraday's confession can give hope to the growing number of literary scholars working with mathematics: 'I was at first almost frightened when I saw such mathematical force made to bear upon the subject *and then wondered to see that the subject stood it so well*' (my emphasis).[14] The novels by Pynchon, Broch and Musil impressively demonstrate that literary fiction stands the force of maths exceedingly well and indeed thrives on it, maybe particularly when exposing this force as, in some aspects, fictitious. Not least, their works, engaging with and at the same time establishing the notion of modernist mathematics, are evidence of the truth of this book's opening statement: 'Mighty are numbers; joined with art, resistless.' Q.E.D.

NOTES.

1. Martin Willis, *Literature and Science* (New York: Palgrave, 2015), p. 166.
2. Astradur Eysteinsson and Vivian Liska, 'Approaching Modernism', in *Modernism*, ed. Astradur Eysteinsson and Vivian Liska (Amsterdam and Philadelphia: John Benjamins, 2007), 1–8 (p. 6).
3. Michael H. Whitworth, 'Introduction', in *Modernism*, ed. Michael H. Whitworth (Malden, MA and Oxford: Blackwell, 2007), 3–57 (p. 6).
4. Qtd in Whitworth, 'Introduction', p. 7.
5. Max Horkheimer, *Eclipse of Reason* (London: Bloomsbury, 2013), p. 2.

6. Horkheimer, *Eclipse of Reason*, p. 2.
7. Camille Falconet qtd in Yves Gingras, 'What Did Mathematics Do to Physics?', *History of Science*, 39 (2001), 383–416 (p. 402).
8. Falconet, qtd in Gingras, 'What Did Mathematics Do to Physics?', p. 402.
9. Falconet qtd in Gingras, 'What Did Mathematics Do to Physics?', p. 406.
10. Jon Lloyd and Elmar Veenendaal, 'Are Fire Mediated Feedbacks Burning Out of Control?' *Biogeosciences Discuss* (2016), 1–20, p. 15.
11. Eugene P. Wigner, 'The Unreasonable Effectiveness of Mathematics in the Natural Sciences', in *Symmetries and Reflections: Scientific Essays* (Cambridge, MA and London: MIT Press, 1970), 222–37 (p. 222).
12. James Clerk Maxwell, *The Scientific Letters and Papers of James Clerk Maxwell*, vol. 1, ed. Peter Michael Harman (Cambridge: Cambridge University Press, 1990), p. 548.
13. Steven Connor, 'Blissed Out – on Hedonophobia', Talk at the Pleasure Symposium, De Montfort University, 25 June 2012. http://stevenconnor.com/blissedout/ (last accessed 10 February 2016).
14. Maxwell, *The Scientific Letters and Papers*, p. 548.

GLOSSARY

Banach–Tarski paradox: A theorem in set-theoretic geometry published by Stefan Banach and Alfred Tarski in 1924. The theorem implies that, in theory, a solid ball can be cut up into a number of pieces and then be reassembled to make a ball of any other size. This inspired the informal phrase that 'a pea can be cut up and reassembled into the sun'. Although contradicting intuition, the Banach–Tarski paradox does not put into question accepted assumptions of modern mathematics. It can be proven using the axiom of choice, an axiom of set theory formulated by Ernst Zermelo in 1904.

calculus: The calculus is a branch of mathematics concerned with change, for example motion. Examples of application are calculations with velocity, acceleration, arc length and centre of mass. Independently from each other, Newton and Leibniz invented the calculus in the seventeenth century.

combinatorial analysis: Combinatorics is a branch of mathematics concerned with the theory of combinations and permutations. It is the study of structures and different ways of arranging objects according to specific rules.

commutativity: Commutativity means that in a calculatory process the order of the elements can be changed without affecting the result. For example: $4 * 3 = 3 * 4$, or $a+b=b+a$. The multiplication of *Quaternions* is not commutative, but: $i * j = -j * i$.

GLOSSARY

complex number: A complex number has the form $x+yi$ and consists of a *real* unit (x) and an *imaginary* unit (yi). A complex number can be interpreted as a *vector* in a plane which starts from the origin and goes to the point $x+yi$ with x units on the real x-axis and y units of the imaginary number axis i, which is the perpendicular y-axis.

continuum, Cantor's continuum: The term 'continuum' refers to *real numbers*. Cantor compared the sizes of infinite *sets* and formulated the hypothesis that there exists no set whose power is between the power of the set of *integers* and the power of the set of real numbers. Cantor could not prove his hypothesis, and it was later shown that Cantor's continuum hypothesis can neither be proved nor disproved in the framework of standard set theory.

delta t, Δt: Delta denotes a small quantity, here the difference in time (t). In calculus, delta t can become *infinitesimally* small, so that delta t corresponds to a moment in time that approaches zero.

fictitious force: Fictitious forces, also called 'pseudo forces', arise when a change in the frame of reference reveals that what is experienced as a 'force' does not exist. For example, a person sitting in an accelerating car feels a 'force' that pushes them into their seat. Viewed from inside the car and its accelerated reference frame, there exists a force. However, an observer from the outside understands that the effect is due to the acceleration of the car and not to an external force. The outside observer does not need to refer to a force to explain the phenomenon, while for the passenger being pressed into the seat, the experience of a 'force' is real. From the inside, the passenger cannot determine whether the force they experience is real or fictitious. See also *Principle of Equivalence*.

function: A function relates an input value to exactly one output value. Functions can be visualised as graphs.

imaginary number: The term 'imaginary number' is sometimes used as a synonym for '*complex number*' which consists of a *real* part (x) and an imaginary part (yi): $x+yi$. More specifically, the term 'imaginary number' refers to the element i of a complex number: $i^2 = -1$, or also: $i = \sqrt{-1}$. Negative squares are defined in the complex number system, but not in the real number system; imaginary numbers were therefore said to 'not exist'. Imaginary numbers can be thought of as set on an axis perpendicular to the real number line.

incompleteness theorem: The incompleteness theorem states that mathematics cannot be proven complete and consistent. There are always statements in mathematics that are regarded as true but cannot be proven. The theorem was formulated by Kurt Gödel in 1931 and ended the hope that the formalist programme could determine the foundations of mathematics.

infinitesimal: An infinitesimal is an infinitely small quantity, a value that is approaching zero but is infinitesimally greater than it.

integer: A whole number, such as 1, 2, 3, . . .

irrational number: An irrational number is a *real* number that cannot be expressed as a ratio of two whole numbers. Examples are π and √2.

law of excluded middle: The law of excluded middle states that either a proposition is true or the negation of the proposition is true. It is also known as 'tertium non datur', meaning that there is no third possibility between the proposition and its negation. Intuitionist mathematics does not accept the law of excluded middle as an axiom.

law of large numbers: The law of large numbers is a theorem in probability theory, stating that over a large number of cases, the average value will be close to the expected value. For example, when flinging a coin, the outcome of a single throw cannot be predicted, but over a larger number of cases, heads and tails will come up equally often.

non-Euclidean geometry: In non-Euclidean geometries Euclid's *parallel postulate* does not hold, that is, parallel lines can meet and, as an implication of the inapplicability of the parallel postulate, the angular sum of a triangle is not necessarily 180 degrees. For example, geometry on the globe is elliptic: on the globe, a triangle can be defined by two longitudinal lines, which meet at the pole, and the equator connecting them. Since longitudes cut the equator at right angles, the two angles at the basis of the triangle already sum up to 180 degrees. When the angle at the pole, where the two longitudes intersect, is added, the angular sum of the triangle is greater than 180 degrees, thus contradicting Euclid's postulate. Non-Euclidean geometries were discovered in the nineteenth century.

normal distribution: The normal distribution is the most common probability distribution. The function is shaped like a bell with the peak at the mean value and probabilities decreasing on both sides of the mean value.

parallel postulate: Euclid's axiom states that in a geometric system there are two straight lines that are at constant distance from each other. In *non-*

Euclidean geometry, which was discovered in the nineteenth century, the parallel postulate does not hold.

Poisson distribution: The Poisson distribution is a probability distribution describing the probability that a given number of events occur in an interval of time or over a number of experiments. For example, if on average two goals occur in a football match, there might be matches with 0 goals and others with 4 goals; the Poisson distribution describes the probability of seeing a match with no goal, 1 goal or 2 goals etc. The Poisson distribution was introduced by Siméon Poisson in 1837.

principle of equivalence: This principle in relativity theory states the equivalence of gravitational and inertial mass. A thought experiment by Albert Einstein illustrates the principle: If an elevator floats in space, a person inside it is suspended in mid-air, while in an elevator on earth, a person stands on the floor due to gravity. If the elevator in space accelerates, the person inside stays at the same spot while the elevator floor comes closer. As the floor pushes into the person, they come to rest on the floor and experience the sensation of a gravitational force – as the person does not accelerate but remains inert, they experience the change in the position of the surrounding elevator as a force pushing them to the ground. This shows that in accelerating surroundings, the effects of a person's inertia is equivalent to the effects of gravity. See also *Fictitious Force*.

Quaternion: Quaternions are hypercomplex numbers and extend the *complex number* system from two to four dimensions. While *complex numbers* describe the location of points on a plane, Quaternions describe the location of points in space. A Quaternion consists of a *scalar* or *real* part (a) and the remaining *vector* or *imaginary* part: $a+bi+cj+dk$, whereby i, j, and k are *imaginary numbers*. Quaternions were discovered by William Rowan Hamilton in 1843.

Quine–Putnam indispensability argument: W. V. Quine and Hilary Putnam argue that mathematics is indispensable to science and that, because we can apply mathematical entities such as numbers, sets and functions to great effect in the empirical sciences, we can believe that these entities exist. In short, the argument states that mathematical objects exist since they are immensely useful in the empirical sciences.

rational numbers: A rational number can be expressed as a ratio of whole numbers, for example ½, 4/7, etc. In contrast, *irrational* numbers cannot be expressed as ratios of whole numbers.

real number: The real number system includes *rational* and *irrational* numbers, but does not include *complex* or *imaginary* numbers. Real numbers can be considered as points on the number line.

Riemann hypothesis: See Zeta-function

Russell's paradox: Russell's paradox was discovered by Bertrand Russell in 1901. It concerns the question of whether the set of all sets that are not members of themselves is a member of itself. As the question cannot be answered but any answer creates a paradox, it demonstrated that *set theory* leads to contradictions.

scalar: 'Scalar' is a term defined by William Rowan Hamilton to describe the scalar or *real* part of a *Quaternion*. A scalar is a *variable* that can be expressed as a real number and has only quantity, not direction. In contrast, a *vector* has both quantity and direction.

set theory: Set theory studies mathematical sets, that is, collections of objects. Nearly all mathematical objects can be formulated in set theory, proposing it as a possible foundational theory of mathematics. Set theory was developed in the nineteenth century, but in the early twentieth century, paradoxes such as the *Russell paradox* were discovered and challenged the belief that a secure foundation of mathematics could be established through set theory.

third law of motion: The third law of motion is one of three physical laws formulated by Newton. It states that to every action there is a reaction of equal force in the opposite direction: '*actio = reactio*'.

indeterminacy principle: The indeterminacy principle, also known as the uncertainty principle, was formulated by the German physicist Werner Heisenberg in 1927. It concerns the smallest scales of nature, subatomic particles, and states that it is impossible to precisely measure the position and momentum of a particle at the same time: the more precisely the position of a particle is measured, the less precisely can its momentum be determined, and vice versa. This is not a practical problem of measurement, but at the subatomic level there is a 'fuzziness' in nature itself.

variable: A variable stands for a value that may vary. It usually refers to *real numbers*. In a *complex number* $x+yi$, the values x and y are variables, whereas i is not a variable but a constant: i is always $\sqrt{-1}$.

vector: A vector is characterised by its length and by its direction. It can be imagined as a directed line in a coordinate system, originating in one point and pointing to another.

Weierstrass function: The Weierstrass function was formulated by Karl Weierstrass in 1872. By proving that there are continuous functions that are nowhere differentiable, the Weierstrass function challenged popular belief in the mathematical community.

zeta-function / Riemann's ζ-function: The zeta-function considers the distribution of prime numbers in a *complex number* system. The famous Riemann hypothesis, formulated by Bernhard Riemann in 1859, is about the distribution of the zeros of the zeta-function. While it can easily be shown that the zeta-function has zeros at the negative even *integers* such as $-2, -4, -6, \ldots$, Riemann conjectured that the non-trivial zeros occur at complex values that vary in their *imaginary* component but all have the *real* part ½. The conjecture has remained unproven to today.

BIBLIOGRAPHY

Adams, Dale, *Die Konfrontation von Denken und Wirklichkeit: Die Rolle und Bedeutung der Mathematik bei Robert Musil, Hermann Broch und Friedrich Dürrenmatt* (St. Ingbert: Röhrig, 2011).
Adorno, Theodor W. and Max Horkheimer, *Dialectic of Enlightenment*, trans. John Cumming (London and New York: Verso, 1997).
Airy, George, 'Supplement to a Proof of the Theorem That Every Algebraic Equation Has a Root', *Transactions Cambridge Philosophical Society* 10 (1858), 327–30.
Alexander, Amir, *Infinitesimal: How a Dangerous Mathematical Theory Shaped the Modern World* (New York: Scientific American/Farrar, Straus and Giroux, 2014).
American Association for the Advancement of Science, *Proceedings of the American Association for the Advancement of Science*, 40 (1891).
Aristotle, *Poetics*, ed. and trans. Stephen Halliwell (Cambridge, MA: Harvard University Press, 1995).
Armstrong, Tim, *Modernism: A Cultural History* (Cambridge and Malden, MA: Polity, 2005).
Attridge, John, 'Introduction: Modernism, Trust and Deception', in *Incredible Modernism: Literature, Trust and Deception*, ed. John Attridge and Rod Rosenquist (Farnham: Ashgate, 2013), pp. 1–20.
Badiou, Alain, *Being and Event*, trans. Oliver Feltham (London and New York: Continuum, 2005).

Badiou, Alain, *Number and Numbers*, trans. Robin Mackay (Cambridge: Polity, 2008).
Badiou, Alain, 'Platonism and Mathematical Ontology', in *Briefings on Existence: A Short Treatise on Transitory Ontology*, ed. and trans. Norman Madarasz (New York: State University of New York Press, 2006), pp. 89–100.
Baez, John C., 'The Octonions', *Bulletin of the American Mathematical Society*, 39.2 (2002), 145–205.
Bartram, Graham, '"Subjektive Antipoden"? Broch's *Die Schlafwandler* and Musil's *Der Mann ohne Eigenschaften*', in *Hermann Broch: Modernismus, Kulturkrise und Hitlerzeit*, ed. Adrian Stevens, Kurt Wagner and Sigurd Paul Scheichl (Innsbruck: Institut für Germanistik, 1994), pp. 63–75.
Beer, Gillian, 'Translation or Transformation? The Relations of Literature and Science', *Notes and Records of the Royal Society of London*, 44.1 (1900), 81–99.
Bell, John L., *The Continuous and the Infinitesimal in Mathematics and Philosophy* (Milan: Polimetrica, 2006).
Bendels, Ruth, *Erzählen zwischen Hilbert und Einstein: Naturwissenschaft und Literatur in Hermann Brochs 'Eine methodologische Novelle' und Robert Musils 'Drei Frauen'* (Würzburg: Königshausen & Neumann, 2008).
Bentley, Richard, *The Works of Richard Bentley*, vol. 3, ed. Alexander Dyce (London: Macpherson, 1838).
Benton, Graham, 'Daydreams and Dynamite: Anarchist Strategies of Resistance and Paths for Transformation in *Against the Day*', in *Pynchon's Against the Day: A Corrupted Pilgrim's Guide*, ed. Jeffrey Severs and Christopher Leise (Newark: University of Delaware Press, 2011), pp. 191–213.
Bergson, Henri, *The Meaning of the War: Life & Matter in Conflict* (London: Fisher Unwin, 1915).
Bernays, Paul, 'Hilbert's Significance for the Philosophy of Mathematics' [1922], in *From Brouwer to Hilbert: The Debate on the Foundations of Mathematics in the 1920s*, ed. and trans. Paolo Mancosu (Oxford: Oxford University Press, 1998), pp. 189–97.
Blasber, Cornelia, 'A City "Under Glass": Vienna in Robert Musil's *The Man without Qualities*', in *Vienna: The World of Yesterday, 1889–1914*, ed. Stephen Eric Bronner and F. Peter Wagner (New York: Humanity Books, 1999), pp. 150–67.
Bloor, David, 'Hamilton and Peacock on the Essence of Algebra', in *Social History of Nineteenth Century Mathematics*, ed. Herbert Mehrtens, Henk Bos and Ivo Schneider (Boston, MA: Birkhäuser, 1981), pp. 202–32.
Bloor, David, *Knowledge and Social Imagery* (London: Routledge & Kegan Paul, 1976).

Boole, George, *An Investigation of the Laws of Thought on Which are Founded the Mathematical Theories of Logic and Probabilities* [1854] (New York: Dover, 1958).

Breger, Herbert, 'A Restoration That Failed: Paul Finsler's Theory of Sets', in *Revolutions in Mathematics*, ed. Donald Gillies (Oxford: Oxford University Press, 1992), pp. 249–64.

Broch, Hermann, *Briefe 1*, ed. Paul Michael Lützeler (Frankfurt am Main: Suhrkamp, 1974–1981).

Broch, Hermann, *Briefe 3, 1945–1951*: *Kommentierte Werkausgabe 9/1*, ed. Paul Michael Lützeler (Frankfurt am Main: Suhrkamp, 1975), pp. 383–4.

Broch, Hermann, *Briefe: Dokumente und Kommentare zu Leben und Werk*, ed. Paul Michael Lützeler (Frankfurt am Main: Suhrkamp, 1981).

Broch, Hermann, *Erkennen und Handeln: Essays, Band II*, ed. Hannah Arendt (Zürich: Rhein-Verlag, 1955).

Broch, Hermann, *Das essayistische Werk und Briefe, 1913–1951: Kommentierte Werkausgabe 9/1*, ed. Paul Michael Lützeler (Frankfurt am Main: Suhrkamp, 1986).

Broch, Hermann, *Geist and Zeitgeist: The Spirit in an Unspiritual Age. Six Essays by Hermann Broch*, ed. and trans. John Hargraves (New York: Counterpoint, 2002).

Broch, Hermann, *Hofmannsthal and His Time: The European Imagination, 1860–1920*, trans. Michael P. Steinberg (Chicago: University of Chicago Press, 1984).

Broch, Hermann, 'Joyce and the Present Age' [1932], in *A James Joyce Yearbook*, ed. Maria Jolas (Paris: Transition, 1949), pp. 68–108.

Broch, Hermann, 'Kommentare', in *Die Schlafwandler: Eine Romantrilogie* (Frankfurt am Main: Suhrkamp, 1996), pp. 719–35.

Broch, Hermann, *Die Schlafwandler: Eine Romantrilogie* [1930–32] (Frankfurt am Main: Suhrkamp, 1996).

Broch, Hermann, *The Sleepwalkers: A Trilogy*, trans. Willa and Edwin Muir (London: Martin Secker, 1932).

Broch, Hermann, 'Die sogenannten philosophischen Grundfragen einer empirischen Wissenschaft' [1928], in *Philosophische Schriften 1: Kritik*, ed. Paul Michael Lützeler (Frankfurt am Main: Suhrkamp, 1977), pp. 131–46.

Broch, Hermann, 'The Spirit in an Unspiritual Age' [1934], in *Geist and Zeitgeist: The Spirit in an Unspiritual Age. Six Essays by Hermann Broch*, ed. and trans. John Hargraves (New York: Counterpoint, 2002), pp. 41–64.

Brouwer, L. E. J., 'Intuitionism and Formalism' [1912], *Bulletin of the American Mathematical Society*, 20.2 (1913), 81–96.

Brouwer, Luitzen Egbertus Jan, 'Mathematics, Science, and Language'

[1928], in *From Brouwer to Hilbert: The Debate on the Foundations of Mathematics in the 1920s*, ed. Paolo Mancosu (New York and Oxford: Oxford University Press, 1998), pp. 45–52.

Brouwer, Luitzen Egbertus Jan, 'On the Foundations of Mathematics' [1907], in *L. E. J. Brouwer: Collected Works*, vol. 1., ed. Arend Heyting (Amsterdam and Oxford: North-Holland, 1975), pp. 15–101.

Brouwer, Luitzen Egbertus Jan, 'Synopsis of the Signific Movement in the Netherlands: Prospects of the Signific Movement', *Synthese*, 5.5 (1946), 201–8.

Brude-Firnau, Gisela (ed.), *Materialien zu Hermann Brochs 'Die Schlafwandler'* (Frankfurt am Main: Suhrkamp, 1972).

Burdman Feferman, Anita and Solomon Feferman, *Alfred Tarski: Life and Logic* (Cambridge: Cambridge University Press, 2004).

Burton, David M., *The History of Mathematics: An Introduction*, 6th edn (Boston, MA et al.: McGraw-Hill, 2007).

Campbell, Lewis and William Garnett, *The Life of James Clerk Maxwell; With Selections from His Correspondence and Occasional Writings*, 2nd edn (London: Macmillan, 1882).

Cantor, Georg, 'Über unendliche, lineare Punktmannigfaltigkeiten V', *Mathematische Annalen*, 21.4 (1883), 545–91.

Carnap, Rudolf, 'The Elimination of Metaphysics through Logical Analysis of Language' [1932], in *Logical Positivism*, ed. A. J. Ayer, trans. Arthur Pap (New York: The Free Press, 1959), pp. 60–81.

Cassirer, Ernst, *The Philosophy of Symbolic Forms 3: The Phenomenology of Knowledge* [1929], trans. Ralph Manheim (New Haven: Yale University Press and London: Oxford University Press, 1957).

Cassirer, Ernst, *Substance and Function and Einstein's Theory of Relativity* [1910], trans. William Curtis Swabey and Marie Collins Swabey (Chicago and London: Open Court, 1923).

Chetwynd, Ali, Review of *The Cambridge Companion to Thomas Pynchon*, ed. Inger H. Dalsgaard, Luc Herman and Brian McHale, *College Literature*, 39.4 (2012), 142–5.

Clairaut, Alexis, 'Du système du monde, dans les principes de la gravitation universelle', in *Histoire de l'Académie royale des sciences, année M. DCCXLV, avec les mémoires de mathématique & de physique* (Paris: L'Imprimerie royale, 1745), pp. 329–64.

Cliver, Gwyneth, 'Maddening Mathematics: The Kinship of the Rational and the Irrational in the Writing of Robert Musil', *Journal of Romance Studies*, 7.3 (2007), 75–85.

Connor, Steven, 'Blissed Out – on Hedonophobia', Talk at the Pleasure Symposium, De Montfort University, 25 June 2012. <http://stevenconnor.com/blissedout/> (last accessed 10 February 2016).

Cooley, Hollis R. et al., *Introduction to Mathematics: A Survey Emphasizing Mathematical Ideas and Their Relations to Other Fields of Knowledge* (London, Bombay and Syndey: Harrap, 1938).

Cooke, Leighton Brett, 'Ancient and Modern Mathematics in Zamyatin's *We*', in *Zamyatin's We: A Collection of Critical Essays*, ed. Gary Kern (Ann Arbor: Ardis, 1988), pp. 149–67.

Corry, Leo, 'How Useful is the Term "Modernism" for Understanding the History of Early Twentieth-Century Mathematics?', in *Science as Cultural Practice: Modernism in the Sciences, ca. 1900–1940*, ed. Moritz Epple and Falk Mueller (Berlin: Akademie Verlag, forthcoming 2020).

Crowe, Michael J., *A History of Vector Analysis: The Evolution of the Idea of a Vectorial System* (New York: Dover, 1994).

Dalen, Dirk van, *Mystic, Geometer, and Intuitionist: The Life of L. E. J. Brouwer; vol. 1: The Dawning Revolution* (Oxford: Clarendon, 1999).

Dalen, Dirk van, *Mystic, Geometer, and Intuitionist: The Life of L.E.J. Brouwer; vol. 2: Hope and Disillusion* (Oxford: Clarendon, 2005).

Darling, David, *Gravity's Arc: The Story of Gravity, from Aristotle to Einstein and Beyond* (Hoboken: Wiley, 2006).

Daston, Lorraine, 'The Doctrine of Chances without Chance: Determinism, Mathematical Probability and Quantification in the Seventeenth Century', in *The Invention of Physical Science: Intersections of Mathematics, Theology and Natural Philosophy since the Seventeenth Century*, ed. Mary Jo Nye, Joan L. Richards and Roger H. Stuewer (Dordrecht, Boston, MA and London: Kluwer Academic Publishers, 1992), pp. 27–50.

De Morgan, Augustus, *On the Study and Difficulties of Mathematics* (Chicago and London: Open Court and Kegan Paul, 1910).

Derrida, Jacques, 'Structure, Sign and Play in the Discourse of the Human Sciences', in *Modern Criticism and Theory*, 2nd edn, ed. David Lodge and Nigel Wood (Harlow: Pearson, 2000), pp. 89–103.

Doob, Joseph L., 'The Development of Rigor in Mathematical Probability (1900–1950)', *The American Mathematical Monthly*, 103.7 (1996), 586–95.

Duyfhuizen, Bernard, 'Starry-Eyed Semiotics: Learning to Read Slothrop's Map and *Gravity's Rainbow*', *Pynchon Notes*, 6 (1981), 5–33.

Earl, James W., 'Freedom and Knowledge in the Zone', in *Approaches to Gravity's Rainbow*, ed. Charles Clerc (Columbus: Ohio State University Press, 1983), pp. 229–50.

Eddington, Arthur, *The Nature of the Physical World* (New York: Macmillan, 1929).

Eddington, Arthur, *The Theory of Relativity and Its Influence on Scientific Thought* (Oxford: Clarendon, 1922).

Edwards, T. R. N., *Three Russian Writers and the Irrational: Zamyatin,*

Pil'nyak, and Bulgakov (Cambridge: Cambridge University Press, 1982).
Einstein, Albert, *Relativity: The Special and the General Theory*, trans. Robert W. Lawson (New York: Henry Holt, 1920).
Eliot, T. S., 'A Commentary', *The Monthly Criterion*, 6.4 (1927), 289–91.
Engelhardt, Nina, 'Mathematics between Totalitarian Order and Revolution: Yevgeny Zamyatin's *We*', in *Imagine Maths 5; Between Culture and Mathematics*, ed. Michele Emmer et al. (Bologna: Monograf, 2016), pp. 91–101.
Engelhardt, Nina, 'Scientific Metafiction and Historiographic Metafiction: Measuring Nature and the Past', in *Twentieth-Century Rhetorics: Metahistorical Narratives and Scientific Metafictions*, ed. Giuseppe Episcopo (Naples: Cronopio, 2014), pp. 145–72.
Engelhardt, Nina, 'Scientific Metafiction and Postmodernism', *Zeitschrift für Anglistik und Amerikanistik: A Quarterly of Language, Literature and Culture*, 64.2 (2016), 189–205.
Epple, Moritz, *Die Entstehung der Knotentheorie: Kontexte und Konstruktionen einer modernen mathematischen Theorie* (Braunschweig: Vieweg und Teubner, 1999).
Epple, Moritz, 'Kulturen der Forschung: Mathematik und Modernität am Beginn des 20. Jahrhunderts', *Wissenskulturen: Über die Erzeugung und Weitergabe von Wissen*, ed. Johannes Fried and Michael Stolleis (Frankfurt am Main: Campus, 2009), pp. 125–58.
Epple, Moritz, 'Styles of Argumentation in Late 19th Century Geometry and the Structure of Mathematical Modernity', in *Analysis and Synthesis in Mathematics: History and Philosophy*, ed. Michael Otte and Marco Panza (Dordrecht and Boston, MA: Kluwer, 1997), pp. 177–98.
Esposito, Elena, *Die Fiktion der wahrscheinlichen Realität* (Frankfurt am Main: Suhrkamp, 2007).
Euripides, *Hecuba. The Plays of Euripides II*, trans. Edward P. Coleridge (London: Bell, 1891).
Eve, Martin Paul, 'Thomas Pynchon, David Foster Wallace and the Problems of "Metamodernism": Post-Millennial Post-Postmodernism?', *C21 Literature: Journal of 21st-century Writings*, 1 (2012), 7–25.
Eysteinsson, Astradur and Vivian Liska, 'Approaching Modernism', in *Modernism*, ed. Astradur Eysteinsson and Vivian Liska (Amsterdam and Philadelphia: John Benjamins, 2007), 1–8.
Falconet, Camille, 'Préface', in Bernard le Bovier de Fontenelle, *Théorie des tourbillons cartésiens* (Paris: Guerin, 1752), pp. iii–xxxi.
Ferreirós Domínguez, José, *Labyrinth of Thought: A History of Set Theory and Its Role in Modern Mathematics* (Basel and Boston, MA: Birkhäuser, 2007).

Field, Hartry, *Realism, Mathematics and Modality* (Oxford: Blackwell, 1989).
Field, Hartry, *Science without Numbers: A Defence of Nominalism* (Oxford: Blackwell, 1980).
Frege, Friedrich Ludwig Gottlob, *Grundgesetze der Arithmetik* (Jena: Pohle, 1903).
Frege, Gottlob, 'Notes for Ludwig Darmstaedter' [1919], in *Posthumous Writings*, ed. Hans Hermes, Friedrich Kambartel and Friedrich Kaulbach, trans. Peter Long and Roger White (Chicago: University of Chicago Press, 1979), pp. 253–7.
Friedman, Alan J., 'Science and Technology', in *Approaches to* Gravity's Rainbow, ed. Charles Clerc (Columbus: Ohio State University Press, 1983), pp. 69–102.
Galilei, Galileo et al., *The Controversy on the Comets of 1618*, trans. Stillman Drake and C. D. O'Malley (Philadelphia: University of Philadelphia Press, 1960).
Gamwell, Lynn, *Mathematics + Art: A Cultural History* (Princeton and Oxford: Princeton University Press, 2016).
Gascoigne, John, 'From Bentley to the Victorians: The Rise and Fall of British Newtonian Natural Theology', *Science in Context*, 2.2 (1988), 219–56.
Giaquinto, Marcus, *The Search for Certainty: A Philosophical Account of Foundations of Mathematics* (Oxford: Clarendon, 2002).
Gingras, Yves, 'What Did Mathematics Do to Physics?', *History of Science*, 39 (2001), 383–416.
Grattan-Guinness, Ivor, 'The British Isles', in *Writing the History of Mathematics: Its Historical Development*, ed. Joseph W. Dauben and Christoph J. Scriba (Basel: Birkhäuser, 2002), pp. 161–78.
Grattan-Guinness, Ivor, 'Does History of Science Treat of the History of Science? The Case of Mathematics', *History of Science*, 28.2 (1990), 149–73.
Graves, Robert Perceval, *Life of Sir William Rowan Hamilton*, 3 vols (Dublin: Hodges, Figgis & Co, 1882–89).
Gray, Jeremy J., 'Anxiety and Abstraction in Nineteenth-Century Mathematics', *Science in Context*, 17.1/2 (2004), 23–47.
Gray, Jeremy J., *János Bolyai, Non-Euclidean Geometry, and the Nature of Space* (Cambridge, MA: Burndy, 2004).
Gray, Jeremy J., 'Modernism in Mathematics', *The Oxford Handbook of the History of Mathematics*, ed. Eleanor Robson and Jacqueline Stedall (Oxford: Oxford University Press, 2009), pp. 663–83.
Gray, Jeremy J., 'Modern Mathematics as a Cultural Phenomenon', in *The Architecture of Mathematics*, ed. José Ferreirós and Jeremy Gray (Oxford: Oxford University Press, 2006), pp. 371–96.

Gray, Jeremy J., *Plato's Ghost: The Modernist Transformation of Mathematics* (Princeton and Oxford: Princeton University Press, 2008).

Griard, Jérémie, 'The *Specimen Demonstrationum Politicarum Pro Eligendo Rege Polonorum*: From the Concatenation of Demonstrations to a Decision Appraisal Procedure', in *Leibniz: What Kind of Rationalist?*, ed. Marcelo Dascal (New York et al.: Springer, 2008), pp. 371–82.

Hacking, Ian, *The Emergence of Probability: A Philosophical Study of Early Ideas about Probability, Induction and Statistical Inference* (Cambridge: Cambridge University Press, 2006).

Hacking, Ian, *The Taming of Chance* (Cambridge: Cambridge University Press, 1990).

Hadamard, Jacques, *The Mathematician's Mind: The Psychology of Invention in the Mathematical Field* (Princeton: Princeton University Press, 1996).

Hamilton, William Rowan, 'Elementary Sketch of the Nature of that Conception of Mathematical Quaternions, which is Developed more in Detail by Sir W. R. Hamilton, in his recently published Volume on Lectures on that Subject', in *Life of Sir William Rowan Hamilton* III, ed. Robert Perceval Graves (Dublin: Hodges, Figgis & Co., 1889), pp. 635–7.

Hamilton, William Rowan, *Lectures on Quaternions* (Dublin: Hodges and Smith, 1853).

Hamilton, William Rowan, 'Theory of Conjugate Functions, or Algebraic Couples; with a Preliminary and Elementary Essay on Algebra as the Science of Pure Time', *The Transactions of the Royal Irish Academy*, 17 (1831), 293–422.

Hankins, Thomas L., *Sir William Rowan Hamilton* (Baltimore and London: Johns Hopkins University Press, 1980).

Hardy, G. H., *A Mathematician's Apology* (Cambridge: Cambridge University Press, 1992).

Hawkes, Rob, 'Bogus Modernism: Impersonation, Deception and Trust in Ford Madox Ford and Evelyn Waugh', in *Reconnecting Aestheticism and Modernism: Continuities, Revisions, Speculations*, ed. Bénédicte Coste, Catherine Delyfer and Christine Reynier (New York and London: Routledge, 2017), pp. 175–86.

Haydon, Benjamin Robert, *The Autobiography and Journals of Benjamin Robert Haydon*, ed. Malcolm Elwin (London: Macdonald, 1950).

Heizmann, Jürgen, 'A Farewell to Art: Poetic Reflection in Broch's *Der Tod des Vergil*', in *Hermann Broch, Visionary in Exile: The 2001 Yale Symposium*, ed. Paul Michael Lützeler (Rochester, NY and Woodbridge: Camden, 2003), pp. 187–200.

Henderson, Linda Dalrymple, *The Fourth Dimension and non-Euclidean Geometry in Modern Art* (Princeton: Princeton University Press, 1983).

Henry, John, *The Scientific Revolution and the Origins of Modern Science* (Basingstoke: Palgrave, 2002).
Herd, Eric W., 'Hermann Brochs Romantrilogie *Die Schlafwandler* (1930–32), in *Hermann Broch*, ed. Paul Michael Lützeler (Frankfurt: Suhrkamp, 1986), pp. 59–77.
Hilbert, David, 'Axiomatic Thought' [1918], in *From Kant to Hilbert: A Source Book in the Foundations of Mathematics*, vol. 2, ed. William Bragg Ewald (Oxford: Oxford University Press, 1996), pp. 1105–15.
Hilbert, David, 'Mathematical Problems', trans. Mary Winston Newson, *Bulletin of the American Mathematical Society*, 8.10 (1902), 437–79.
Hilbert, David, 'On the Infinite' [1925], in *Philosophy of Mathematics: Selected Readings*, ed. Paul Benacerraf and Hilary Putnam (Oxford: Blackwell, 1964), pp. 134–51.
Hofmannsthal, Hugo von, *Selected Prose*, trans. Mary Hottinger (New York: Pantheon Books, 1952), pp. 133–4.
Hoheisel, Claus, *Physik und verwandte Wissenschaften in Robert Musils Roman Der Mann ohne Eigenschaften. (dmoe) Ein Kommentar*, Diss. (Berlin et al.: European University Press, 2004).
Horkheimer, Max, *Eclipse of Reason* (London: Bloomsbury, 2013).
Hume, Kathryn, 'The Religious and Political Vision of Pynchon's *Against the Day*', *Philological Quarterly*, 86.1–2 (2007), 163–87.
James, William, *Pragmatism: A New Name for Some Old Ways of Thinking; Together with Four Related Essays Selected from The Meaning of Truth* (New York, London, Toronto: Longmans, Green, 1949).
James, William, *The Principles of Psychology* (New York: Holt, 1910).
Jenkins, Alice, 'George Eliot, Geometry and Gender', in *Literature and Science*, ed. Sharon Ruston (Woodbridge: D. S. Brewer, 2008), pp. 72–90.
Jolley, Nicholas, *Leibniz* (New York: Routledge, 2005).
Kaku, Michio, 'Theory of Everything', *Nova Science Now*. <http://www.pbs.org/wgbh/nova/blogs/secretlife/physical-science/michio-kaku/> Transcript at <http://p-i-a.com/Magazine/Issue6/MichioKaku.htm> (last accessed 21 June 2017).
Kant, Immanuel, *Critique of Pure Reason*, trans. Norman Kemp Smith, 2nd edn (Basingstoke: Palgrave Macmillan, 2007).
Klein, Felix, 'The Present State of Mathematics', in *Mathematical Papers Read at the International Mathematical Congress held in Connection with the World's Columbian Exposition Chicago 1893*, ed. Eliakim Hastings Moore, Oskar Bolza, Heinrich Maschke and Henry White (New York: Macmillan, 1896), pp. 133–5.
Könneker, Carsten, 'Moderne Wissenschaft und moderne Dichtung: Hermann Brochs Beitrag zur Beilegung der "Grundlagenkrise" der

Mathematik', *Deutsche Vierteljahrsschrift für Literaturwissenschaft und Geistesgeschichte*, 73 (1999), 319–51.

Kraus, Justice, 'Musil's *Die Verwirrungen des Zöglings Törleß*, Cantor's Structures of Infinity, and Brouwer's Mathematical Language', *Scientia Poetica*, 14 (2010), 72–103.

Kreutzer, Leo, *Erkenntnistheorie und Prophetie: Hermann Brochs Romantrilogie 'Die Schlafwandler'* (Tübingen: Niemeyer, 1966).

Küppers, Bernd-Olaf, *Physik der Geschichte? Zur Annäherung von Natur- und Geisteswissenschaften* (Paderborn: Universität-Gesamthochschule Paderborn, 1991).

Laplace, Pierre-Simon Marquis de, *A Philosophical Essay on Probabilities* [1814], ed. E. T. Bell (New York: Dover, 1951).

Latour, Bruno, 'Why Has Critique Run out of Steam? From Matters of Fact to Matters of Concern', *Critical Inquiry*, 30.2 (2004), 225–48.

Leibniz, Gottfried Wilhelm, 'The Art of Discovery' [1675], in *Leibniz: Selections*, ed. Philip P. Wiener (New York: Scribner's, 1951), pp. 50–8.

Leibniz, Gottfried Wilhelm, *Briefwechsel zwischen Leibniz, Arnauld und dem Landgrafen Ernst von Hessen-Rheinfels*, ed. C. L. Grotefend (Hanover: Hahnsche Hof-Buchhandlung, 1846).

Leibniz, Gottfried Wilhelm, *The Leibniz–Des Bosses Correspondence*, ed. and trans. Brandon C. Look and Donald Rutherford (New Haven and London: Yale University Press, 2007).

Leibniz, Gottfried Wilhelm, *Philosophical Writings*, ed. G. H. R. Parkinson, trans. Mary Morris and G. H. R. Parkinson (London and Vermont: Everyman, 1995).

Lloyd, Jon and Elmar Veenendaal, 'Are Fire Mediated Feedbacks Burning Out of Control?' *Biogeosciences Discuss* (2016), 1–20.

Leibniz, Gottfried Wilhelm, *Sämtliche Schriften und Briefe*, 1/13, ed. Akademie der Wissenschaften Göttingen (Berlin: Akademie Verlag, 2010).

Lützeler, Paul Michael, *Hermann Broch – Ethik und Politik: Studien zum Frühwerk und zur Romantrilogie 'Die Schlafwandler'* (Munich: Winkler, 1973).

Lützeler, Paul Michael, *Hermann Broch und die Moderne: Roman, Menschenrecht, Biografie* (Munich: Fink, 2011).

Lützeler, Paul Michael and Michael Kessler (eds), *Hermann Broch Handbuch* (Berlin and Boston, MA: De Gruyter, 2016).

Lyotard, Jean-François, *The Postmodern Condition: A Report on Knowledge*, trans. Geoff Bennington and Brian Massumi (Manchester: Manchester University Press, 1984).

MacMillan, Margaret, *The War That Ended Peace: The Road to 1914* (New York: Random House, 2013).

Malet, Antoni, 'Isaac Barrow on the Mathematisation of Nature: Theological

Voluntarism and the Rise of Geometrical Optics', *Journal of the History of Ideas*, 58.2 (1997), 265–87.

Mancosu, Paolo, *Philosophy of Mathematics and Mathematical Practice in the Seventeenth Century* (New York and Oxford: Oxford University Press, 1996).

Marinetti, Filippo Tommaso, 'The Founding and Manifesto of Futurism' [1909], in *Manifesto: A Century of Isms*, ed. Mary Ann Caws (Lincoln, NE and London: University of Nebraska Press, 2001), pp. 187-9.

Maxwell, James Clerk, *The Scientific Letters and Papers of James Clerk Maxwell*, vol. 1, ed. Peter Michael Harman (Cambridge: Cambridge University Press, 1990).

McHale, Brian, 'Change of Dominant from Modernist to Postmodernist Writing', *Approaching Postmodernism*, 21 (1986), 53–79.

McHale, Brian, 'Modernist Reading, Post-Modern Text: The Case of *Gravity's Rainbow*', *Poetics Today*, 1.1–2 (1979), 85–110.

McHale, Brian, *Postmodernist Fiction* (London and New York: Routledge, 1996).

McHale, Brian, 'Pynchon's Postmodernism', in *The Cambridge Companion to Thomas Pynchon*, ed. Inger H. Dalsgaard, Luc Herman and Brian McHale (Cambridge: Cambridge University Press, 2012), pp. 97–111.

McLaughlin, Robert, 'After the Revolution: US Postmodernism in the Twenty-First Century', *Narrative*, 21.3 (2013), 284–95.

Mehrtens, Herbert, *Moderne Sprache Mathematik: Eine Geschichte des Streits um die Grundlagen der Disziplin und des Subjekts formaler Systeme* (Frankfurt am Main: Suhrkamp, 1990).

Mehrtens, Herbert, 'Modernism vs. Counter-Modernism, Nationalism vs. Internationalism: Style and Politics in Mathematics, 1900–1950', in *L'Europe mathématique: histoires, mythes, identités*, ed. Catherine Goldstein, Jeremy Gray and Jim Ritter (Paris: Éditions de la Maison de l'homme, 1996), pp. 518–29.

Menand, Louis, 'Do the Math: Thomas Pynchon Returns', review of *Against the Day* by Thomas Pynchon, *The New Yorker*, 27 Nov. 2006.

Molloy, Seán, 'Escaping the Politics of the Irredeemable Earth-Anarchy and Transcendence in the Novels of Thomas Pynchon', *Theory & Event*, 13:3 (2010), n. pag. Literature Online, Web, 14 Apr. 2014.

Moore, Thomas, *The Style Connectedness: Gravity's Rainbow and Thomas Pynchon* (Columbia: University of Missouri Press, 1987).

Moritz, Robert Édouard, *Memorabilia Mathematica; or the Philomath's Quotation-book* (New York: Macmillan, 1914).

Musil, Robert, *Diaries, 1899–1941*, ed. Mark Mirsky, trans. Philip Payne (New York: Basic Books, 1998).

Musil, Robert, *Gesammelte Werke II. Prosa und Stücke. Kleine Prosa,*

Aphorismen, Autobiographisches, Essays und Reden, Kritik, ed. Adolf Frisé (Reinbek bei Hamburg: Rowohlt, 1978).

Musil, Robert, *The Man without Qualities*, vol. 1, trans. Sophie Wilkins and Burton Pike (London, Basingstoke and Oxford: Picador, 1995).

Musil, Robert, *The Man without Qualities*, vol. 2, trans. Sophie Wilkins and Burton Pike (New York: Vintage, 1996).

Musil, Robert, *Der Mann ohne Eigenschaften*, 2 vols, ed. Adolf Frisé (Reinbek bei Hamburg: Rowohlt, 2001).

Musil, Robert, 'The Mathematical Man' [1913], in *Precision and Soul: Essays and Addresses*, ed. and trans. Burton Pike and David S. Luft (Chicago and London: University of Chicago Press, 1990), pp. 39–43.

Musil, Robert, *Precision and Soul: Essays and Addresses*, ed. and trans. Burton Pike and David S. Luft (Chicago and London: University of Chicago Press, 1990).

Musil, Robert, 'Sketch of What the Writers Knows', in *Precision and Soul: Essays and Addresses*, ed. and trans. Burton Pike and David S. Luft (Chicago and London: University of Chicago Press, 1990), pp. 61–7.

Musil, Robert, Eithne Wilkins and Ernst Kaiser, 'A Conversation with Robert Musil', *The Transatlantic Review*, 8 (1961), 9–24.

Nahin, Paul J., *An Imaginary Tale: The Story of $\sqrt{-1}$* (Princeton: Princeton University Press, 1998).

Newton, Isaac, *The Mathematical Principles of Natural Philosophy*, vol. 2, trans. Andrew Motte (London: H. D. Symonds, 1803).

Nicolson, Marjorie Hope, *Newton Demands the Muse: Newton's Opticks and the Eighteenth Century Poets* (Princeton: Princeton University Press, 1966).

Nicolson, Marjorie Hope, *Science and Imagination* (Hamden: Archon Books, 1976).

Nietzsche, Friedrich, *Beyond Good and Evil*, trans. R. J. Hollingdale (London: Penguin, 2003).

Nietzsche, Friedrich, *The Gay Science* [1882], ed. Bernard Williams, trans. Josefine Nauckhoff (Cambridge: Cambridge University Press, 2001).

Nietzsche, Friedrich, 'Posthumous Fragments', NF 1885, Gruppe 38 [2], in *Nietzsche Source; Digital Critical Edition*, ed. Paolo D'Iorio (1885), n. pag., Web, 30 May 2012.

Nietzsche, Friedrich, *Twilight of the Idols, or How to Philosophize with a Hammer* [1889], trans. Duncan Large (Oxford and New York: Oxford University Press, 1998).

Nietzsche, Friedrich, *The Will to Power*, ed. Walter Kaufmann, trans. Walter Kaufmann and R. J. Hollingdale (London: Weidenfeld & Nicolson, 1968).

Parshall, Karen V. H. and David E. Rowe, 'Embedded in the Culture:

Mathematics at the World's Columbian Exposition of 1893', *The Mathematical Intelligencer*, 15.2 (1993), 40–5.

Pickering, Andrew, *The Mangle of Practice: Time, Agency, and Science* (Chicago: University of Chicago Press, 1995).

Pickering, Andrew and Adam Stephanides, 'Constructing Quaternions: On the Analysis of Conceptual Practice', in *Science as Practice and Culture*, ed. Andrew Pickering (Chicago: University of Chicago Press, 1992), pp. 139–67.

Pöhlmann, Sascha, 'Introduction: The Complex Text', in *Against the Grain: Reading Pynchon's Counternarratives*, ed. Sascha Pöhlmann (Amsterdam and New York: Rodopi, 2010), pp. 9–34.

Poincaré, Henri, *Science and Hypothesis*, trans. W. J. G. (London and Newcastle on Tyne: Walter Scott, 1905).

Pope, Alexander, 'Intended for Sir Isaac Newton', in *Collected Poems*, ed. Bonamy Dobrée (London, Melbourne and Toronto: Dent, 1983).

Pound, Ezra, *Literary Essays of Ezra Pound*, ed. T. S. Eliot (London: Faber & Faber, 1954).

Pound, Ezra, 'Meditatio' [1916], in *Pound/Joyce: The Letters of Ezra Pound to James Joyce, with Pound's Essays on Joyce*, ed. Forrest Read (London: Faber & Faber, 1967), pp. 69-74.

Pynchon, Thomas, *Against the Day* (London: Vintage, 2007).

Pynchon, Thomas, *The Crying of Lot 49* (London: Picador, 1979).

Pynchon, Thomas, *Gravity's Rainbow* (London: Vintage, 2000).

Pynchon, Thomas, *Mason & Dixon* (New York: Picador, 1997).

Pynchon, Thomas, 'Nearer, My Couch, to Thee', *The New York Times Book Review* (6 June 1993), p. 57.

Pynchon, Thomas, *Slow Learner* (New York: Penguin, 1984).

Quigley, Megan, *Modernist Fiction and Vagueness: Philosophy, Form, and Language* (New York: Cambridge University Press, 2015).

Quigley, Megan, 'Modern Novels and Vagueness', *Modernism/Modernity*, 15.1 (2008), 101–29.

Rice, Adrian, 'Inexplicable? The Status of Complex Numbers in Britain, 1750–1850', in *Around Caspar Wessel and the Geometric Representation of Complex Numbers*, ed. Jesper Lützen (Copenhagen: Reitzels, 2001), pp. 147–80.

Richards, I. A., *The Principles of Literary Criticism* (London and New York: Routledge, 2003).

Riemer, Willy, 'Mathematik und Physik bei Hermann Broch', *Hermann Broch*, ed. Paul Michael Lützeler (Frankfurt am Main: Suhrkamp, 1986), pp. 260–71.

Rogers, Janine, *Unified Fields: Science and Literary Form* (Montreal and Kingston: McGill-Queen's University Press, 2014).

Rotman, Brian, 'Mathematics', in *The Routledge Companion to Literature and Science*, ed. Bruce Clarke and Manuela Rossini (London and New York: Routledge, 2011), pp. 157–68.

Russell, Bertrand, *My Philosophical Development* [1959] (London: Routledge, 1993).

Russell, Bertrand, 'The Philosophy of Logical Atomism', in *Logic and Knowledge: Essays, 1901–1950*, ed. Robert Charles Marsh (London and New York: Routledge, 2004), pp. 175–281.

Russell, Bertrand, 'Vagueness', in *Russell on Metaphysics: Selections from the Writings of Bertrand Russell*, ed. Stephen Mumford (London and New York: Routledge, 2003), pp. 211–20.

Salter, William Mackintire, 'Nietzsche and the War', *International Journal of Ethics*, 27.3 (1917), 357–79.

Sanders, Walter, 'The Seer of Space: Lifetime of Rocket Work Gives Army's Von Braun Special Insight into the Future', *Life* (18 November 1957), pp. 133–9.

Schachterle, Lance, 'Introduction', in Joseph W. Slade, *Thomas Pynchon* (New York: Peter Lang, 1990), pp. vii–x.

Schachterle, Lance and P. K. Aravind, 'The Three Equations in *Gravity's Rainbow*', *Pynchon Notes*, 46–9 (2000), 157–69.

Schlant, Ernestine, *Hermann Broch* (Boston, MA: Twayne, 1978).

Schlant, Ernestine, 'Hermann Broch and Modern Physics', *The Germanic Review*, 53.2 (1978), 69–75.

Sebastian, Thomas, *The Intersection of Science and Literature in Musil's* The Man without Qualities (Rochester, NY: Camden House, 2005).

Shapiro, Barbara J., *Probability and Certainty in Seventeenth-Century England: A Study of the Relationships between Natural Science, Religion, History, Law, and Literature* (Princeton: Princeton University Press, 1983).

Sigmund, Karl, *Sie nannten sich der Wiener Kreis: Exaktes Denken am Rand des Untergangs* (Wiesbaden: Springer, 2015).

Simmel, Georg, *The Philosophy of Money*, trans. Tom Bottomore and David Frisby (London and New York: Routledge, 1978).

Snapper, Ernst, 'The Three Crises in Mathematics: Logicism, Intuitionism and Formalism', *Mathematics Magazine*, 52.4 (1979), 207–16.

Spengler, Oswald, *The Decline of the West: Form and Actuality*, trans. Charles Francis Atkinson (London: Allen & Unwin, 1922).

Stark, John O., *Pynchon's Fictions: Thomas Pynchon and the Literature of Information* (Athens: Ohio University Press, 1980).

Stevens, Adrian, 'Hermann Broch as a Reader of James Joyce: Plot in the Modernist Novel', in *Hermann Broch: Modernismus, Kulturkrise und Hitlerzeit*, ed. Adrian Stevens, Fred Wagner and Sigurd Paul Scheichl (Innsbruck: Institut für Germanistik, 1994), pp. 77–101.

Stone, Marshall, 'The Revolution in Mathematics', *The American Mathematical Monthly*, 68.8 (1961), 715–34.

Tait, Peter Guthrie, 'On the Intrinsic Nature of the Quaternion Method' [1894], in *Scientific Papers*, II (London: Forgotten Books, 2013), pp. 392–3.

Tegmark, Mark, *Our Mathematical Universe: My Quest for the Ultimate Nature of Reality* (London: Penguin, 2015).

Thiher, Allen, *Understanding Robert Musil* (Columbia: University of South Carolina Press, 2009).

Thomas, Samuel, *Pynchon and the Political* (New York: Routledge, 2007).

Turner, Henry S., 'Lessons from Literature for the Historian of Science (and Vice Versa): Reflections on "Form"', *Isis*, 101.3 (2010), 578–89.

Vaihinger, Hans, *The Philosophy of 'As If': A System of the Theoretical, Practical, and Religious Fictions of Mankind* [1911], trans. C. K. Ogden (London: Routledge, 2000).

Van Stigt, Walter P., 'Brouwer's Intuitionist Programme', in *From Brouwer to Hilbert: The Debate on the Foundations of Mathematics in the 1920s*, ed. Paolo Mancosu (New York and Oxford: Oxford University Press, 1998), pp. 1–22.

Vollmer, Gerhard, *Wieso können wir die Welt erkennen? Neue Beiträge zur Wissenschaftstheorie* (Stuttgart and Leipzig: Hirzel, 2003).

Weir, David, *Anarchy and Culture: The Aesthetic Politics of Modernism* (Amherst: University of Massachusetts Press, 1997).

Wells, Herbert George, *Experiment in Autobiography: Discoveries and Conclusions of a Very Ordinary Brain (Since 1866)* (Philadelphia and New York: J. B. Lippincott, 1967).

Weyl, Hermann, 'Mathematics and Logic', *The American Mathematical Monthly*, 53.1 (1946), 2–13.

Weyl, Hermann, 'On the New Foundational Crisis of Mathematics' [1921], in *From Brouwer to Hilbert: The Debate on the Foundations of Mathematics in the 1920s*, ed. Paolo Mancosu (New York and Oxford: Oxford University Press, 1998), pp. 86–118.

Weyl, Hermann, *Philosophy of Mathematics and Natural Science* (Princeton: Princeton University Press, 2009).

Whitworth, Michael H., *Einstein's Wake: Relativity, Metaphor, and Modernist Literature* (Oxford: Oxford University Press, 2001).

Whitworth, Michael H., 'Introduction', in *Modernism*, ed. Michael H. Whitworth (Malden, MA and Oxford: Blackwell, 2007), 3–57.

Wiener, Norbert, *I Am a Mathematician* (London: Gollancz, 1956).

Wigner, Eugene P., 'The Unreasonable Effectiveness of Mathematics in the Natural Sciences', in *Symmetries and Reflections: Scientific Essays* (Cambridge, MA and London: MIT, 1970), pp. 222–37.

Williams, Raymond, *Keywords: A Vocabulary of Culture and Society* (New York: Oxford University Press, 1983).
Willis, Martin, *Literature and Science* (New York: Palgrave, 2015).
Wittgenstein, Ludwig, *Tractatus Logico-Philosophicus*, trans. D. F. Pears and B. F. McGuinness (London and New York: Routledge, 2014).
Wolfson, Susan J., 'Reading for Form', in *Reading for Form*, ed. Susan J. Wolfson and Marshall Brown (Seattle and London: University of Washington Press, 2006), pp. 3–25.
Zamyatin, Evgeny, *We*, trans. Clarence Brown (New York: Penguin, 1993).
Ziolkowski, Theodore, 'Hermann Broch and Relativity in Fiction', *Wisconsin Studies in Contemporary Literature*, 8.3 (1967), 365–76.

INDEX

Against the Day, 19, 24–58, 151, 158
analytic philosophy *see* philosophy, analytic
anarchism, 26, 31–2, 38–9, 45–50
   transformation into cultural realm,
      45–50, 53, 159
Axiom of Choice, 44–5

Bergson, Henri, 101–2, 118
Bloomsbury, 71
bookkeeping, 65–70, 75, 81
Broch, Hermann: *The Sleepwalkers*, 19,
   59–92, 93, 158
Brouwer, Jan Egbertus Luizen, 8–9, 32–3,
   73–5, 105; *see also* intuitionism

calculus, infinitesimal, 138–42, 150–1
Cantor, Georg, 25–6, 29–30
Cassirer, Ernst, 16
causality, 129–33, 138–9, 143, 145–8;
   see also correspondence; function,
   mathematical
Chandos Letter, 71–2, 76
combinatorial analysis, 143
complex numbers, 34–8, 50–5; *see also*
   imaginary numbers; Quaternions
correspondence, 130–3, 138–9; *see also*
   function, mathematical
counter-modernism, mathematical, 8–9,
   86, 87–8, 158; *see also* Brouwer;
   intuitionism
credit *see* money
crisis of mathematics, 7–10, 14–16, 25–6,
   27–33, 33–5, 69–70, 113–14, 158, 160
   and metafiction, 30–1, 41, 111–12
   see also Brouwer; formalism; Hilbert;
   intuitionism

Derrida, Jacques, 87–8
determinism *see* causality
disintegration, 14, 61–2, 62–5, 72, 75–6,
   82–5, 88, 106–7, 115, 118; *see also*
   fragmentation; mathematics: uncertainty

Einstein, Albert *see* theory of relativity
Enlightenment, 1, 6, 127, 129, 138, 140
   critique of, 25, 44, 127, 129, 138–40,
      143, 150, 152, 158–9, 161
epistemology, 4–5, 16, 63, 77, 94–6,
   100–4, 110–12, 114, 116, 147
essayism, 119–22, 158; *see also*
   pragmatism; vagueness
ethics, 9, 46–8, 64, 68, 94–5, 97–100, 102,
   103–4, 106, 110, 116, 118–19, 122,
   128–31, 131–8, 142, 150, 152, 159,
   162; *see also* gravity; inertia
excluded middle *see* middle state

fictionalism, mathematical, 17–18; *see also* mathematics: fiction
First World War, 14, 19, 25, 70, 101–2
force, 130–7, 151–2
form, 4, 18–19, 51–4, 59, 62, 70–3, 76–81, 82–5, 87–8, 119–22, 146–50, 158; *see also* formalism
formalism
   literary 59, 65, 71, 85, 87, 88
   mathematical, 7–10, 32, 73–4, 80, 82–5, 100, 105, 158
foundations of mathematics *see* crisis of mathematics
fragmentation, 47–8, 64, 94; *see also* disintegration; uncertainty
Frege, Gottlob, 8, 29–30, 65, 70, 71
function, mathematical, 138–9

Gödel, Kurt, 10
gravity, 128–9, 130, 131–8, 151–2
Gravity's Rainbow, 2, 19, 126–56, 158

Hardy, G. H., 13–14, 33, 41
Hilbert, David, 8–10, 29–30, 32, 51, 80, 83; *see also* formalism
Hofmannsthal, Hugo von, 71–2, 76

imaginary numbers, 7, 15, 17, 34–7, 39–40, 54, 65n; *see also* complex numbers; Quaternions
incompleteness theorem, 10
inertia, 135–6, 152
infinitesimals, 140–1; *see also* calculus, infinitesimal
intuitionism, 7–10, 32, 73–6, 77, 81, 85, 105–8, 158

James, William, 110, 112–14, 115–16, 121

Klein, Felix, 28
Kute Korrespondence *see* correspondence

Language
   artificial, 65
   philosophy of, 65–6
   scepticism of, 48, 71–6, 106–7
Leibniz, Gottfried Wilhelm, 129, 131–3, 136–7, 140–3, 149
literature and mathematics studies, 2, 3–4, 11–12, 157
logical positivism *see* Vienna Circle
logicism, 7–10, 65, 70–1, 97–8, 100, 105, 106–7
Lord Chandos Letter, 71–2, 76

The Man without Qualities, 19, 93–125, 158
Mason & Dixon, 44
'The Mathematical Man', 113–16
Mathematical Universe Hypothesis, 18
mathematics
   as art, 13–14, 16, 37
   British, 12
   cultural dimension of, 4–5, 8, 10–18, 40–4, 85
   and fiction, 13–18, 113, 131–8, 138–42, 142–6, 146–50, 152, 158, 160, 161
   and freedom, 8, 9, 16, 17, 45, 136–7, 142, 148, 158; *see also* mathematics: fiction; possibility; self-referentiality
   German, 12, 33, 126–7
   history of, 4–5, 13, 28–30, 51, 55, 85, 161
   as language, 5–6, 10, 16, 37, 40, 65–76, 80, 86–7, 96, 98, 106–7, 109, 162
   and metafiction, 30–1
   as model, 3, 4, 17, 54, 60–1, 67, 70, 86, 87–8, 94, 103, 114, 117, 121–2, 158
   and modernism *see* modernism, mathematical
   and morality *see* ethics
   and natural sciences, relation to, 1–2, 4, 158–9
   and nature *see* mathematics: reality, relation to
   as non-rational, 67, 75–6, 86, 88, 104–6, 109, 113–14, 159; *see also* intuitionism; mysticism
   and reality, relation to, 1–2, 4–7, 10, 26, 39, 44–5, 66–70, 74, 86, 97–8, 144–6, 149, 160–1; *see also* mathematics: as art; modernism, mathematical; self-referentiality
   schools of, 7–10
   sociology of, 4–5, 43–4
   as structural science, 4, 18, 61, 87, 158
   and uncertainty, 10, 14, 25–6, 69, 98–100, 113–14, 121, 138–42, 142–6, 158, 160; *see also* crisis of mathematics; disintegration; mathematics: and fiction; probability; vagueness
   unreasonable effectiveness of, 18, 161
metafiction, 30–1, 41, 111–12; *see also* self-referentiality
middle state, 58n, 95, 99–100, 117
modernism and science, 1, 3–4, 20, 161
modernism, mathematical, 2, 7–13, 13–20, 45–55, 88, 122, 157–9, 160, 161, 162; *see also* formalism; mathematics: and

modernism, mathematical *(cont.)*
    freedom; mathematics: and reality, relation to; ontology; self-referentiality
money, 115–16, 118–19
Musil, Robert
    The Man without Qualities, 19, 93–125, 158
    'The Mathematical Man', 113–14, 116
mysticism, 40–1, 45, 73, 88, 94–6, 100–4, 104–9, 110–11; *see also* transcendence

Newton, Isaac, 127, 128–9, 131, 132–3, 134–7, 140–1, 149
Nietzsche, Friedrich, 14–15
non-Euclidean geometry, 6–7, 31–2

ontology, 5, 7, 18, 39–40, 44–5, 84–5, 86, 146–50, 152, 160

perspectivism, 15, 77–80, 137; *see also* theory of relativity
philosophy, analytic, 65–7, 109
physico-theology, 128-131, 131-8, 152, 162; *see also* ethics
politics, 16, 24–7, 31–3, 43, 45–50, 53, 54, 58n, 142–3; *see also* anarchism
possibility, 25, 28, 33, 35–6, 42, 44–5, 58n, 81–5, 88, 112–13, 115, 121, 133, 136–8, 139–42, 142–6, 149, 152, 160, 162; *see also* mathematics: and reality, relation to; ontology; probability
postmodernism, 26, 43, 54, 50–5, 87–8, 128, 146–50, 151, 152, 158, 162
post-structuralism, 87–8
pragmatism, 109–10, 112–19, 121, 158
probability, 108, 142–6, 147–8, 151
Pynchon, Thomas
    Against the Day, 19, 24–58, 151, 158
    Gravity's Rainbow, 2, 19, 126–56, 158
    Mason & Dixon, 44

quantum physics, 148
Quaternions, 33–43
    and time, 36–7
    in sociology of mathematics, 43–4

rationalisation, 25, 65, 68, 101–2, 111, 118–19, 159
reason, 1, 6, 9, 25, 29, 61–2, 67, 70, 93, 95, 99–100, 104–5, 114, 116, 158–60

relativity theory *see* theory of relativity
Riemann, Bernhard, 7, 31–2, 41, 51; *see also* zeta-function
Riemann hypothesis *see* zeta-function
Russell, Bertrand, 25–6, 29–30, 66, 70–1, 96, 109

science fiction, 24, 148–50
Science Wars, 43, 45, 151
self-referentiality, 10, 16, 29–31, 41, 53, 54, 68–70, 72–3, 82–4, 86, 97–8, 111–12, 118, 157
September 11 attacks, 26, 50, 53
set of all sets, 29–30
Signific Movement, 74
The Sleepwalkers, 19, 59–92, 93, 158
sloth *see* inertia
Spengler, Oswald, 15–16
statistics, 103, 108, 143–6, 148
structural science, 4, 18, 61, 87, 158
structuralism, 72–3, 87–8; *see also* formalism
structure, 18, 59–61, 69–70, 76–89, 158
synthesis, 95, 100–1, 103–4, 108–9, 117; *see also* unity

theory of relativity, 77–9, 134–7
time, 36–7, 41–2, 44
transcendence, 40–1, 45, 88, 94–6, 100–4, 104–9, 107–8; *see also* mysticism
trust, 69, 72, 107, 115–19, 121–2, 146, 158

uncertainty *see* mathematics: uncertainty
unity, 68, 72, 75–6, 78–9, 81–3, 85, 87–8, 99, 104–5, 107, 110–11; *see also* synthesis

vagueness, 109–10, 120–1, 158; *see also* pragmatism
Vaihinger, Hans, 16–17
vector, 38–9, 42–3
Vienna Circle, 13, 63, 73

Weierstrass, Karl, 25, 28–9
Wittgenstein, Ludwig, 73–4

Zermelo, Ernst *see* Axiom of Choice
zeta-function, 51

EU representative:
Easy Access System Europe
Mustamäe tee 50, 10621 Tallinn, Estonia
Gpsr.requests@easproject.com

www.ingramcontent.com/pod-product-compliance
Lightning Source LLC
Chambersburg PA
CBHW051117230426
43667CB00014B/2621